WO
ORGANISATIONS

Don Davison, BA (Hons), MCIT, Cert Ed
Head of Business and Commerce,
Rockingham College of Further Education
Wath upon Dearne, Rotherham

PITMAN
150 YEARS

Pitman Publishing
128 Long Acre, London WC2E 9AN

© Don Davison 1987

First published in Great Britain 1987

British Library Cataloguing in Publication Data

Davison, Don
  Working in organisations.
  1. Organization
  I. Title
  302.3′5′024658   HM131

  ISBN 0-273-02761-1

Printed and bound in Great Britain

This book is dedicated to the
memory of my late friend and colleague
Alan Taylor

CONTENTS

PREFACE

This book is intended to help those people who are either still at school or college and are planning a business career or who are being retrained for office work.

Basically it has been written with the needs of BTEC First Certificate/ Diploma in mind. I hope it will meet this aim. However, additional relevant material has been included. Students following other basic courses should therefore find it useful. Overall the pattern is based on the BTEC First Course Core Studies. The sequence in which the various topics are presented in the classroom is, of course, the prerogative of the teacher. I do nevertheless suggest that the order I have used has many virtues.

Don Davison 1987

ACKNOWLEDGMENTS

The various people and organisations named below have given helpful advice, constructive criticism and, in many cases, material during preparation of this book. For all this help I am most grateful. Any errors are, of course, my responsibility.

G Le Andre, J Blackshaw, AD Carroll and PA Saunders – all of the Faculty of Education, Huddersfield Polytechnic

Julia Bailey, Lecturer in Law, Business Faculty, Huddersfield Polytechnic

Public Relations Department, Kirklees MDC

The Environmental Health Officers Association

PB Sharman, formerly Director of Finance, Kirklees MDC

PC Kelly, Directorate of Finance, Kirklees MDC

SD Storr, Kirklees Area Health Authority

RE Hancock, Head of Intelligence, Electricity Council

The Royal Society of Health

T Megahy, MBE, MEP (formerly Leader of Kirklees MDC)

A Killarney

A Green

B Stancliffe, formerly Yorkshire Regional Water Authority

Information Division, Office of Fair Trading

Bob Finch, Schools Liaison Officer, Public Relations Department, ICI

Mrs B Brown, Librarian, *Huddersfield Examiner*

Bulmber and Lumb Ltd, Bradford

Radio, Electrical and Television Retailers Association Ltd

Roneo Vickers Business Forms Ltd, Clayton West and DG Rangeley, Sales Administration Manager

Hartlepool BC

Chief Amenities and Recreation Officer, Calderdale MBC

Halifax Building Society and PR Thornton

N Blackburn, Rowntree Mackintosh Ltd

SB Ross, Public Relations Officer, Cadbury Schweppes Ltd

Royal Society for the Prevention of Accidents and JA Hart

The Post Office

National Girobank

Roneo Vickers Ltd

IBM (UK) Ltd

Gestetner Ltd

Air Products Ltd, London

Cadbury Ltd

CP Printers Ltd, Barnsley
Copystatic Ltd
Management Control Systems, Manchester
DH Green
K Stephenson, Whitwood Mining and Technical College, Castleford
SA Lipscombe, Barnsley College of Technology
Peter Cafferty, RH Robertshaw, Jim Taylor, Ken Taylor, JR Willans, all
    of Huddersfield Technical College
Advertising Standards Authority
British Telecom
Cardkey Systems Ltd, Reading
The Building Societies Association
WA Crabtree and C Charlesworth, K and W (Chamber of Commerce) Ltd
Granville Clay, TASS
K Handy, Huddersfield District Secretary, AUEW
RB Hesselden, JP, formerly Director, Holset plc
A Kay, Clerk to the Justices, Huddersfield
R Levesley, Deputy Unit Administrator, Huddersfield Royal Infirmary
John Graystone, Education Department, TUC
Midland Bank plc, 'Cheque In' and the Communications Centre Group
Barry Sheerman, MP for Huddersfield
WG Smith, Regional General Manager, CRS Ltd, Yorkshire Region
GG Taylor, Manager, Marks and Spencer plc, Huddersfield Branch
P Taylor and CG Williams, both of the Finance Directorate, Kirklees
    MDC
Harry Theobalds, Head, Advertising Control, IBA
Yvonne Millwood, IBA
Triumph Adler GB Ltd
K Welton, Kirklees and Wakefield Chamber of Commerce and Industry
Addressing Systems International Ltd
We offer our apologies in advance to anyone who has helped, and whose
name we have, in error, omitted from this list.

Don Davison

Yorkshire, April 1987

INTRODUCTION

If you were asked the question 'why do we need to work?', most would immediately say 'to earn money to buy what we need'.

While that is important there are many other reasons. Perhaps some or all of the following apply to you:

- a sense of belonging and being needed
- development of confidence
- being successful
- variety
- meeting a challenge
- job satisfaction
- being part of the adult world
- making a contribution to society.

The reasons for working or wanting to work may be varied and complex for each and every one of us. In discussion with your group try to identify and list all the possible reasons for working. Whatever our reasons we need to develop our personal skills and understanding of the world around us. Some of you who read this book will already have a job. The others will be looking forward to getting one in the near future. Quite rightly you will want well paid, regular and, if at all possible, interesting employment. In time you will be thinking about providing yourself with a pleasant house, comfortable furniture, a car and good holidays. You will expect sound medical care if and when you need it. When you become a parent you will expect educational facilities and opportunities for your family and yourself. The wonders of modern technology such as audio-visual equipment and access to computer facilities in the home, will also not have escaped your notice. Eventually, these might also possibly be yours.

But all these things simply do not grow on trees. The resources needed for their production have to be made available by somebody. Factories, raw material, and a skilled labour force, all working together, are needed before the user can have them.

This book is about the world of work – which makes all the things we have mentioned possible. It is from this world that the material things which we eat, use and enjoy are generated. There are many different kinds of organisations existing in the world of work. Some provide goods. Others provide services. I aim to help you to understand these various organisations, their relationships with each other and with people such as their customers, their employees and those who finance their activities.

You will also be examining in detail one part which is vital to the successful operation of most organisations – the office.

1 EMPLOYMENT OPPORTUNITIES AND YOUR CAREER

Objectives

At the end of this chapter you should be able to:

- List some of the major sources of information about jobs
- Understand the importance of correct completion of job application forms
- Prepare for an interview for a job
- Be aware of the need for personal development.

As stated in the introduction to this book, some students using this book will already have a job. If you do, knowledge of career development and other job opportunities will be important. In the future you may change jobs if you wish to do something completely different. Others will not yet have started work but will still find the services and sources of information about jobs of great importance.

Job information

Careers service

In school you had the advice of a careers teacher and before, or shortly after, leaving school you had the advice of the careers service. Most towns have a Careers Office, and the staff are there to advise and help you to find work, or to find a suitable training scheme or full-time course at college to gain qualifications before looking for a job. They would want to know about you and about the type of work you would like to do. Through their links with industry and commerce they receive information about job opportunities. They then look in their records for details of people registered with them, who may be interested in this type of work. The careers service does not confine its services to just the school-leaver.

Newspapers

Local and national newspapers carry advertisements of vacancies. The 'situations vacant' columns give details of jobs available but it is important to get into the habit of looking at the paper regularly. If you don't get a copy of the paper then your local library will have one. The most important one for local jobs will be the local evening paper published each day or weekly.

Trade magazines

If you are looking for a special kind of work or promotion in a certain area of work then many special trade magazines have vacancy columns. A look in the magazine section of your local library will give you an idea of the specialist magazines available, or you may ask to look at Willing's Press Guide for information on specialist magazines.

Employment agencies/vacancy boards

There are employment agencies in many towns. They are advised of vacancies by employers and provide a service, for a fee, by matching applicants in their records with the vacancy. One of the most important job areas for which agencies operate is office work. You will need to have qualifications or some experience for most of these jobs. Some firms have noticeboards outside their premises giving details of vacancies. These were more popular 10 or 20 years ago and many firms have found other ways of recruiting staff.

Job centres

Employers advise the government-run job centres of vacancies and they display cards giving full details. You can call in regularly and look at the different jobs on offer. You should make frequent visits as vacancies can become available daily.

In addition to the many organised sources of information about jobs you can help yourself by asking friends and relations to let you know if they hear of any opportunities. Find out about local firms in your area and apply direct to them. They may not have a vacancy when you apply but may be prepared to keep your application on file for the future. It is important for you to seek out your local sources of information and use them – they will not come to you.

Job applications

When applying for a job take care. If you are writing in reply to an advertisement take some trouble with the letter. It needs to be neat, correctly spelt and contain what you want to say. It should be clear and easy to understand. Instead of putting all the facts about yourself and your qualifications in the letter attach a CV (curriculum vitae). This will give a straightforward list of information about you, your qualifications and interests and saves the person receiving your application from having to 'pick' it out of the letter. If you telephone the organisation about a job then spend a little time before you do to prepare what you intend to say and any questions you have to ask.

Job application forms

Many firms ask you to fill in an application form. It is at this stage that many applications for jobs fail. Some application forms are easy to complete and some are lengthy and difficult. Before you start, read the form carefully. Make notes about the information you need, like dates and examination boards. If the form tells you to complete a section in BLOCK CAPITALS then do so. It is important to you that the form is correctly completed. The person dealing with your application will instantly have a poor impression of you if you have filled in the form incorrectly.

Interviews

This is not supposed to be a guide to exactly how you should conduct yourself during an interview, but it should help you to some extent. It is up to you to present yourself in the best possible light, to illustrate that you have the qualities which the employer wants.

The employer will think more of you if you attempt to find out something about the firm before you go for the interview. It may well be the case that you want a job, any job. If you simply tell the employer that one job is as good as another then he or she may well feel upset at your answer. The employer will undoubtedly feel that a future employee will be more suitable if they really *want* the job offered, rather than just any old job.

Try to look at yourself in the ways that an employer will look at you. If you have some deficiencies then think how you can remedy them. Be positive. Walk into the interview wanting the job and showing this clearly to the interviewer. A lot of people have failed to get jobs because they have given the interviewer the impression that they didn't really want them. So let the employer be certain that you really want the job and that it is not simply a matter of you having been 'sent for an interview'.

Attend the interview on time; dressed properly for the occasion; hairstyle not too much out of place. Be polite and courteous, and show an interest in the employer and their organisation. Don't let them ask all the questions. Ask some yourself.

In Chapter 2 we look at the employer's expectations of the employee and your rights in employment. When you have been successful in obtaining a job, your employer will expect you to develop those skills necessary to carry out the work required of you. It will be in your interest as well as your employer's to look to the future for promotion or career changes.

Further education

It is suggested by many that the opportunities for personal advancement through further education and training have never been greater. It is true that many opportunities exist but this in itself brings problems. The range and complexity of educational opportunities means you must seek advice. If you look at the world in which we live you will notice the amount of change that is taking place. As these changes occur, new jobs will appear with new skills to learn so that any training that helps you to prepare for the future will be valuable. Look at the prospectus for your local college and see the range of courses available, in addition to yours. Some of them will be full-time courses, some evening courses, some part-time during the day, and some will be block release where the student attends college for a length of time and then returns to work, alternating work and college.

Training opportunities

Some companies have their own training departments and others use the courses available at the local college to train staff in the skills they require. Perhaps if you are in employment you are attending college as part of your job training, or you may be on a Youth Training Scheme and attending college as part of the off-the-job training. The Youth Training Scheme is now a two-year programme leading to trainees obtaining qualifications for the job they would like to do on completion of the scheme.

Assignments

1 Below are the comments made by several candidates during interviews. If you were an interviewer, what would the comments tell you about the individuals who had made them?

(a) 'Yes, my father does run his own small business. It is growing. I spend a lot of my spare time helping him out, especially as he has promised to hand the business over to me when he retires.'

(b) 'Before the interview ends may I ask some questions please? What are the holiday pay, sick pay, overtime pay, and discount arrangements for your employees? Is there any leave of absence for study? If so, does one get full pay when absent?'

(c) 'I want this job mainly because I don't like working in a big city. I like to be near the countryside. I spend practically all my spare time walking.'

(d) 'My father always told me to finish any job I was doing before I broke off. So I do just that. I don't care what the others think of me.'

(e) 'With my school record and examination successes, I want a job that challenges me. I'm not conceited but I am ambitious. I think I'm worth a job demanding plenty of initiative. I don't want to stay in a groove. I like to work things out on my own. What are the promotion prospects if I get this job, please?'

(f) 'I quite liked the people I worked with but, like my boss, they were inefficient and not very bright.'

2 Draft an advert for an office job. During the interviews the comments listed in Assignment 1 were made by different candidates for the post. In the light of the requirements for the job you have described in the advert, how do you think the employer will interpret the comments? Give reasons for your answer.

3 If you have not yet started work, talk to a friend who has a job. What do they think of the employer's expectations of them? What is your opinion of what they told you?

4 Examine the various sources of information about jobs in your area during the next two weeks. Make a file on the jobs advertised that are suitable for someone on your course.

5 (a) Working in sub-groups of two or three, select a job advertised in any of the sources of information available.

(b) After discussion draw up a list of duties you consider a person in such a job might do.

(c) Circulate the vacancy among all your group of students asking them to apply in writing with a CV.

(d) Discuss in your sub-group the applicants and select a short list of at least four candidates.

(e) Allocate responsibilities for questions to members of your sub-group and interview the candidates.

(f) Select the successful applicant and give your reasons – discuss the selection with all the candidates.

6 (a) Obtain three advertisements for clerical staff from local newspapers.

(b) Write a letter of application in reply to one of the advertisements.

2 EMPLOYERS AND EMPLOYEES

Objectives

At the end of this chapter you should be able to:

- Recognise employers' expectations of loyalty, commitment, consistent work, good timekeeping and acceptable appearance.
- List the legal obligations in employment to the employee.
- Give examples of the rules concerning discipline at work, dismissal and redundancy.
- Understand payment systems.
- Distinguish between 'gross' and 'net' pay.

Employers' expectations

Job interviews will be extremely important to you. Even if you are in a job, it is unlikely that you will stay in it for the rest of your life. Indeed, you may change jobs several times during your working life, and each time you will be subject to a job interview. It is therefore essential that you should be aware of what employers expect of employees.

So that you can get this in perspective, it is necessary for you to understand how the employers' minds will work. For instance, their views of the world, of their business, and particularly, their views of young people. For their part employers should maintain the rights and conditions of employees. It is in the interests of employers to have contented employees who enjoy their work.

There is no doubt about it, the attitudes of older people towards the young have always been somewhat strained. Clay tablets dating back to 4000 BC were found some years ago, and on one of them the words (translated) 'We don't know what the young are coming to' were found. It has always been so throughout the ages. It may seem strange to you now, but it is more than likely that you will be saying the same sort of thing in thirty or forty years time.

There is almost certainly a greater outward difference between your generation, and that of your mother and father, than there was between their generation and that of your grandmother and grandfather. Change has speeded up in the last thirty years or so, both as regards clothes and general appearance, and also the work situation, or lack of it. Such a speed of change is not easy for either the old or the young to tackle.

In recent years there has been a swing towards 'being judged for what I am' rather than 'being judged on the basis of how I dress or appear'. Dressing 'decently' for older men might well be to wear a three piece suit, a shirt and tie, and highly polished shoes. Dressing 'decently' for you is possibly quite different from that. The arguments about what 'acceptable' clothes should be could continue indefinitely. Nonetheless, if, because of your dress, you failed to get a desirable job it would be very disheartening for you.

Let us put it another way. Suppose you were the employer and you were interviewing two people for a job. Suppose that ability, education and achievements were the same. One of the candidates dressed the same as you do, liked the same kind of music, and supported the same football team. The other candidate was completely the opposite in dress and hobbies, and hated your sort of music. It is highly likely that you would choose the person similar to yourself. If it would be in order for you to do that, then why shouldn't an employer with different tastes from you choose someone in his own image?

It may be the case that your employer likes the way that you dress, but that the customers would object most strongly if you appeared at work with your particular style of clothes and hairstyle. In such a case the employer would have to insist that keeping customers happy is more important than you keeping your present appearance.

One piece of advice which has proved useful over the years is that a candidate should try and present an 'acceptable' appearance when turning up for an interview. Once you get the job, and the employer gets to know and respect you for what you are, then you may find that you can dress and present an appearance rather more to your own liking.

Put yourself again in the place of the employer. You have started a business, it is expanding, and you want to find some people to work for you. What would YOU expect from them? The first thing you will find from having your own business is that no-one owes you a living. You will have to work for what you get, and you will have to risk your money. This is *your* money that is at risk, not that of anyone else. If you lose customers you may become bankrupt. If your employees waste your money you may also end up in the bankruptcy court. If your employees do a shoddy job you may be sued for negligence by your customers or the public, and your own reputation could be destroyed, as well as losing most of your money. Similarly employees stealing the firm's cash and postage stamps, taking home stationery for personal use, making private phone calls without permission, wasting time, arriving late at work and leaving early, will hardly endear themselves to you.

We can now examine the various facets of an employer's expectations in greater detail, bringing in some aspects not considered so far.

Loyalty

A dictionary definition of this is 'being faithful and true'. The employer has trusted you by giving you the job in the first place. In return he or she feels entitled to expect that you will not damage the interests of the company in any way and that you work reasonably hard and conscientiously. This most certainly is not easy to measure. Loyalty, of course, is a two-edged thing in that the employee is also entitled to feel that the employer is loyal to the work-force as far as possible. In an ever-changing world, and with increasing foreign competition, this cannot mean that the employer is able to guarantee the continued existence of any job in the organisation. The employer should, as far as is possible under the circumstances, have the welfare of the employees at heart and should show that he or she realises that employees are human beings, and not just people to be paid. Some workers complain that, although they may be well paid, they still feel that they are not treated as real people with their own thoughts and feelings, but are instead regarded as just a number on the payroll.

In a number of ways 'loyalty' can be upheld by the law. An employee is liable in law for revealing trade secrets or other confidential information to others – unless the employer agrees. Similarly, an employee should not canvas customers for any firm other than the one they are employed by. An employee, from the most junior employee up to the chairperson of a large company, should not make 'secret profits' out of their employment which are not disclosed to the employers.

Many employing organisations issue a handbook to their employees, in which are stated the conditions of service and what is expected of them.

Commitment

Employers when taking on a new employee, are committed in law to all sorts of responsibilities. They are committed to paying salaries or wages on time, and to paying whatever national insurance and sick pay is due. They also commit themselves not to discriminate against the employee or dismiss them unfairly, and that on redundancy of an employee, certain statutory payments will be made. They may also voluntarily commit themselves to pay for a pension fund for the employee, and to give the employee paid leave to attend classes.

Such a commitment on the part of employers leads them to think that they are entitled to commitment from the employee. They feel that the employee should be committed to giving the interests of the employers a high priority in their actions. 'A fair day's work' is what is called for here. This means not just that someone should work reasonably hard, but also that the standard of work should be a reasonable one.

The amount of commitment shown by an employee is most obviously reflected in the standard and quality of their work. How then do we measure commitment? Where a person does a routine, mechanical job their output is easy to measure, as is the standard of work produced. Measurement is more difficult where non-routine work is involved, because the level of output might not be a fair reflection of the effort or commitment. Examples of such jobs are nursing, supervisory jobs, and people who handle varying kinds of queries and difficulties fall into this category.

As with loyalty, commitment depends on various factors. An employee is more likely to be committed to the job if they think that their work is appreciated and that they are being fairly treated.

Consistency

Just as employers consistently pay the employee's wages, and look after the employee's other interests, in return employers look for consistent work from employees. They do not expect good work one day, followed by slip-shod work the next. Obviously no one can be exactly consistent in their work. Illness, private worries, the time of the year, boredom, can all affect performance no matter how hard someone tries to keep up a consistent performance. The word that should be applied is that of 'reasonably' consistent work, in that there may be variations but they will not be very marked ones.

Honesty

Obviously, honesty is expected from any employee who handles cash on behalf of the firm. Usually, the theft or mishandling of cash by such a person will result in dismissal and prosecution.

There are other kinds of dishonesty than stealing cash, but most of them leave the employer financially worse-off. For example, the theft or goods or stores by employees; making private phone calls at the firm's expense without permission; falsifying in some way the time records on which wages are based and using the firm's motor vehicles without permission.

The annual audit carried out by the professional accountant may trace some, or even all of these things. When dishonesty is rife, without any proper check by management, then the firm can soon run into severe difficulties. There have been various cases over the years where widespread dishonesty has brought about the financial collapse of a firm.

When employees are dishonest they are not only likely to lose their job but they will probably find it hard to get future employment. Even where an employer cannot prove dishonesty there are still problems for the employee. He or she may well find that promotion prospects are not very good. If they want to change to another job they may find it difficult to get a good reference from the old employer.

Good timekeeping

An employer cannot make plans and get the work performed efficiently if the workforce – *without permission* – turn up to start work when they feel like it and cease work when they want.

In many cases, such as on a production line, in a dentist's surgery, or with a railway line, work cannot even begin unless a sufficient number of people are there at a given time. They would also have to close down if above a certain number left early.

If bad timekeeping was not frowned upon, then the workers who had maintained good timekeeping would probably start to become poor timekeepers themselves. There certainly would not be much incentive to get to work on time and stay there until the correct closing time.

Many organisations require their employees to 'clock on', as this provides a reasonable measure of time-keeping. However, in some sorts of organisations it is not essential that fixed times are adhered to. These firms may offer some sort of 'Flexitime' to their employees, so that they can choose for themselves exactly when they come to work and when they leave, subject to a given number of hours being worked per week. This system and its advantages are described on page 22.

Of course, bad timekeeping may be another form of dishonesty. If payment is made for 38 hours, but only 36 hours attendance has been made, then the payment for 2 hours, without work, is a case of the employee being dishonest. Bad timekeeping can also lead to customers being kept waiting. This can mean that the customers will move their custom to other firms, or they will order fewer goods or services. This will lead to the firm finding it more difficult to pay the reasonable wages and salaries that the employees expect.

Adaptability

The world of work is changing at an ever-increasing rate. To survive, businesses must also learn to adapt themselves to changing conditions in the world outside. An employer will therefore look for workers who can, and who will also be willing to adapt themselves, to meet the new challenges ahead. Someone who can only do one thing, and is only willing to do that one thing, will be frowned upon by a good many employers. There are however, instances of jobs where the tradition of never-changing is important, but that is not true of the vast majority of jobs.

Similarly, employees expect that their employer will adapt in order to survive in the business world and keep them in their jobs, paying them reasonable remuneration while doing so.

Routine work

The person who has a fascinating and exciting job is fortunate indeed. To most people international footballers, film stars, pop groups and the like come into this category. Everyone imagines that these people are fascinated by their jobs all the time, and that everything is different and exciting all the time. But is it really so?

Footballers have to spend a lot of time exercising, running, jumping, and practising ball control, day after day after day. They simply will not get to the top if they do not do all of this routine work. The flash of genius you see on the pitch is the result of many thousands of hours of routine work to bring such perfection.

A film star spends a great deal of time in very routine work, learning lines, and waiting on set to be called. A full day on the set, waiting for all the various technicians and others involved to get their functions co-ordinated, can result in maybe a couple of minutes of film being made. They may have to do a scene again and again, possibly 20 times or more, before it meets with the approval of the director of the film. A pop group will practise for hours, and repeat their songs many times over, before they are satisfied with a recording.

Because most jobs consist of a great deal of routine work it does not mean that they are boring jobs. Whether or not a job is boring for an employee, will often depend on their attitude. If you approach a job knowing that there is bound to be quite a lot of routine work connected with it, and that routine applies with the great majority of jobs, then you have accepted the routine of the work in your own mind. You will be far less bored than the person who somehow expects that there should be no routine in jobs at all.

There is a responsibility on the part of employers to help reduce boredom experienced by employees. It is one thing to do routine work of a repetitive type when there is no alternative to it, but quite frequently the work could be so arranged to make it more interesting for the employees. Some car manufacturers, for instance, have workers operating in groups, assembling cars, rather than on production lines. A person in the group, instead of doing one simple repetitive job, may have responsibility for a large number of different functions, bringing greater job satisfaction.

Co-operation

There will be jobs where co-operation with colleagues is highly essential. One can imagine the problem in an operating theatre if the nurse would not hand the scalpel to the surgeon doing your operation because of a personal dislike for the other. The ability to get on well with your working colleagues is desirable in most jobs. In all of these cases employers will be looking for someone who they think can get on well with fellow-workers and co-operate with them.

Following instructions

An employee who will not follow instructions will not be welcomed by most firms. The instructions are given so that the work to be performed can be understood, and will fit properly into the total workload of the firm. Failure to carry out instructions may well hold up a piece of work needed urgently by a customer. It may also completely wreck the work performed by everyone else. Sometimes it may endanger the lives or health of other workers or customers. Ignoring instructions as to how to operate a machine, or not to smoke in certain prohibited places, can cost others their lives.

It is also true that employees should expect that employers should give proper instructions at the right time, in the right manner, and in the right place. Failure to do so can mean that the workers might lose pay bonuses because they are unable to complete the work within a prescribed time. It can also lead to bad morale because of workers arguing about what should be done, rather than being fully aware as to what should be done. In addition, instructions to protect employees' physical well-being, which are not given properly, or not given at all, can result in disability or even death.

Asking for clarification

It is possible for instructions to be genuinely misunderstood. Again it is possible for completely wrong instructions to be given. At any such time the employee should ask for clarification of the instructions. Simply to carry on with the job when the instructions are not clear, or where they are obviously the wrong instructions, can cause all sorts of problems. An employer would therefore expect his employees to question the instructions in such cases.

It is, of course, possible to be simply obstinate and obstructive by deliberately trying to misinterpret instructions. You must be careful to ensure that an employer understands your concern at the lack of clear instructions, and does not mistakenly assume that you are being unnecessarily awkward.

An employee has legal rights and employers have obligations to their employees. A far-sighted employer will not only provide for their obligations under the law but will also create a working environment that provides the best possible facilities and opportunities for employees. We have looked at the expectations of employers in the early part of this chapter and these are much more likely to be realised where there is mutual regard and understanding.

The contract of employment

1 A contract exists as soon as a worker has agreed to work for an employer and the employer has agreed to pay them wages or a salary. Each 'side' promises to do something in return for a promise from the other side.

2 No later than 13 weeks after a person starts a new job they must receive a written statement showing details of:

(a) the grade or title of the job;

(b) the date the job started;

(c) the rate of pay and method of calculating it;

(d) hours of work and holidays;

(e) sickness benefits

(f) when wage payments are to be made;

(g) the pension scheme provisions (if there is one);

(h) grievance procedures;

(i) the worker's rights concerning membership of a trade union;

(j) the organisation's discipline rules;

(k) the notice each side must give to end the employment. This varies with the amount of time an employee has been with the organisation (12 years or more service attracts 12 weeks' notice).

3 If you start work in a place where terms and conditions of employment have already been agreed between union(s) and management, then your contract contains those terms and conditions. These terms may be modified by government policy. During recent years national incomes policy has meant the 'freezing' of, or limitations on, some wage increases. In the past it was usual for agreements dealing with a whole industry to be made. Now more local arrangements (e.g. at company level) are made.

4 Where the employers' or trade union organisation is too weak a Wages Council for the trade or industry is set up. The Council deals with wages

and conditions for those aged 21 years and over, in that particular industry. The powers of the Wages Councils is governed by the 1986 Wages Act, Section 12.

5 A worker's wages had to be paid in bank-notes and coins. The Truck Acts have been repealed by the Wages Act 1986, and methods of paying wages will in future be included in the contract of employment.

6 Deductions from wages can be made for:

(a) food and board provided by the employer (e.g. hotel workers);

(b) National insurance contributions and PAYE ('pay as you earn') income tax deductions;

(c) trade union subscriptions – if the worker has, in writing, requested the employer to make such deductions from his wages.

7 *(a)* For jobs which are the same, or roughly similar, men and women must receive equal pay.

(b) It is now illegal to advertise a job as for 'man (or woman) only'.

(c) A woman having a baby is now, by law, allowed 29 weeks leave, six of them paid. This does not apply to anyone adopting a baby.

(d) No longer may women be discriminated against as regards job promotion, selection, training, or dismissal – or any other benefits of employment. (discriminate = deal or distinguish unfairly).

8 *(a)* Discrimination against anyone on the grounds of race, colour or national origin is forbidden. This also applies to recruitment, conditions of work, promotion, training or dismissal.

(b) A trade union cannot refuse membership to anyone on the grounds of race or colour.

(c) The Commission for Racial Equality was set up to promote equality and issue codes of practice and non-discrimination notices to employers not complying with the terms of the Race Relations Act, 1976.

(d) Complaints of discrimination in employment are heard by industrial tribunals who may award compensation, or make an order, instructing the employer to stop the discriminating practice.

9 Absence from work because of sickness is a serious matter for most people. Apart from their illness are they going to suffer a drop in income? (*See* Statutory sick pay, page 26.)

(a) In many jobs, arrangements regarding payment of wages while off sick have been agreed between unions and employers.

(b) The Employment Protection (Consolidation) Act 1978 provides for payment of normal wages up to a maximum of 26 weeks when a person is suspended on medical grounds.

'Suspended on medical grounds' applies to those jobs covered by special health and safety regulations. Such jobs include exposure to lead or other chemicals, to ionising radiation, or where the manufacture of paints and colours, vitreous enamelling and the tinning of metal hollow-ware take place. It also applies where for a variety of medical reasons a person cannot continue to carry out their duties or be transferred to suitable alternative work.

To obtain medical suspension pay an employee must have been employed continuously for four weeks before suspension begins and to have worked not less than 21 hours per week. (According to the length of an employee's service this is reduced to 16 hours or 8 hours after 5 years continuous service. Employees who do not get pay to which they consider they are entitled on suspension for medical grounds, or who think that they have been underpaid, can complain to an industrial tribunal. If the tribunal finds the complaint justified, it will order the employer to pay the amount it thinks is due.

(c) Similarly, provision is made for paid leave for the first six weeks of absence when having a baby. Women in such cases are also protected from dismissal because of pregnancy and they have a right to return to work.

Hours of work

The five day working week is now very common in the UK. Remember, hours of work have to be stated in the contract of employment. They vary between different jobs. The average is 39/40 hours per week (manual workers) and 36/38 hours per week (non manual employees).

With rising unemployment there have been demands for a shorter working week. Actual hours worked, because of overtime, are often greater than normal hours.

For a shorter working week it is argued that it would help solve the unemployment problem; that hours of work in the UK are longer than those of workers in most other EEC countries; that it would improve people's health and happiness and that too much expensive overtime is worked already.

Against the shorter week some people say that those who do work long hours are skilled and not easily replaceable, that it would be very costly, and that many people would not know what to do with more leisure time. What are your opinions?

(a) The law prevents children under 13 years of age from being employed in any capacity.

(b) Until they are 16 years old, children cannot work in an industrial job.

(c) School children working in jobs such as newspaper delivery, and assisting in shops at the weekend, are a very familiar sight. Their hours and conditions are largely determined by local authorities.

(d) Women and young people cannot work underground. Dangerous jobs (e.g. manufacture of lead) are also forbidden to them.

Holidays

Holiday entitlement has to be stated in the contract of employment. Nearly all employees get at least 15 working days as holidays plus statutory public holidays such as Christmas Day, Boxing Day and Good Friday. Many agreements between unions and management relate length of holidays to years of service. Details of additional payments (overtime) and/or time off in lieu for working on public holidays is given in the contract. Think of the different groups of workers who have to work these days, e.g. nurses, police, etc.

Exercises

1 Make a list of any six of the items which must be in a contract of employment. When you have checked your answer make sure that you also know the items you did not write down.
2 You start a new job and for your first pay you receive a cheque. There are deductions from your salary for national insurance, PAYE and trade union subscriptions. You have been told nothing by the firm about these deductions.
  What action would you take?
3 Working with a fellow student, write a radio script for a discussion on the shorter working week. Try and illustrate the points each of you makes by actual examples from your own knowledge.

Health and safety

1 In some jobs (e.g. Post Office engineering) agreements between employers and unions regulate safety at work. However, in general, it is the law which sets the basic standards.
2 Some unions (e.g. National Union of Mineworkers) have been very active in getting safety standards 'written into' the law. As a result the Mines and Quarries Act 1954 is one of the strictest pieces of safety legislation there is.
3 For all workers, except domestic employees in private households, the Health & Safety at Work Act 1974 now provides legal protection.
4 Now all employers have certain duties regarding health and safety. Thus:
  (a) Plant and work systems must be provided and maintained so that they are, 'as far as is reasonably practicable,' safe and offer no health risks (e.g. contracting a chest disease).
  (b) The same rule applies to the use, handling, storing and transporting of substances or articles. For example, one of the most frequent types of accident involves the operation and cleaning of food slicing machines. The

causes of such accidents include the provision of inadequate safety guards, the removal of guards while the machine is running and the use of the hands to push forward the food being sliced.

(c) All employees have to be given information, training and supervision – to ensure health and safety.

(d) The whole working environment must be free from health risks. This includes the provision of adequate entrances and exits to premises.

(e) Welfare arrangements (e.g. first aid facilities) must be provided.

5 *(a)* Under the 1974 Act a Health and Safety Commission has been appointed. It includes representatives of employers, workers and local authorities.

(b) Those who carry out the rules are the body of inspectors maintained by the Health and Safety Executive. They can serve a notice on an employer to improve standards. They can also issue a prohibition notice to an employer, ordering the employers to stop any operation carrying a risk of serious personal injury, until it is put right.

6 The standards generally expected are those of a prudent (i.e. cautious, worldly wise) employer. This means the employer must take reasonable care in choosing workers who are not a danger to others, e.g. the shopfloor practical joker or the incompetent van driver.

7 The equipment must come from reputable makers. If it is faulty and an accident happens, the manufacturer is liable if the fault was not evident from an examination.

8 The employer also has the duty of planning and supervising the work so that safety risks are avoided.

9 If there is a court case and it is decided that the worker has not shown enough care for his or her own own safety, the damages the employer has to pay to the worker will be reduced (e.g. industrial injury: employee entitled to £400 compensation – court decides worker is 25% to blame for accident – employer pays £300).

10 Employers insure themselves:

(a) in respect of the disease contracted, or injury suffered at work by any of their workers and

(b) in respect of injury caused by one worker to another. This is known as 'vicarious (i.e. acting on behalf of another) liability'.

11 Rightly, health and safety are now regarded as important matters. Nevertheless, society is very complacent about the number of workers killed and injured while at work.

There is now a network of Works Safety Committees. Safety Officers are appointed by many large concerns. Local accident prevention groups affiliated to the Royal Society for the Prevention of Accidents or the British Safety Council also exist. See also Chapter 18 regarding various safety hazards in the office.

12 The Companies Act 1980 (now incorporated in the Companies Act 1985) enacted that company directors now owed a duty not only to the shareholders but also to the interests of employees. This is very much in line with the growing demand for more knowledge and involvement by employees in the organisations in which they work. The EEC tends to support such developments.

Discipline and dismissal

What can employers do if they think a worker's behaviour is unsatisfactory and they wish to punish or dismiss them?

The worker may persuade fellow workers that he or she should not be punished or dismissed; they may take industrial action on his or her behalf. The employer, to avoid a work stoppage, may 'give in'. Cases of this sort have occurred. They are not our concern here.

What are the employer and employee legally allowed to do in such circumstances? That is the question.

1 Contracts of employment contain information of the disciplinary rules the organisation has made and of any system of appeals there may be. Often these are the results of collective bargaining between management and trade union. Employers may only lawfully do what the contract of employment allows them to do.

2 For a serious offence a worker can be suspended on pay. Remember, in these circumstances, the worker has the right to wages but not the right to work.

3 Fines can only be imposed if there is a term in the contract of employment saying so. Fines, which are so large as to be out of all proportion to the seriousness of the misconduct, are unlawful. Fines can sometimes operate unfairly, e.g. if you lose a half hour's pay for being one minute late and you are fined the same amount for being 29 minutes late. If the contract of employment provides for fines where a worker damages his employer's property or materials, then the fine must not be greater than the loss which has occurred – or the estimated loss.

Dismissal

1 Workers cannot be dismissed because of their race, colour or sex.

2 Dismissal without notice can operate for dishonesty, misconduct and in some cases for 'talking back to the boss'. But this is a very difficult area. Before legal proceedings have been brought and a decision given by the courts, it is hard to say when dismissal without notice will be allowed. The more serious the misconduct, the more likely is immediate dismissal to be approved.

An example of serious misconduct would be of a worker found deliberately setting fire to a storeroom in their work place.

Unfair dismissal
This occurs unless employers can show one of several reasons for their action. These include:
1 Misconduct (*see* above).
2 The worker lacking the qualifications or the ability to do the job for which they were employed.
3 If keeping a worker in a particular job means the employer would be breaking, for example, the terms of a 'closed shop' agreement. (A 'closed shop' is one where only members of a certain union can be employed.)
   In such cases, a worker who refuses to join the union can be dismissed. Otherwise the employer would be acting illegally, i.e. breaking the terms of the Employment Protection (Consolidiation) Act 1978, which permits a trade union by agreement to stop an employer hiring a non-unionist.
4 Redundancy (*see* below).
5 Personal considerations, e.g. psychological incompatibility, i.e. 'not being able to get on at all with', between the worker and certain members of the management team.
6 If a person is dismissed for striking, unfair dismissal only occurs if the striker can prove that he or she has not been treated in the same way as other·strikers (e.g. the others may all have got their jobs back).
7 In all these cases the employer has to prove that the reasons for the dismissal were genuinely sufficient for it to occur. This rule does not operate if a worker is dismissed for reasons of national security.

Redundancy
1 Workers are entitled to redundancy pay if they are dismissed when the employer closes down the business (or the part where the workers are employed). Redundancy also occurs where there is a drop in the demand for the skills offered by the workers (e.g. because of the introduction of some new labour saving machinery).
2 No redundancy payment is made to a worker who has been with a firm less than two years or who has reached state retirement pension age (65 years of age for both men and women).
3 The lump sum payment is calculated on the worker's age, number of years in the job and present earnings.

Notice
1 The Employment Protection (Consolidation) Act 1978 lays down minimum periods of notice which must be given when a person is dismissed (except in misconduct cases).

These are:
- after 4 weeks employment – one week's notice
- after 2 years employment – 2 weeks notice
- for every additional one year of employment – an additional one week's notice
- maximum – after 12 years employment or more – 12 weeks notice.

2 Anyone who has worked 26 weeks or more before they are dismissed has the right to receive a written statement giving the reasons for their dismissal.

3 You have no doubt heard the phrase 'wages in lieu of notice'. It applies usually where an employer wants to end the employment of a worker quickly. Instead of the terms of the agreement being carried out, the employee is paid the wages equivalent of the notice and asked to leave.

Now workers can insist on the contract not ending until the period of notice has run out. Even if the employer wants them off the premises, workers can insist on being paid weekly until the end of the notice period.

Exercises

1 Complete the following sentence in your workbook:
Plant and work systems must be provided and ....(1)
so that they are, as far as is ....(2)
safe and offer no ....(3)
2 What are the usual causes of accidents with food slicing machines?
3 What dangers to health and safety do you think can arise from working in an office?
4 A dismissal is unfair unless the employer can show that the reason for the dismissal was misconduct, redundancy or .....
Give the other reasons.

ACAS

In order to improve industrial relations the government, in 1974, set up the Advisory Conciliation and Arbitration Service (ACAS). Workers and employers are represented and some 'independent' persons also serve on it. ACAS may offer conciliation where disputes occur and it is thought it may help in reaching an agreement. It can also appoint single arbitrators to settle differences.

If workers feel their rights have not been properly recognised in such matters as unfair dismissal, redundancy pay, racial or sex discrimination, they can appeal to an industrial tribunal. These tribunals sit in all areas of the country. They have a legally qualified chairperson and two other members, one nominated from employers' associations and one nominated by trade unions.

EEC

The entry of the UK into the European Economic Community (Common Market) on 1 January 1973 resulted in both benefits and obligations regarding employment.

'The constant improvement of the living and working conditions of the peoples' was a stated aim of the EEC when it was established by the Treaty of Rome in 1957. Under it workers have the right freely to move between member states for the purpose of employment. They are subject to the laws and regulations of the country in which they work.

You are likely now to be at work or it is hoped that you will soon be. It is important for you to know something of your rights and your obligations. These may appear to be somewhat complicated. They often are! Many Acts of Parliament relating to workers' rights and conditions have been passed in the last 20 years.

If you are not sure on any point seek advice, preferably from the Personnel Officer of the organisation for which you work, or from your union, or professional association representative.

Payment systems

The earnings paid to employees are often the result of agreements between the firms and trade unions. The method of calculating wages or salaries can vary between different employees within the same firm. Some may be paid on an hourly basis calculated weekly, others may receive an annual salary paid in weekly or monthly amounts. The amount paid for a normal working week is referred to as a 'basic' wage or salary. In many cases additional payments are made. Not all workers receive a wage or salary. Some may be paid on a commission basis. This means they are paid by results and do not have a guaranteed basic wage.

Usually an agreement is made so that the costs saved as a result of additional work performed will be shared between the employer and the employee.

Piece rates
As an incentive to employees to work more quickly a rate of pay is agreed for each article produced. The more articles employees produce, the more wages they will earn. This is a popular method of payment in manufacturing industries.

Commission
Payments are sometimes made as a percentage of the sales (e.g. by mail

order companies). This can be in addition to a basic salary or instead of a salary.

The methods used in calculating additional payments vary from firm to firm.

Additional payments

Additional payments to basic wage or salary can be made for a variety of reasons. These include:

Overtime
If employers want employees to work longer than usual hours they will offer extra payment for each additional hour worked.

Bonus scheme
Additional payments are also made to employees for extra work done. The employer will fix a time in which a job is to be completed. If the job is finished in less time, additional money, dependent on the amount of time saved, will be paid to the employee.

Attendance records

In calculating wages employers need to have records of employee attendances, particularly for hourly paid workers. Attendances are recorded by:

1 *Time sheets.* An employee conpletes a time sheet indicating the hours of attendance each day. This is often done when staff work away from their base on contract work such as road repairs, and industrial painting. The foreman in charge usually signs the time sheet as an accurate record.

2 *Time books.* Some firms keep a time book. As employees arrive for work they sign the book.

3 *Clock cards.* Because they have many employees large firms find the use of a time book difficult. Thus many firms have a time clock. As employees report for work they insert a card with their name and clock number on it into the machine. Their arrival times are punched on the cards. On departure the process is repeated. Attendance time is then the difference between the time of 'clocking on' and 'clocking off'. This method of recording attendance is popular in factories and large industrial complexes. It is also used in some offices.

4 *Flexitime.* In recent years there has been a move away from rigid hours of attendance, particularly in office work. Employees are allowed to vary their arrival and departure times. A specified block of time in the day, say 11 am to 3 pm has to be worked by all employees. Thus, if the employees

work a 35 hour week of 7 hours a day for 5 days, it is possible for them to vary their attendance times between 8 am to 6 pm, providing they are in attendance daily from 11 am to 3 pm, and work a total of 35 hours in the week. For example, if the employees wished, they could work from 8 am to 4 pm daily with an hour for lunch. Alternatively, they might work from 10 am to 6 pm with an hour for lunch, or any combination of time they choose between these hours. The arrangements for flexitime vary from firm to firm. Nevertheless, advantages to both employers and employees result. Thus, employees can work hours to suit their domestic arrangements, e.g. dental, optical, and medical appointments, appointments at the hairdressers, and shopping trips. Busy weekend times can then be avoided. Employers benefit by fewer casual staff absences.

As with additional payments, hours of attendance vary between firms. Often they are the result of negotiations between trade unions and employers. Employees of firms that are on continuous production seven days a week, 24 hours a day (e.g. glass works and chemical processing plants) often each work six days and then have two days rest. Service 'industries' (e.g. hospitals) also frequently use this system. Many industrial firms and commercial offices normally work from Monday to Friday.

Gross wage and net wage

The gross wage is the total pay earned by an employee. It is the basic wage plus any additional payments such as bonus and/or overtime. The employer deducts certain items from the gross wage such as income tax (PAYE), and national insurance. After the total of the deductions has been subtracted from the gross wage, the net pay is what is left. This is the amount of money to be paid to the employee. The deductions made from an employee's earnings can be divided into two broad categories: *(a)* compulsory deductions and *(b)* voluntary deductions. Employees are given a 'pay slip' with their wages. This shows gross wage, deductions and net wage.

Compulsory deductions from wages

1 *Income tax (Pay As You Earn – PAYE)*. This is a statutory deduction, i.e. a deduction made by law. The amount paid in income tax depends on the allowances to be 'set' against earned income. These include personal allowances (more for a married man than a single person), and various other allowances.

(a) All employees complete a claim form for tax allowance. After completion of the claim form the Inland Revenue allocates a tax code number to each employee. By referring to the Free Pay Table issued by

COMPANY UK Stores Ltd		EMPLOYEE Lam, Kim Ms.				
CUMULATIVE TO DATE						
DATE 23.8. ...	GROSS 1834	GROSS TAXABLE 1834	TAX 306.50		N I CONTRIBUTIONS 164.85	
TAX CODE		PREVIOUS EMPLOYMENT				
PERIOD TAX 21	BASIC CODE 200L	GROSS	TAX		ANALYSIS CODE 613	EMP 5
GROSS PAY		DEDUCTIONS		HOURS 35 p.w.	OVERTIME 2 hrs	
Basic	87.00	Tax	16.40	RATE 2.41	ADDITIONAL 7.26	
		Nat. Ins.	7.85	HOLIDAY CREDITS -		
				EMPLOYERS CONTRIBUTIONS N.I. Current 9.12 N.I. Cum. 191.52		
				Payments Cheque	Carried Forward	
BROUGHT FORWARD						
TOTAL PAY	94.26	TOTAL DEDUCTIONS	24.25	NET PAY 70.01		

Fig. 2.1 Earnings statement

the Inland Revenue, the employer can calculate the amount of tax-free pay allowed to the employee each week. Any earnings in excess of this tax-free pay are taxable.

(b) The amount of income tax paid depends on the levels of taxation proposed by the Chancellor of the Exchequer and approved by Parliament. Rates of income tax vary and are set in 'bands', i.e. first £X above the free pay allowances is calculated at a certain percentage to the next 'band' at a higher percentage and so on.

When an employee leaves a job the employer completes the P45. This shows the employee's tax code, earnings to date, and tax deducted. The P45 must be given to the new employer who can continue tax deductions without any problems. At the end of the tax year, each employee is given a form P60 showing total earnings and total tax paid for the year. This document is important and must be kept safely. It may be needed as evidence of earnings if sickness benefit or other allowances are claimed in the following year. These payments can be related to previous earnings.

(c) An employee without a code number or form P45 will have tax deducted at emergency rates. Any adjustment of over-deductions for income tax will then be made when a code number or P45 is obtained.

2 *Related national insurance* is another statutory deduction. All employees earning above a minimum wage pay a percentage of their gross earnings

as national insurance contributions. These contributions are for sickness and unemployment benefits, old age pension, national health service and other welfare benefits. Deductions are not made from employees' wages when they are off ill, provided medical evidence (a doctor's note) is produced. Contributions are not made when a person is registered as unemployed. A married woman had the choice of paying a full or a reduced contribution if her husband already paid the full contribution. Since 1977 this option is no longer available and the appropriate full contributions are paid. In such cases the benefits received were less than those received by a married woman paying the full contribution. If an employee already contributes to an occupational pension scheme that satisfies certain conditions then it is possible for the employer to contract his employee out of part of the state scheme, and the percentage deduction made is less than that of an employee who does not belong to such a scheme or who has not been 'contracted out' by his employer.

3 *Superannuation/private pensions.* Many employees now belong to private pension schemes run by their employers. Contributions in such cases are not statutory deductions, but they are usually a condition of employment. An employee's contributions to such a scheme are usually based on a percentage of earnings. The employer also makes a payment into the fund for each employee. These contributions provide retirement pension benefits in addition to the basic old age pension provided by the state. The pension is usually based on earnings on, or near to, retirement and on the number of years employed.

Voluntary deductions

In addition to the compulsory deductions mentioned above, provisions are frequently made for many other deductions from earnings. These are at the request of the employee and include trade union subscriptions, social clubs, savings (Save As You Earn), rent, insurance policy premiums and private medical schemes.

Payroll

Each firm prepares a master list of all its employees' earnings, deductions and net pay. This is used by the wages department for statistical and record purposes. Each week the amount of money to be paid to each employee is analysed into the different notes and coins required for payment (e.g. £95.30 = one £50 note, four £10 notes, one £5 note and three 10p pieces).

This cash analysis is used to withdraw the amount of money required to pay wages. A wage packet is completed for each employee. The necessary notes and coins, together with the pay slip, are put into a sealed envelope. These envelopes are usually transparent. The contents are so arranged that an employee can check the contents before opening the envelope. A dispute about the actual cash in a wage packet is then not entertained if the packet has been opened. Salaries and wages can also be paid by cheque or by credit transfer (*see* Chapter 12) and this method is most commonly used for monthly paid staff. Computers and accounting machines are increasingly used for the calculation of wages. Constant information such as income tax and national insurance deductions, and other deductions for each employee, together with wage rates, can be included in a computer program. After variable information (such as hours worked or bonus and commission earned) has been fed in, the computer will calculate and print out the necessary payroll and payslips.

Clock No.	Name	Wage	£10	£5	£1	50p	10p	5p	2p	1p
102	A. Franklin	65.20	5	2	5		2			
103	S Fish	46.32	3	3	1		3		1	
104	J Goodyear	28.43	2	1	3		4		1	1
105	E Maddison	78.16	7	1	3		1	1		1
106	D Smith	48.37	4	1	3		3	1	1	
107	A Strawther	33.52	3		3	1		1		
Total		£300.00	24	8	18	1	13	2	4	2

Summary of cash required:

			£	p
24 @ £10	=		240.00
8 @ £ 5	=		40.00
18 @ £ 1	=		18.00
1 @ 50p	=		.50
13 @ 10p	=		1.30
2 @ 5p	=		.10
4 @ 2p	=		.08
2 @ 1p	=		.02
			300.00

Fig. 2.2 Wages cash analysis

Statutory sick pay

Employers have now been made responsible for paying some of the sickness benefit to employees previously paid by the Department of Health and Social Security. This is called statutory sick pay (SSP). The employer has to keep a record of absences through illness and to pay sickness benefit based on average weekly earnings. The payment is only made for what are called qualifying days, i.e. days in which the employee qualifies for sickness pay. A qualifying day is a day in the normal working week, e.g. Monday to Friday – agreed between the employer and the employee.

The first three qualifying days are not counted for sick pay and are called 'waiting days'. Payments for further qualifying days are based on the average weekly wage including bonus and other payments on which National Insurance contributions are paid. The maximum SSP payment an employer has to make is for eight weeks in any one tax year. Further payments to the employee are made by the Department of Health and Social Security. The employer can reclaim any payments made to employees by deducting this amount from the total National Insurance contribution that has to be paid for all employees.

Computer based systems

Computerised wages systems are not new. One of the advantages of so using a computer is its ability to carry out a large number of calculations very quickly. The computer needs a program specially designed to calculate wages. All the permanent information for each employee (i.e. name, clock or works number, personal tax code, together with related National Insurance contribution and Income Tax calculations), is stored on magnetic tape or disk. The variable information, such as hours worked, bonus payments, and allowances is fed into the computer (input), which has already been programmed with the permanent information. The computer combines both sets of information and calculates each employee's wages and deductions for that period. It prints out a wage summary and wages slips. The permanent information is updated to include items such as the correct 'gross wage to date' and 'tax paid to date' ready for the next period.

There are different input devices (ways of feeding in information) available and the more common methods are:

(a) punched card (see Fig. 17.3)

(b) paper tape (see Fig. 17.4)

(c) visual display unit (see Fig. 17.5)

(d) optical character recognition – OCR – where clock or works numbers and hours worked are handwritten on specially designed forms read by the Optical Character Reader.

It is important to keep information secure and to avoid loss of wages data. If any problems do occur during the operations of the wages program, causing damage to the tape or disk, considerable work would be involved in retracing payments made to employees and re-calculating the figures used during the current period. To avoid these problems, a firm usually operates a 'grandfather', 'father', 'son' system. This is where three disks or tapes are kept. The 'son' is the current period; the 'father' the previous period and so on. When the new disk or tape is complete it becomes the 'son' and the previous week becomes the 'father'. The 'father' becomes the 'grandfather' and the previous 'grandfather' tape or disk is used for something else. Therefore if a problem such as loss of data occurs, the wages program will only need to be run again from the previous period.

Exercises

Write the answers in your workbook.

1 What do we call the total wage earned by an employee?
2 Name two compulsory deductions from wages.
3 Name two voluntary deductions from wages.
4 What do the initials PAYE mean?
5 Name two methods by which an employee can earn additional payments.
6 What tax form does an employer give to employees when they leave their job?
7 What tax form does an employee receive at the end of the tax year?
8 Name two methods of paying wages to employees.
9 What document do employees receive with their wages?
10 How can employers ensure that they have just the right amount of notes and coins to pay employees' wages?

Assignments

1 Write a report for employers warning them of the particular risks to the health and safety of employees included in the following types of employment:

(a) Shop assistant
(b) Garage mechanic
(c) Copy typist

2 Find two advertisements for jobs from your local or national newspaper and decide:

(a) Do the advertisements break the existing law?
(b) What types of persons are, in your opinion, most suitable for the jobs?

3 (a) Calculate the gross wage of AJ Smith from the following information. His normal working week is 40 hours. Any additional hours worked are paid at time plus a half.

Monday	9 hours
Tuesday	8 hours
Wednesday	8 hours
Thursday	10 hours
Friday	9 hours

The rate of pay is £3.50 per hour.

(b) Having completed AJ Smith's gross wage calculate his net wage from the following information:

PAYE		£9.20
National insurance		£3.40
Other deductions		£1.00

4 Calculate the gross wage for R Roberts from the clock card opposite. The normal working week is 40 hours (eight hours a day for five days). Any time worked over 40 hours is paid at time plus a half, except Sunday which is paid at double time. An allowance of five minutes per day is allowed for lateness at the beginning of the day without penalty, after which the starting time is calculated from the next quarter hour, e.g. arrival at 0808 hours, time paid from 0815 hours, arrival time 0820 hours, paid from 0830 hours. The normal eight hour day must be completed before overtime can be paid. The rate of pay is £1.60 per hour.

Name R. Roberts				Clock No. 108	
Day	Arr	Dep	Arr	Dep	Daily hours
Sunday	0800	1201	1300	1700	
Monday	0758	1200	1300	1800	
Tuesday	0810	1200	1300	1745	
Wednesday	0800	1200	1300	1700	
Thursday	0820	1202	1300	1830	
Friday	0757	1200	1258	1700	
Saturday	0800	1200	–	–	
Basic hours	Overtime hours	Additional hours	Total hours		
Total Hours			@		= £

5 If you are employed or on placement in an organisation investigate the following:

(a) Does the method of paying wages differ between groups of workers or are all employees paid by the same method?

(b) Are there any trade unions in your organisation?

(c) Look for notices on Health and Safety.

(d) What additional payments are made above basic wage rates – are there any bonus schemes – what payments (if any) are made for overtime?

(e) What method or methods are used for recording attendance at work?

6 At a recent meeting of your Staff Social Club it was agreed that the Staff outing would be on the 6 June. You have been asked to make preliminary enquiries about cost of travel, meals etc. for approximately 45 Staff. The outline of the outing suggested by the Committee is:

A visit to a place of historical interest with lunch either en route or at the place to be visited. Then free time until early evening and return approximately 6.30 pm. It is suggested that the place to be visited should be a city or town to allow for shopping, etc. in the free time available.

KM MOTORS LTD

CONFIRMATION   CONTRACT No.

We have pleasure in confirming your booking of coach hire as detailed below:

	Starting Points	Time
Name of Organiser:		
Address		

Date of Hire _____ Coach Size
Destination and Route

Special Instructions   Coach Hire Charge
£

- -

KM MOTORS LTD

INVOICE/REMITTANCE ADVICE

CONTRACT No.

Date of Hire ....   To Hire of Coach

Organiser's Name ....

Address ....

....

....   Organiser's

....   Signature ....

**PLEASE COMPLETE AND RETURN THIS SLIP WITH FULL AMOUNT
OR DEPOSIT
VAT REG. NO.**

(a) Select a suitable place in which it is not early closing day. State which reference books you have used to help you make your choice.

(b) Write a suitable letter of enquiry asking for a coach quotation. Address it to K M Motors (use a suitable local address).

(c) Complete the Confirmation form and Remittance Advice on page 30.

(d) Select a suitable hotel or restaurant for lunch en route. Make brief notes of what you will say when you telephone and make a booking.

(e) For the benefit of those who are going on the outing write a brief description of the place to be visited including special points of interest.

(f) Give the second class rail fare and train times as an alternative to coach travel for those who cannot go by coach.

(g) Prepare a specimen itinerary to submit to the Social Committee together with the average cost per person by coach and by rail.

(h) Draft a suitable notice for the Staff Notice Board for consideration by the Committee.

7 You are employed as the wages clerk at the firm of A Jones & Co. Ltd. From the information provided below complete the payrolls for a period of two consecutive weeks. The company employs four hourly-paid workers:

(a)   301 E Johnson, Foreman, Tax Code 210
Rate of pay £5 per hour.
302 S Wilson, Fitter, Tax Code 190
Rate of pay £3 per hour.
303 F Ward, Fitter, Tax Code 184
Rate of pay £3 per hour.
304 D Thomas, Electrician, Tax Code 115
Rate of pay £3.50 per hour.

(b) Hours to be paid are:

		Week 1	Week 2
301	E Johnson	46	48
302	S Wilson	46	42
303	F Ward	46	46
304	D Thomas	44	48

Overtime is included in the hours shown. No other calculation is required other than number of hours x rate per hour.

(c) The tax weeks are 1 and 2. The total voluntary deductions per employee each week are:

301	E Johnson	£4.80
302	S Wilson	£2.70
303	F Ward	£3.60
304	D Thomas	£6.20

Each payroll must be totalled and balanced where appropriate. Prepare a cash analysis statement for each week in order to draw the cash required from the bank.

State *(i)* The total Income Tax to be paid by the company to the Inland Revenue for the two weeks.

(ii) The total amount of National Insurance contributions to be paid by the company to the Ministry of Health and Social Security for the two weeks.

8 The following staff are paid weekly from the following annual salaries (52 weeks):

A Jones	£6700
C Johnson	£8450
K Bullars	£11240
M Nussey	£7300
R Barker	£6460

They have all received a 5% salary increase. Calculate each person's new annual salary. What will be each employee's new weekly pay?

9 Complete the cash analysis form below in your workbook.

Name	Amount		£10	£5	£1	50p	10p	5p	2p	1p
	£	p								
A Brown	62	42								
W Chapman	41	20								
W Cooke	53	42								
H Davis	23	84								
R Gregory	34	75								
S Williams	76	19								
P Young	48	18								
Total										

Check that the total values of each note and coin required agrees with the total cash required.

10 Some of the employees of the firm for whom you work are finding it difficult to get to Head Office to collect their wages. Your company has recently expanded. Some employees are working away from the firm, somtimes for several weeks at a time. Your employer has asked you to examine methods of paying wages other than in cash. Advise the employer how this could be done. State any advantages to both the employer and employees of the alternative methods you suggest.

3 TRADE UNIONS AND EMPLOYERS' ASSOCIATIONS

Objectives

At the end of this chapter you should be able to:

- Describe the functions performed by trade unions and staff associations in an organisation.
- Identify the different kinds of trade unions and employers' associations now in existence.
- Outline the roles played in trade union activity by union branches, shop stewards and the TUC.
- Describe the functions performed by employers' associations and identify their impact on organisations.
- Describe the machinery which has been established by government for the settlement of disputes.
- Recognise the role of employers and trade unions in the establishment and operation of disciplinary and disputes procedures.
- Define collective bargaining, picketing, gross and serious misconduct.

It is important that employers and employees work well together. If an organisation is to continue in existence, let alone flourish – particularly when it may be a firm which is fighting to survive in a fiercely competitive market – then management and workers cannot constantly be in conflict. Both trade unions and employers' organisations are composed of people of different outlooks and ideas. Some are unselfish. Some are the reverse. Few of them are either saints or devils. They are all human beings and like all other human beings they are liable, from time to time, to make mistakes. Probably the most important aspect of trade unions for you to remember is that they are accountable to their members who are nearly all employees. They are not responsible to the government, nor to any organisation with whom they may be negotiating on behalf of their members.

There are about 11 million trade unionists in the United Kingdom. Indeed, union cards are carried by more people than those who hold cheque and credit cards. About a half of all employees are members of trade unions. In some cases, employees are forbidden to belong to a union (e.g. civil servants at the Cheltenham, government intelligence gathering organisation). Unions vary in size from the TGWU (1.7 million members) to the Cloth Pressers Society (18 members). Over 100 unions are affiliated to the TUC.

What do the unions do?

1 They negotiate (i.e. bargain) with employers about wages, salaries, hours, meal breaks, safety precautions and working conditions generally. Other matters which may well be the subject of negotiation include the way wages are paid; retirement and pension arrangements; fringe benefits (e.g. the discounts available to employees when they buy the firm's products for themselves), and holidays.

2 They work with employers to sort out problems at work (e.g. how jobs are organised); to make the organisation and the industry generally more efficient; and the implications for the employees if the organisation expands or if it closes down or its activities are reduced (e.g. redundancies, unemployment).

3 Unions always try to see that their members get the rights to which they are entitled, e.g. sick pay, or time off for training.

4 They give advice to their members. If a union member feels that they have been unfairly treated (i.e. victimised) or unfairly dismissed, the union will help when the matter is discussed with management. If the case is a serious one, the union will obtain legal advice and probably arrange for the member to be represented. Large unions often have lawyers on their full-time staff.

5 When it is alleged that a breach of discipline has been committed by a member, the union will advise and probably represent them when a hearing takes place.

6 The union will oppose racial or sex discrimination against individuals or groups of members.

7 If an accident occurs, and a member is injured, the union will take action to ensure that appropriate compensation is awarded.

8 Not all union members have jobs. In general, unions campaign to protect the living standards of the unemployed and for policies to reduce the levels of unemployment.

9 Most unions have associations which cater for their retired members. Again, the unions try to bring pressure on the government to make sure

that pensioners have decent incomes.

10   At the opposite end of the age scale, the unions work to protect young people on government work experience and training schemes, e.g. they will try and ensure that the training provided is of good quality.

Where groups of employees are not in a union, a number of these functions will be carried out by some other body such as a staff association. Staff associations are usually organised by the employers and they are not affiliated to the TUC. They are often to be found in large organisations among clerical and sales staff.

Organisation of trade unions

There is no simple way of describing the principles on which trade unions are organised. Thus:

1   Some are organised on the basis of a single skilled trade or craft, e.g. The Association of Patternmakers and Allied Craftsmen.

2   Some are industrial unions. They cater for workers in a particular industry, irrespective of their jobs. An example of this type of union is the NUM. But note that even in mining, colliery overmen, deputies and shotfirers have their own separate national association. Similarly the NUR may be classified as 'industrial' but some employees in the railway industry have their own union, e.g. ASLEF which caters for drivers.

3   General unions cater for all classes of workers – especially the unskilled. The TGWU is an example of a general union.

4   The AEU began as a craft union. It now includes skilled and semi-skilled workers. Indeed the AEU is a loose federation embracing engineering, white collar, foundry and construction workers. TASS is one of the sections of the AEU.

Mergers

In recent years there has been a number of union mergers. The TUC embraces 90% of all trade union membership. Thus, the comparatively large number of unions which are not affiliated to the TUC (there are over 300 of them) account for only one million members. Obviously they are relatively small unions. The Professional Footballers Association with 2000 members is one such union. British trade unions still reflect the craft basis on which many of them were formed a century ago. After the Second World War (i.e. post-1945), European trade unions were reformed mainly on an industrial basis. During the period of industrial decline of the late 1970s and early 1980s, many British craft unions were forced to seek amalgamation with other unions. These moves were caused by the decline in the membership of a number of the older craft unions due to the replacement of the old craft jobs by the introduction of new technological methods.

Finance

The unions are financed by regular subscriptions from their members. These subscriptions usually vary with members' wages and salaries. The bigger the wage, the bigger the payment to the union. A union's income will be used to pay for the Head (or National) office; regional offices and possibly area or district offices where they exist. All these offices have to be staffed appropriately with organisers, clerical support, administrative assistance and often education sections as well. Smaller unions usually only have a Head Office. General Secretaries of the large unions, who work from the Head Office, are often well known to the public. They are frequently contacted by the media, particularly when a union is in the news for some reason or other (e.g. a strike). Often, too, a Union's President or Chairman will play an active role in the union's affairs nationally. The union's income will also be used in some cases to pay sick and strike pay to members and in paying affiliation fees to the TUC.

The TUC

The TUC, a voluntary association of trade unions, was founded in 1868. It has limited formal powers and no individual union needs to be bound by its decision. Nevertheless, it is regarded as speaking for the whole trade union movement. As a result of this, the TUC enjoys considerable authority. Delegates of the member unions meet together every year to consider matters of common interest to all their members. Congress is made up of these delegates. The number of delegates per union varies with the union's membership strength.

Through the General Council of the TUC, and its various committees, relationships on an organised basis are maintained with the government and also with employers' associations such as the CBI. The TUC has representation on a variety of national organisations e.g. the Health and Safety Commission, the Manpower Services Commission, NEDC – and many others.

Unions retain full control of their own affairs. Nonetheless, the TUC General Council has been given the responsibility of intervening in disputes and differences between unions which are affiliated to it. The only sanction the TUC can apply is to suspend or expel a union from membership.

Membership

Note that a trade union is an industrial organisation. It is not a political party, even though through its political fund it may support the Labour Party. It will accept as a member anybody whose job or trade entitles them to join. This is irrespective of race, colour, and political or religious beliefs.

The branch

The branch is the unit of organisation where most union business is conducted. Through the branch, union subscriptions are collected and benefits paid out. Nowadays, many employers co-operate with trade unions and deduct union subscriptions directly from the wages of those employees who so wish it. The money deducted is paid directly to the union(s), thus saving administrative costs and preventing arrears. This procedure, widely used in the USA, is known as the 'check-off' system. The branch members elect their own officials (usually chairman, secretary, treasurer and a small committee). It is the branch which takes part, by direct voting, in the election of the union's national officials. By voting, the branch also selects those of its members who are to represent them at regional and national meetings of the union.

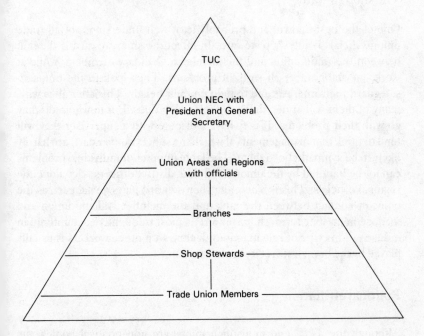

Fig. 3.1 Structure of the trade unions

The branch may also submit proposals on matters which it considers affect the union. Usually, branch meetings are held monthly. Often, the attendance at them is poor. Members who complain and yet stay away from branch meetings really have much of the solution to their problems in their own hands. Attendances usually improve when wages and conditions of service and redundancies are discussed. Motions which have been submitted by branches will, time permitting, be debated at the union's national and annual conferences. (Note: a *motion* is a proposal or viewpoint *before* it has been debated. If it is accepted, it then becomes a *resolution*). Resolutions passed at the Union's annual conference then become part of the union's policy for the ensuing year. The branches also often elect, by direct vote, the President or National Chairperson, and the General or National Secretary.

The branch is the unit to which the individual member belongs. Often they are based on the area in which members work (not where they live) but not always. Thus, the NUM has colliery branches and the NUJ has branches based on individual newspapers. NUJ branches are called 'chapels' and the Chairperson is described as Father or Mother. Union branches are the 'grassroots' of the trade union movement.

The shop steward

One of the best known, and probably least well understood, of all trade union officials is the shop steward. In effect the shop steward is the link between the trade union and the members. Ordinary members, while at work, inevitably meet all sorts of problems. They look to the union to safeguard their interests and to fight on their behalf. This after all is why, many of them will argue, they pay their union dues. But to whom do they go with their problems? If they have a dispute with a supervisor they will tend to think that management (of which the supervisor is a part) are hardly likely to be sympathetic to them. The large number of individual problems cannot be handled by the union's full time district officers – let alone the regional officials. This is where the shop steward plays a vital part, as the point of contact between the rank and file member and the union and management. The term 'shop steward' is most frequently encountered in industry. This type of role in unions dealing with office workers is usually played by the branch secretary or chairperson.

Political affiliation

Although the TUC and individual unions are non-political bodies, the Trade Union Act of 1913 allowed unions to finance 'political' objectives provided they set up a special fund for that purpose. Such a fund had to be created by special contributions from members, provided a ballot of the members had decided to do so. Members could opt out (i.e. 'contract out') of subscribing to such a fund if they so wished. A union's political fund can be used in a variety of ways, e.g. to pay the expenses of a Parliamentary candidate, before, during and after the election; to help in the maintenance of an MP; and in holding political meetings. Most unions also affiliate to the Labour Party and pay subscriptions to the Party's funds based on the numbers on which they have decided to affiliate. This is a highly controversial area.

It is worth noting that some limited companies also make contributions to political parties (usually the Conservative party). Legislation has, from time to time, altered the rules relating to the use of trade union funds for political purposes.

Employers' associations (EAs)

These associations are no easier to analyse than are the trade unions. In general, British employers have preferred to work on their own rather than acting with their colleagues. Often they have not wished to become involved with matters which have not affected them directly. Also, a number of them have been anxious to keep the control over matters affecting them in their own hands. Again the attitudes of employers towards these associations have tended to differ. Some employers have regarded them as a means for the discussion with fellow employers of problems of mutual interest. Others have regarded effective joint action as desirable, e.g. in negotiating rates of pay throughout an industry.

As with the unions, there are different kinds of EAs. Some have concentrated their attention on relations with employees; others on industrial and commercial matters. Chambers of Commerce do not become involved in relationships with trade unions. These non-political and non-profit-making bodies exist rather to protect and further the trading interests of their members who are merchants, professional people and manufacturers. Note that Chambers of Trade draw their membership mainly from the retail trade.

In general, EAs have developed as a sort of reaction to trade union suggestions and actions. Some EAs deal with a whole industry. They are national in scope. Others are purely local and deal with only a portion of an industry. There are roughly 1000 EAs and 40 national federations of employers. They range from the Engineering Employers' Federation to the Glass Manufacturers' Federation; from the National Association of Port Employers to the Textile Employers' Association.

In addition to the employers' associations, many employers are members of professional bodies usually through their own qualifications. There are many such professional organisations, e.g. Chartered Institute of Transport, Chartered Accountants. Their responsibilities include the professional conduct and standard of their members, qualifications and examination standards for entry, etc. Through their local branches and committees they provide the opportunity for members to get together to discuss matters of common interest and often provide social occasions for members to meet each other.

The CBI

The CBI is to employers roughly what the TUC is to the unions. Founded in 1965, it is a voluntary association which took over the functions which used to be carried out by three separate bodies. These were (*a*) The British Employers' Confederation (which represented employers in industrial relations matters); (*b*) the Federation of British Industries (which dealt with a wide range of business interests and activities – other than industrial relations) and (*c*) The National Association of British Manufacturers. This latter body was concerned with employers' trading and commercial interests and tended to concentrate its attentions on smaller firms. With its chain of regional offices throughout Britain, the CBI has five different kinds of members. They are trade associations, employers' organisations and industrial, commercial and public sector organisations. Seventy-five per cent of the CBI membership is concentrated in the industrial companies group. The CBI is also widely represented in overseas countries with which we trade.

The functions of the CBI

1 It makes representations to (i.e. it 'lobbies') the country's law makers – MPs, the government, government departments and the civil service. This activity is aimed at influencing legislation – either in trying to get it changed or in ensuring that it is in line with what the CBI may regard as desirable. The TUC engages in similar activities although obviously the legislation which the two bodies wish to influence – and how – is scarcely likely, on a number of occasions, to be the same.

2 It issues a useful Survey of Industrial Trends. From time to time references to these Surveys are used in media presentations.

3 It issues various publications dealing with the country's trading and economic position.

4 The CBI does not conduct day to day negotiations with the unions. These are left to the various associations and federations of employers. Nor does it interfere in the internal affairs of the organisations which are

affiliated to it. Its position in these respects is then, very similar to that of the TUC.

5 It holds an annual conference, which is usually televised (as is the TUC's annual meeting). This conference provides an opportunity for employers to discuss the CBI publications and for their views on national issues to be put forward and discussed. Differing views, at these meetings of both the TUC and the CBI, are often heard.

6 Both the CBI and the TUC are bodies of considerable influence. Their suggestions have certainly been reflected in the legislation enacted by different governments.

7 Many employers are also members of the Institute of Directors. As its name implies, this association aims to cater for and look after the professional interests of Directors.

Collective bargaining

'The regulation of relations between employers and workers or trade unions' is how the law describes the main purpose of both EAs and unions. The process they use is called 'collective bargaining'. Discussions are held and collective agreements made covering a whole range of topics – wages, hours, overtime, holidays, amenities, incentive schemes, safety, health and welfare and the interchange of ideas. Approximately three-quarters of all employees are covered by collective bargaining agreements.

Usually there are two stages in collective bargaining. First, national agreements dealing with items such as minimum wages and hours are made. Then other items are settled through company or shop negotiations. Some large companies (e.g. ICI, BP and Shell) do not join with any other organisations when they negotiate arrangements with the unions. They have their own arrangements.

In general, voluntary settlement of wages and other matters, rather than legally binding and enforceable wage settlements, are favoured in this country. This is called 'free collective bargaining'. Agreements arrived at by this method are not legally binding. This means the parties are free to raise any matter for renegotiation at any time. In some countries the parties may, by law, be forced to settle disputes whilst an agreement is in operation. Collective bargaining is a continuous process. It is not like a definite binding contract between two sides. Different parts of the bargain may be renegotiated whenever one or other of the parties so wishes. Compare this with the system in the USA where agreements are reached and they exist, virtually unaltered, for a stated period of time.

Difficulties obviously arise when differences continue to exist between

EAs and unions and they cannot be resolved by the usual collective bargaining machinery. The general rule in Britain is that the parties to disputes settle them themselves. It is only after all the agreed methods of negotiation have been tried and have failed that intervention from outside takes place. The Code of Practice which accompanied the Industrial Relations Act 1971 was drafted in order to provide helpful guidelines for dealing with disputes procedures.

The role of the government

There is nothing new in central government being involved in dealing with matters relating to employment. In the time of Elizabeth I laws relating to apprenticeship were passed.

Department of Employment

The main government department now concerned with industrial relations is the Department of Employment. Its Secretary of State is responsible for the bulk of employment policy matters. Remember though, that under our system of government, the introduction of any new major policies and important changes in the existing law are the concern of the government as a whole. They will be decided at the highest level. Specialised bodies involved with aspects of employment have originated from the Department of Employment. These include the MSC, which co-ordinates public policy on training; the Health and Safety Executive (*see* page 16) and ACAS (*see* page 20 and below).

ACAS

The Advisory, Conciliation and Arbitration Service, as its name indicates, provides advice and conciliation and it will arbitrate when required. ACAS often comes into the news, when deadlock has been reached in the settlement of a dispute which has led to a strike. The Council which controls ACAS is composed of an independent chairperson, with representatives from the unions and the employers together with some independent persons. ACAS was created by the Employment Protection Act, 1975. It was given the job of improving industrial relations and encouraging the extension of collective bargaining. It deals essentially with disputes concerning pay, conditions at work and individual rights (e.g. unfair dismissal).

The Central Arbitration Committee was also created in 1975. It arbitrates in industrial relations cases; is broadly representative of employers and employees, and has an independent chairperson. It works closely with ACAS. On occasions it has referred cases back to ACAS where it has been thought possible to obtain a voluntary agreement.

Industrial tribunals

Industrial tribunals exist basically to deal with the hearing and settlement of disputes. Their procedures are quicker, less expensive, and more informal than are those of the courts. Each tribunal has a qualified lawyer as chairperson and there are also two lay members who have relevant experience (i.e. from the employers' and from the unions' sides). These tribunals deal with unsettled disputes where rights have been granted by law. They deal with equal pay, redundancy payments, sex discrimination and employment protection cases. They are often faced with difficult questions involving the interpretation of the wording of statutes. Appeals from the decisions of tribunals go to the Employment Appeals Tribunal. Judges of the High Court sit there with experienced laymen. From any decision of the EAT appeal is to the Court of Appeal and finally to the House of Lords.

Wages Councils

Where the organisations of employers and employees are not sufficiently developed to permit collective bargaining, Wages Councils are in operation. They consist of an equal number of representatives of employers and employees, (and independent members). They set minimum wages and deal with other matters such as holidays. They were established to deal with low wage industries. Where it has been shown that they were no longer necessary, some Wage Councils have been abolished. Under the Wages Act 1986 they only deal with employees 21 and over and their powers are being reduced.

Disciplinary matters

The dictionary definition of discipline includes 'the promotion of order, regularity and obedience'. Basically discipline revolves around the following of agreed rules. Rules regarding conduct are needed in any organisation. Orderly arrangements are vital if there is to be efficiency. The employees want to know what the rules of the organisation are. Furthermore, they are entitled to know that the stated rules will be followed. Arbitrary (depending on the will of one person) rules, made up as events occur and on the spot, are not efficient. Rules relating to discipline often relate to certain expected standards of conduct. Such rules *must* be made known to the employees. They must also be certain (i.e. not subject to sudden changes) and they must be reasonable.

It is obviously better if such rules are put into operation after they have been agreed by both sides. The employer may (and usually does) take the initiative in framing them. But if they are imposed without consultation, and employees regard them as unfair, they will almost certainly be a source of future friction and disagreement.

The Code of Practice

An Industrial Relations Code of Practice, relating to disciplinary matters in employment has now been in existence for over a decade. This Code was introduced along with the Industrial Relations Act of 1971. It is not legally binding but it has to be taken into account by adjudicating bodies. The Code of Practice says for example that the disciplinary procedures should be in writing; that they should state to whom they apply; provide for matters to be dealt with as quickly as is possible; and state which levels of management have been given the authority to take which forms of disciplinary action. The Code also says that individuals should be given the right to be accompanied by a trade union representative when any disciplinary matter is being decided upon. The offending employee must also be told why any penalty has been imposed and of their right of appeal.

Offences by employees vary, particularly as to the degree of their seriousness. 'Gross misconduct' often includes fighting at work, thieving, smoking in a prohibited place and being intoxicated while at work. Such offences usually involve immediate suspension and can often lead to dismissal. Poor timekeeping, noisy behaviour and wasting material may be regarded as misconduct of a serious nature but not as serious as gross misconduct. Usually, unless gross misconduct is involved, a first offence is likely to lead to a verbal warning, followed by a written warning, and, if the misconduct persists, eventually to dismissal.

The adequacy and fairness of such disciplinary rules can only be judged when a breach of one of them occurs. What is important is that the penalties for the various kinds of offence must be clear and they must be known by all concerned. That removes the danger of an offending employee turning round and saying 'Nobody ever told me that'.

A particularly sensitive area is where a union official is disciplined for some alleged offence. Inevitably the feeling can arise that the employer wants to get rid of the individual because of their involvement in union activities. Such cases may well be regarded as an attack on the union.

What about offences of a criminal nature committed outside working premises and hours? The test here is often whether or not the offence has

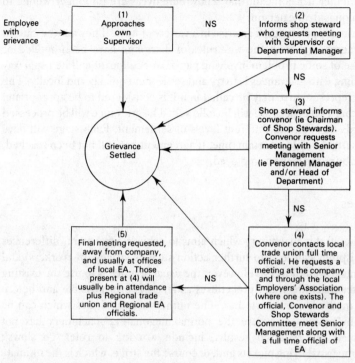

SETTLEMENT OF EMPLOYEE GRIEVANCES

NS = If no settlement is reached.

Fig. 3.2 The author wishes to acknowledge the help given him by Mr Granville Clay of TASS in the preparation of this Figure.

(a) The people present at each stage will depend on the importance of the grievance. Most minor grievances are settled at stages 1, 2 or 3.

(b) A general grievance, covering all workers, e.g. a wage claim, will start at stage 3.

(c) Outside arbitration (or the use of an industrial tribunal), can be resorted to without going through the procedures shown in Fig. 3.2. Usually, arbitration is in the hands of one individual. But if a highly controversial matter arises, a board of arbitration will be used. This has three members – an independent chairperson, one member with an employer's background and another with a union background. If there is a disagreement within the arbitration board, then the chairperson has the power to decide the issue. Where voluntary arbitration is used those involved in effect give up their rights to settle the dispute. What they have really done is to invite in an outsider to make the decision.

(d) Many agreements have a 'status quo' clause, where the employer agrees not to change any working practice or agreement without going through the agreed procedures.

made the individual concerned unsuitable to do the job (or unavailable) and whether it has meant that fellow employees are no longer willing to work alongside the person.

Obviously grievances can arise in a variety of ways. They may be caused by disagreement with the way rules of discipline have been applied or because of some problem involving pay or work allocation. The usual way of dealing with grievances is to try and settle them quickly and locally. The union representative may be called in if it is considered to be appropriate. After that a set procedure will be followed. The grievance will be processed upwards through the different levels of settlement. Each stage will have to be settled within a certain time. If agreement has still not been reached, then arbitration may be employed.

Strikes

Despite all this machinery which aims to achieve agreement, differences and disputes can lead to further action such as strikes (by workers) and lockouts (by employers). However, the usual practice is to use the existing disputes machinery and procedures as far as is ever possible and before other methods are resorted to. The numerous techniques which can be used by employees where the normal negotiating machinery has not produced the required results, include working to rule; 'go slows'; overtime bans; flying pickets and, of course the strike, which is the ultimate weapon.

Many false ideas about strikes exist. In a survey of strikes covering some 19 countries during the 1970s, Britain lay about half-way in terms of days lost through strikes. Indeed far more days are lost in Britain through accidents and absence from work because of the common cold than are ever lost because of strikes. It should be remembered too that, as an eminent judge once pointed out, the right to strike is an essential part of collective bargaining.

Picketing involves placing men and women ouside a workplace, in order to try and persuade others to stop working there. 'Crossing a picket line' means in effect ignoring the pleas of pickets and going into work. Picketing is a highly controversial area of employer-employee relations. Peaceful picketing has been legally defined. Thus, trade unionists must picket at or near their own place of work. Their sole purpose must be peacefully to obtain or communicate information or peacefully to persuade a person to work or not to work. Difficult situations can arise where large numbers of flying pickets are brought in from other areas to try and persuade people not to work. In such cases allegations of intimidation may be made (e.g. NUM strike 1984). The number of pickets allowed is restricted by law.

Union rules

The rules by which trade unions conduct their own affairs are another aspect of discipline and its impact on the world of work. These rules have been developed and refined over many years. They aim, overall, to establish a democratic system where the rights and duties of individual members, elected committees and full time officials are clearly stated. Members are expected to abide by the union's rules and the majority decisions of elected bodies.

Those who flagrantly break these rules can be subject to disciplinary action such as suspension from union membership, a fine or expulsion from the union.

Note that 'Closed Shop' refers to an agreement made between the employer and the employee. The agreement means that it will be a condition of employment that an employee must belong to his appropriate trade union and that the employer will enforce this condition.

Exercises

1 State the matters about which trade unions negotiate with employers.
2 What do trade unions aim to do for young people?
3 What is the main difference between an industrial union and a general union?
4 What role does the branch play in trade union activities?
5 Explain the term 'contracting out'.
6 What are the differences between Chambers of Commerce and other forms of employers' associations?
7 Define 'collective bargaining'.
8 What are the functions of ACAS?
9 Name three rules you would expect to find in a trade union rule book.
10 What does the Code of Practice say about disciplinary procedures?

Assignments

1 In a number of places in this chapter the initials of organisations have been used instead of their full names. These organisations are all well known. Find out the full names of these organisations. Write a brief note about each one stating:
  (a) the number of members it has;
  (b) the address of its Head Office;
  (c) the names of any of its leading officials which you can find (i.e. the President or National Chairperson, the General or National Secretary).
2 Over a period of a week make a note of any references in the media (press, TV and radio) to any type of activity involving trade unions, employers' associations or staff associations. In any three instances you care to select,

describe the matters to which reference was made and add any personal comments you wish.

3 (a) Look at your own place of work and find out if there are any trade unions.

(b) Ask members of your family and friends who are working if they are members of a trade union.

(c) Ask them what benefits they feel they get from being members of a trade union.

4 TYPES OF ORGANISATION – THE PRIVATE SECTOR (I)

Objectives

At the end of this chapter you should be able to:

- State the main features of the following organisations in the private sector – the sole trader and the partnership.
- Describe how each such organisation is formed.
- Explain the advantages and disadvantages of each such organisation.

There follows a brief account of the first venture into sole trading of Roy Carroll. Read it carefully then make a list of what you consider to be the main features, advantages and disadvantages of this type of organisation. Then turn to pages 50, 51 and 52. With your teacher's guidance, check your answer.

The story of Roy Carroll

After 12 years of hard working life, Roy Carroll had managed to accumulate in his building society account a comfortable 'nest egg'. He had always been ambitious.

For at least three years he had had his eye on a shop which he felt he could run successfully. The owner of the shop, Jim Duggan, was 70 years old. Since the death of his wife eight years before, Duggan had run the business completely on his own. Suddenly he decided to sell his business and to retire. Carroll decided that the time to strike out on his own had now arrived. He had always wanted to be his own boss. He had also asked the advice of his friend, Jeremy Ashmore, who ran his own business under the name of 'JA Window Cleaning'. Ashmore warned him of the need to have enough capital with which to start his own business.

Carroll found that he was £2000 short of Duggan's selling price. His brother Joe promised to lend him this sum, provided he paid interest at 1% below the rate the bank charged on an overdraft. Joe wanted nothing to do with the running of the business.

After the business had been brought from Duggan and all the legal formalities completed, Carroll set about 'moving in'. He contacted some wholesalers about goods he wished to sell. In addition, two representatives called on him and he made arrangements with them for their products to be delivered to him.

For a time all went well. Carroll did his best to meet his customers' requirements. He soon got to know them all and had a good idea of who were 'good' payers and who were not. This helped him when he gave credit. His wife helped him by keeping the accounts. His daughter occasionally lent him a hand in the shop. Then, an old furniture warehouse 50 yards from his shop was converted into a supermarket. Carroll found that his trade declined. He was not able to get the same large discounts as the supermarket when he bought goods in order to sell them later in his shop. His prices were not competitive with those of the supermarket. Furthermore, he did not have enough money to stock the same wide range as his competitors.

Carroll worked hard in trying to deal with these difficulties. He never managed to get any proper holidays. He worried as his sales continued to drop. Whilst all this had been happening, trade had improved at the firm where he had worked originally as a carpenter and joiner. The owner, knowing of Carroll's skill and conscientiousness, offered him a job of foreman if he would return. Carroll said 'No thanks'. In the meantime, his wife rejected the offer of a part-time job as clerk/typist in the office of a local solicitor.

Eventually Carroll found he simply could not pay his debts. Despite all the care he had taken in economising in every possible way, he was declared bankrupt. The sad end to this tale is that his shop, his stock and all his personal possessions (except his carpenter's tools and the clothes and bedding of his family and himself) were sold to pay his creditors. His old boss took him back – doing his old job.

The sole trader*

The following are the main features of sole trading together with the advantages and disadvantages of this type of organisation.

From your study of Roy Carroll, how many did you spot?

1 The term 'sole trader' does not mean there is only one person in the business though there can be. Often in a small retail shop the owner and probably other members of the family will work. Also many sole traders employ people from outside their own family circle to work for them.

2 The sole trader is the only owner. He or she provides the capital from savings or by borrowing some of it.

*The term 'sole proprietor' is often used. There is little difference in meaning between the two terms.

3 The sole trader does all the organising and takes all the risks. Any profit is theirs.

4 If the business fails the sole trader is liable for all the debts. They then face bankruptcy. Most private possessions as well as the assets of the business can be sold in order to pay the debtors, i.e. they will face 'unlimited liability'.

Advantages

1 The sole trader has the chance to become their 'own boss'.

2 Customers' personal wants can sometimes be met more easily than by a larger concern.

3 They know their customers. They should therefore be in a better position than a big concern to avoid bad debts and to give credit.

4 They have every incentive to be efficient and to cut out waste, e.g. they pay for the light accidentally left on – nobody else does!

5 It is the easiest type of business to form. There are few legal requirements. (*See* page 52).

6 They do not have to spend time consulting other people before deciding what to do.

7 They provide a service where bigger concerns will not because it is not profitable enough for them (e.g. remote country areas), thus saving customers the cost and inconvenience of travelling to the nearest town.

8 There is no need to reveal capital or profits, other than to individuals such as the bank manager and to HM Inspector of Taxes. (Anyone can read the balance sheet of a public limited company.)

Disadvantages

1 Unlimited liability. (*See* page 50).

2 Expansion can be difficult. The sole trader cannot invite the public to invest in their business.

3 Payment of taxes on death, known as Capital Transfer Tax, can cripple the business.

4 They cannot gain the benefits enjoyed by a bigger concern (e.g. large discounts when buying large quantities).

5 Stocks are often limited in range.

6 Prices are often higher than those of large scale competitors. Recently there have been instances of corner shopkeepers being able to buy goods at supermarkets to sell to their customers more cheaply than they could get them from their usual suppliers.

7 They often work long hours with few holidays. If they were not running

their own business they could be earning wages elsewhere – and finishing work at 5 pm!

Small shopkeepers are not the only sole traders. There are others such as window cleaners, jobbing builders and plumbers. Many professional people (e.g. doctors, accountants and dentists) also operate in the same way.

Partnerships

It is likely that if a sole trader decides to expand they will go into partnership with one or more persons. Those joining the business usually bring in capital. They help to run the business and share the risks.

It is wise to have a legally binding agreement between the partners drafted. This document is known as the Articles of Partnership. In these Articles the following points are usually covered:

1 The capital to be contributed by each partner.
2 The ratio in which profits (or losses) are to be shared. If the Articles of Partnership say nothing on this matter (or there is no other form of agreement) then profits or losses are shared equally.
3 The rate of interest, if any, to be given on capital before the profits are shared.
4 The rate of interest, if any, to be charged on partners' drawings. (Drawings are cash – sometimes goods – taken out of a business by the proprietor for his personal use.)
5 Salaries to be paid to partners.

Firm's name: Part II, Company and Business Names of the Companies Act, 1981 came into force on 26 February, 1982. Thus:

1 If a person trades under a name other than their own then they must state in legible characters the details of the proprietors of the business on all business documents, and give an address in Great Britain at which service of any document will be effective.
2 If the business name contains a 'sensitive' name, e.g. 'National' 'European', 'United Kingdom', then the approval of the Secretary of State must be obtained.
3 If the business name would give the impression that the business was connected with local or central government then the approval of the Secretary of State must be obtained.

Therefore the registration of business names has been abolished by the Companies Act, 1981 (incorporated in the Companies Act, 1985). A person or partnership trading under a name other than their own, need take no action, other than that mentioned in 2 and 3 above.

A partnership must not consist of more than 20 persons. This restriction no longer applies to accountants, solicitors and members of a recognised stock exchange.

Like a sole trader, a partnership faces unlimited liability. A limited partnership can be formed (though few are nowadays). Then, there must be at least one (fully liable) general partner. If the business fails the limited partner is only liable to pay what they have agreed to invest. They cannot take part in running the business.

Advantages

1 It meets the need for more capital and makes expansion beyond the resources of a sole trader possible.
2 The worries of running a business can be shared.
3 The former sole trader can retire and yet remain as a partner and keep an interest in the business.
4 If one of the partners is away ill, there is somebody else to carry on.
5 Some specialisation is possible. Jobs can be shared according to abilities and tastes.

Disadvantages

1 Partners' liability for the firm's debts is unlimited (except for a limited partner).
2 Quick decisions are not so easily made as in the case of the sole trader. Time may be spent in discussion and argument.
3 A partnership is dissolved automatically if a partner is made bankrupt, retires or dies. If any one of the partners wants the partnership to finish then it will be ended – provided the partnership agreement does not provide otherwise. The partner leaving the business is entitled to take out their share of its market value. Such circumstances can ruin the business. To guard against their occurrence, partners often take out insurance policies. The full dissolution of a partnership (involving settlement of all debts, sale of the assets and distribution of the proceeds among the partners), occurs only rarely. Such a situation may arise when there is a disagreement among the partners which cannot be settled amicably or when the court has ordered that the partnership should be dissolved.
4 There is the risk of one of the partners being foolish or dishonest and thereby ruining the business – and all the other partners as well.
5 The number of owners cannot normally exceed 20 (*see* page 52). This can halt the expansion of the business.

Government help

Recently, there has been a growth of interest in the development and establishment of small firms. There is now a special unit of the Department of Trade and Industry called the Small Firms Centre, with offices located in different parts of the country.

The purpose of the SFC and its out of London offices is to provide advice and counselling to small firms, either in existence or about to be formed. In rural areas COSIRA (the Council for Small Industries in Rural Areas) assists small businesses by giving advice, technical and managerial consultancy service, limited loan facilities and specialised training. Initial contact can be made through the Small Firms Centre.

There is also an employers' association catering for the self-employed.

Exercises

1 Name three disadvantages of running a business as a sole trader.
2 Are T Smith and P Brown, both chartered accountants, along with 20 other chartered accountants, allowed to form a partnership for the purposes of entering into public practice? Give reasons for your answer.
3 F England, a successful sole trader, cannot decide whether or not to enter into partnership with P Molyneux. He asks your opinion as to any difficulties you think he might meet if he takes this step. What would you say?

Assignment

Select any three businesses in your area which are partnerships. Why do you think they use this type of organisation?

Limited liability

As you already know the partnership as a form of business organisation has certain disadvantages. Probably, the most important of these is that the partners' liability (except for that of a limited partner) is **not** limited to the amount they have invested in the business. Their liability also extends to nearly all their private possessions.

To meet this difficulty limited liability was introduced in England in 1855. Before then, people who invested capital in a business ran great risks, particularly if they lived a distance from the business and were not able to play a full part in its supervision. After limited liability had been introduced much capital, which until then its owners had not been keen to invest, became available to help in the expansion of industry and trade.

Another major disadvantage of a partnership is that the number of

Public and private companies differ in a number of ways:

Public Co (e.g. XYZ plc)[1]	Private Co (e.g. ABC Ltd)[1]
1 It must have at least two shareholders. There is no maximum limit.[2] 2 Shares are freely transferable. *Note:* The Stock Exchange provides the mechanism whereby shareholders can turn their holdings into cash by selling them to others. See Note 6 on p. 56. 3 It must have at least two directors. All directors must retire when they are 70 years of age (unless the shareholders decide otherwise). 4 *(a)* Via a prospectus it can invite the public to subscribe capital. *(b)* Must now have a minumum authorised and allotted share capital of £50 000. *(c)* At least one quarter of the nominal or authorised value of its shares and the whole of its premium *must* be paid on allotment. *(d)* Shares of a company may no longer be offered at a discount. *(e)* When making a public issue of shares, the company must issue a prospectus which gives full particulars of the history, capital structure, loans, profit record, directors and many other matters calculated to assist the intending shareholder to assess the possibilities of the company. The directors are liable to penalties for fraud, misrepresentation or failure to disclose the material information as required by Schedule 3 of the Companies Act 1985.	1 It must have at least two shareholders.[3] 2 A Private Company can, in its Articles of Association, provide for a restriction on the transfer of its shares but it is not obliged to have such a restriction.[4] 3 It need only have one director although normally there are at least two directors. They can continue in office to whatever age they like. 4 It cannot offer its shares or debentures for sale to the public. 5 Under Section 81 of the Companies Act 1985 the private company cannot go to the public for subscriptions for its shares.

owners cannot usually be more than 20 (*see* page 52). Thus the amount of capital a partnership can raise is restricted.

The type of business organisation to which these two important disadvantages do not apply is the limited liability company. From this point any reference to a 'company' means a 'limited company'. (Note the differences between a *public* limited company and a *private* limited company. *See* page 55.) It is worth remembering that only rarely does a company start its life as a public company. Often an individual or a small group of people will start a business in a small way, providing some good or service which they feel people will want. The form of organisation used in such cases may be sole trader, partnership or a private company. Often businesses develop from sole trader/partnership into private companies. Many family businesses have grown in this way. Development into a public company, where the public are invited to buy shares, follows later. Many private companies never grow into public companies. There are some 15000 public companies in this country whilst there are over 500 000 private companies. The combined capital of the public companies, however, is far more than that of the private companies. In some cases, private companies are taken over by bigger and wealthier public companies. It is only worth 'going public' when a relatively large business, needing much capital, is created. Floating a public company is a very costly business indeed.

Notes

1 Before the Companies Act 1980 came into operation both public and private companies used to have 'Limited' as the last word in their names. Now a public company must have the initials 'plc' as the last part of its name, while a private company still uses 'Limited' (Ltd).

2 Before 1980 a public company had to have at least seven shareholders. The minimum number is now two.

3 The maximum number of shareholders for a private limited company used to be 50. This rule was removed by the Companies Act 1980.

4 Formerly, and for the purposes of obtaining the privileges of a private company (e.g. directors need not retire at 70 years of age), the Articles of Association *had to state* that the transfer of shares was restricted, e.g. shares could only be transferred to members or to the sons and daughters of members.

5 To bring the United Kingdom into line with other members of the EEC, the profit and loss accounts and balance sheets published by companies now have to be drawn up in a set pattern. Previously such accounts, provided they gave certain information, could be drawn up in any way.

6 Previously, companies, except in very restricted circumstances, could not buy back their own shares from shareholders. This has now been made

very easy for a company to do. It will make the financing of private companies, in particular, much easier to manage.

7 Formerly, any company which did not satisfy the requirements for a private company, had to register as a public limited company. *The reverse is now the case.* The law now defines a public company. Any company which does not fall within this definition of a public company is necessarily a private company.

Shares and shareholders

The capital of a company is divided into shares. These can be of any value e.g. £1 or £5 shares. To become a member (or shareholder) of a company, a person must buy one or more shares. They may pay in full for the shares when they buy them. Alternatively, the shares may be partly paid. The balance outstanding on partly paid shares is then paid when the company demands it. The liability of a member of a company is limited to the shares they bought. Where a share is only partly paid, they are liable to pay only the amount owing on those shares.

If a company fails, it is likely to be 'wound up' (the term 'bankruptcy' is not used for a company). In such circumstances a shareholder's private possessions *cannot* be taken to help pay the company's debts. The only amount for which shareholders are liable in such a situation is for the amount unpaid on any partly paid share they may hold. If the shares are already fully paid, then they have no liability for the company's outstanding debts. For example, if you hold 200 fully paid £1 ordinary shares in a company which is being wound up, all you can lose is the £200 you have already paid for them. Indeed, you may still be repaid a part of your £200 (e.g. 10p per share) if there is sufficient cash left to pay the shareholders anything after all the company's debts have been settled. If you hold 200 £1 ordinary shares on which you have only been asked to pay 60p per share (we say these are '60p called') then in the event of the company being wound up all you can be asked to pay is £80 (i.e. 200 × 40p). Note that when a company has issued partly paid shares, it may call up any outstanding sums, provided it follows the proper procedures, as and when it so decides. Such a decision may be taken because the company requires more capital in order to expand – or just to carry on the business.

Ordinary and preference shares

At this stage it is worth noting that companies issue different classes of shares. Shareholders differ. Some regard security as the most important feature of any investment they make. Others do not mind risk if a high dividend is paid.

Ordinary shares (called the Equity of the company) carry most of the risks. Their normal voting rights are one vote per share. The other main class of shares issued by companies are called *preference shares*. If they have a vote it can be as low as one vote per one hundred shares held.

Dividends

Ordinary shares earn a dividend only after the preference shares have been allocated their fixed rate. In effect, they control the company. In poor years they get nothing. In prosperous times they fare much better than the preference shares. As their name implies, preference shares have preference (i.e. they come before) other shares when dividends are to be paid. Similarly, if a company is wound up (i.e. ended) they have preference when capital comes to be repaid. Preference shares have a fixed rate of dividend expressed as a percentage and usually no voting rights.

An illustration of the payment of dividends from profits can now be examined. We can see that, after preference dividends have been paid, then the whole of the remainder of the profits available for dividends will go to the Ordinary shares.

If a company had 10000 five per cent preference shares of £1 each and 20000 ordinary shares of £1 each, then the following dividends would be payable:

Years	1	2	3	4	5
	£	£	£	£	£
Profits appropriated for dividends	900	1300	1600	3100	2000
Preference dividends (5%)	500	500	500	500	500
Ordinary dividends	400	800	1100	2600	1500
	(2%)	(4%)	(5½%)	(13%)	(7½%)

You may well ask what happens when there are just enough profits to cover the preference dividend but there is nothing left after that. The answer simply is that the ordinary shareholder will get no dividend at all.

There are two main types of preference share, these being *non-cumulative preference shares* and *cumulative preference shares*. A non-cumulative preference share is one which is entitled to a yearly percentage rate of dividend. Should the available profits be insufficient to cover the percentage dividend then the deficiency cannot be made good out of future years' profits. On the other hand, any deficiency on the part of cumulative preference shares can be carried forward as arrears, and such arrears are payable before the ordinary shares receive anything.

Illustrations of the two types of shares should make this clearer.

Illustration 1 A company has 5000 £1 ordinary shares and 2000 five per cent non-cumulative preference shares of £1 each. The profits available for dividends are: Year 1 £150; Year 2 £80, Year 3 £250; Year 4 £60; Year 5 £500.

Year	1	2	3	4	5
	£	£	£	£	£
Profits	150	80	250	60	500
Preference dividends					
(limited in years 2 and 4)	100	80	100	60	100
Dividends on ordinary shares	50	–	150	–	400

Illustration 2 Assume that the above preference shares had been cumulative, the dividends would have been:

Year	1	2	3	4	5
	£	£	£	£	£
Profits	150	80	250	60	500
Preference dividends	100	80	120*	60	140*
Dividends on ordinary shares	50	–	130	–	360

*including arrears. See page 58.

Another feature of a company (and in which it differs from a sole trader or partnership) is that, in law, it has a life of its own. This life continues irrespective of how many of its original shareholders are still alive. Obviously in long established companies the first shareholders are all dead. This separate legal existence means that a shareholder may sue the company, even though he or she is one of its owners.

1 Public Companies must include the letters 'plc' as the last part of the firm's name. All documents which the company issues (e.g. letterheads, invoices, receipts, etc.) must bear its name-ending with 'plc'. All its premises must similarly show the firm's name, again ending with 'plc'. The purpose of this is so that anybody who deals with the company knows that the liability of the owners is limited.

2 Private Companies must include the word 'Limited' as the last word of the firm's name. The rules stated above relating to premises and documents apply also to private companies – but the last word of the name in such cases must be 'Ltd'.

Directors

Shareholders are the owners of the company. In large public companies there are too many of them for all to help in running the company. Directors are therefore elected by the shareholders.

The directors deal with management and day-to-day matters. Unless something very important or unusual occurs (e.g. the company suffers serious losses), the shareholders' opportunities for questioning or criticizing the directors are limited to the Annual General Meeting. Every member is entitled to receive a notice (i.e. to be informed) as to when and where general meetings of the company are to be held. At each AGM the directors report to the shareholders on the state of the company and their conduct of its affairs. This report is accompanied by a set of financial accounts for the year.

The Registrar of Companies

Every year, the company must send to the Registrar of Companies:
1 An Annual Return, which among other things contains information about the company's capital.
2 Copies of the profit and loss account and balance sheet.
3 The directors' report.
4 The auditors' report. (The function of the auditors is to examine the books of account. They then report to the shareholders on the correctness or otherwise of these accounts.)

Exercises

1 'Shareholders in a company suffer none of the disadvantages facing a sole trader'. State the reasons why you agree and/or disagree with this statement.
2 (a) If you are the holder of 500 fully paid £1 shares in a company and it gets into financial difficulties, can the company ask you to pay anything further on your shares?
 (b) If your shares are 75p paid, what can the company then ask you to pay?
3 Why must the name of a company always end with 'plc' or 'Ltd'?
4 What documents must a company send to the Registrar of Companies every year?
5 A company has 10 000 £1 ordinary shares and 4000 six per cent cumulative preference shares of £1 each. The profits available for dividends are:

Year 1 £350; Year 2 £500; Year 3 £200; Year 4 £400; Year 5 £500.

Draw up a table (as on page 59) showing the dividends paid in each of the five years to the ordinary and preference shareholders.

6 A company has 20 000 non-cumulative five per cent preference shares of £1 each and 50 000 £1 ordinary shares. The profits available for dividends are:

Year 1 £4000; Year 2 £8000; Year 3 £6000; Year 4 £900; Year 5 £1750.

Draw up a table (as on page 58) showing the dividends paid in each of the five years to the preference and ordinary shareholders.

Forming a company

The oldest method is by obtaining a royal charter. Hudsons' Bay Company (incorporated in 1670) is the oldest surviving chartered company. The BBC (1927) is one of the most recent examples. Formation by Act of Parliament was widely used in the eighteenth and nineteenth centuries in establishing railway and canal companies. It is still available.

The Joint Stock or Registered Company is most often found where trading and commercial operations are involved. This is the kind of company with which we are concerned.

Before such a company comes into being a number of arrangements must be made. These will include the obtaining of assets such as buildings, offices, machinery and land. In addition, the proposed directors have to sign their consent to act as directors.

When a public company is being created, with its invitation to the public to buy shares, it must provide certain information. This includes the history, profit record and other details of any business which is being acquired and converted to a public company. Usually this is a private company.

The names of the directors, auditors and solicitors of the new company must also be given, as well as a statement of the sum of money needed to cover initial expenses and provide enough cash with which to run the business. All this information is contained in the prospectus.

The aim of this document is to help anybody who is thinking of buying shares in the company to form a sound judgment as to the company's likely prospects. Where untrue statements are published in a prospectus, legal remedies (including damages) are available to anyone who has been persuaded to buy shares on the faith of such statements.

After all these preliminary arrangements have been made, certain documents and fees must be forwarded to the Registrar of Companies. The most important of these are the Memorandum of Association and the Articles of Association.

The Memorandum of Association

The Memorandum is the means by which the company, as it were, 'presents itself' to the outside world. It governs its dealings with other firms and individuals. In the case of a public limited company it must include:

1 The name of the company which must include the words public limited company usually abbreviated to 'plc'.

2 The objects of the company. These state the types of business in which the company is allowed to engage. If the company does something it has not been given powers to do, then it has acted 'Ultra Vires' (This Latin phrase means 'beyond the powers of'). Thus if it makes an Ultra Vires contract, such a contract cannot be enforced. However, since Parliament passed an Act in 1972, this ruling does not apply to anyone who has acted in good faith and was, at the time, ignorant of the limitations of the objects clause. In this respect contrast the company with a private individual who can do anything provided it is legal.

3 The address of the registered office of the company.

4 A statement that the liability of the shareholders is limited.

5 A statement that the company is to be a public company.

6 The amount of capital the company wants to have power to raise. This is known as the Nominal or Authorised Capital and must be at least £50 000.

7 The number of shares each of the promoters has agreed to buy.

8 A statement by the two people who have signed the Memorandum that they wish to be formed into a public company.

The Articles of Association

These regulate the internal affairs of the company. They cover a wide range of topics including the arrangements for the various meetings of shareholders; the appointment, powers and duties of the directors; the voting rights of each class of shares, and the appointment of auditors. Those who have signed the Memorandum must also sign the Articles.

When the Registrar is satisfied that all the documents are in order, a Certificate of Incorporation will be issued. From that time the company has come into existence and has a legal life of its own. A private company may then start business immediately. A public company, however, has to meet other requirements, and be issued with a Trading Certificate before it can start business.

Many of the provisions of the Companies Act 1985 are framed to ensure the maximum degree of disclosure by the directors of information calculated to keep the members acquainted with the affairs of the company.

Assignments

1 Draft a table showing:

(a) Vertically (i.e. down the side of the page) – the types of business organisation you have studied so far (i.e. sole trader, partnership, private company and public company).

(b) Horizontally (i.e. across the top of the page) – source of capital; methods of control; liability of owners; number of members; how profits are shared and losses borne.

Complete all the 'boxes' appearing in your table. For example, in the 'Sole trader/sources of capital' box you will write – 'own savings plus anything borrowed'.

The first part of the table is shown below. Leave plenty of space for your answers.

Type of business organisation	Sources of capital	Methods of control
Sole trader	Own savings plus anything borrowed.	
Partnership		

2 Examine any firm in your area in the private sector (your own if employed or on a training scheme) and try to find out:

(a) Who owns the business;

(b) When did it first start in business;

(c) How many people are employed;

(d) If the staff have any trade union representation;

(e) If you are in a job or a trainee, list a description of the work you do at present. Show by means of a chart your position in your own office (if you are at college on a full-time course ask a member of staff if they would assist you to answer this question by using their position in a department of the college as an example).

Note: The figures used in the illustrations on page 58 and in the Exercise on page 60, have been kept 'low' for ease of understanding. Usually, a company's capital and dividends are considerably greater than those shown.

5 TYPES OF ORGANISATION – THE PUBLIC SECTOR (II)

Objectives

At the end of this chapter you should be able to:

- Give at least four examples of how public sector activities affect the lives of ordinary citizens.
- Identify the different types of organisations found in the public sector.
- Summarise the main features of central government, public corporations, regional authorities and local government.
- Explain the principal functions of the elected and permanent elements found in public sector organisations.
- Outline at least three arguments in favour of public sector activities.
- Explain the term 'privatisation'. Outline three arguments in its favour and three arguments against it.
- State the objectives of the EEC and the main functions of the Council of Ministers, the Commission, the European Parliament and the European Court of Justice.

Every day, often on many occasions, most of us come into some kind of contact with the activities of organisations in the public sector. Here are some examples:

1 Making our homes comfortable (electricity, gas, water, and waste disposal) and safeguarding them and their inhabitants (fire, police).

2 The transport of people and goods (roads, railways, harbours, bus and freight transport and air services).

3 Guarding us against illness (National Health Service, control of pollution).

4 Helping employers and workers (grants to industry, Job Centres, vocational training, ACAS).

The list is almost endless. Write in your workbook as many other examples as you can discover or already know.

Public sector organisations are in one of these three groups:

1 Central government.
2 Public corporations and regional authorities.
3 Local government.

Central government

The United Kingdom is governed by the Queen in Parliament, i.e. a constitutional monarch, (who is also Head of the Armed Forces and of the judicial system), the House of Commons and the House of Lords.

A parliamentary constituency is an area which elects a Member of Parliament (MP) to the House of Commons. There is a total of 650 constituencies in England, Wales, Scotland and Northern Ireland.

To have a vote in a parliamentary or general election, you must be 18 years of age. Peers cannot vote in a general election – but they do have a vote at a local election. Certain people do not qualify for a vote. (*See* page 69).

To stand as a candidate at a general election, you must be 21 years of age or more and be a British subject. Unlike local government you do not need to live in the area for which you are standing. You cannot stand for election if:

1 You hold an 'office or place of profit' under the Crown, i.e. a judge, a member of the police, or armed forces, or a civil servant, when you stand for election.
2 You are a clergyman of the Church of England, or of Scotland or of Rome.
3 You are a peer or a lunatic.

The House of Lords, with over 1100 members is not elected. The great majority are hereditary (i.e. their seats have been 'handed down' to them). There are 337 Life Peers and Peeresses (whose seats do not pass to the next generation); nine Law Lords (i.e. Lords of Appeal in Ordinary – the most senior judges in the land) and two Archbishops and 24 Bishops of the Church of England. The powers of the Lords have been curtailed in this century. The majority party in the Commons provides the Prime Minister and Cabinet. Government departments, controlling and operating a range of services are headed by Ministers of the Crown. Senior Ministers are members of the Cabinet. Ministers are accountable to Parliament (often through debates and questions from MPs) for the activities of the departments for which they are responsible. Certain people believe that in reality, power lies to a considerable extent with the civil servants who staff and 'run' the various departments.

The main government departments and their principal functions are

Department	Has responsibility for
Ministry of Agriculture, Fisheries and Food	Food supplies, agricultural policy, relations with EEC.
Ministry of Defence	Defence policy, HM Forces.
Department of Education and Science	Schools, colleges, teacher training, libraries, the arts.
Department of Employment	Industrial relations, pay, measures to deal with unemployment and redundancy.
Department of Energy	Oil, coal, gas, electricity, nuclear energy.
Department of the Environment	Local government, roads, pollution, planning and land use.
Foreign and Commonwealth Office	UK's relationships with other countries.
Department of Health & Social Security	National Health Service, Social Security, pensions, Social Services run by local authorities.
Home Office	Law and order, police, prisons, fire, race relations, firearms, immigration.
Northern Ireland Office	Responsible for government administration in the province.
Scottish and Welsh Offices	Scottish and Welsh affairs.
Department of Trade and Industry	International trade policy, promotion of UK exports, assistance to industry, regional and small firms policies, consumer protection, company legislation, Business Statistics Office.
The Treasury	The financing of government activities, powerful role in the control of the economy and the preparation of the Budget.
Department of Transport	Land, sea and air transport, HM Coastguard, Vehicle Registration, driver licensing, construction and maintenance of motorways and trunk roads.

listed opposite. They are listed alphabetically and not in order of influence. Indeed, at the bottom of the list is the highly important Treasury which is involved with all departments through its control of spending. During the last half century the Treasury's role in the control and operation of the economy has also grown in importance.

Public corporations and regional authorities

Public corporations and regional authorities represent a sort of 'half way' house between central and local government. This group is concerned with services run neither by government departments nor by local councils. Much attention has been paid to the public corporation form of organisation since concerns supplying coal, gas, electricity, and rail facilities were nationalised (i.e. taken into public ownership and control) after 1945. But public corporations have existed for over 100 years, e.g. the Mersey Docks and Harbour board (1858), the Port of London Authority (1908) and the BBC (1927) are among earlier examples. The British postal service was operated by a government office, under a Postmaster General, from 1657 to 1969, when it became an independent corporation. It is now solely responsible for postal services and the National Girobank.

The main features of public corporations are:

1 Established by Act of Parliament.

2 The Minister responsible for the industry appoints the chairperson and board members of each corporation. They are not elected by the people (as, for instance, are MPs and local councillors).

3 In theory, each board has responsibility for day to day operations in its own field. How far, in fact, the influence of the appropriate Minister extends, is a controversial aspect of public corporation operation.

4 Through the Minister, Parliament is presented by each corporation with an annual report and financial statement.

5 A considerable measure of control and influence over these bodies exists through an annual House of Commons debate, Ministerial influence, Select Committees, parliamentary questions, Consumers' Councils and public opinion. You may care to contrast this with the control over a public limited company, largely exercised by shareholders' meetings (usually held annually) and the various government controls (e.g. regulations governing working conditions of employees).

A number of important services (e.g. water, sewerage and health) are now provided by regional authorities. These bodies, both in the areas they cover and the ways they are controlled, lie half-way between local authorities and government departments which provide national services (e.g. Social Security).

There are nine Regional Water Authorities (RWAs) for England and one for Wales. They do many vital jobs. Water services although often taken for granted, are vital to life and health. Each RWA has the duty of supplying water within its area. It also has to conserve (i.e. protect from loss), redistribute, and add to water supplies as well as ensuring that water, which must be of adequate quality, is properly used. The RWAs also deal with sewerage and sewage disposal; prevent river pollution, attend to land drainage and the use of water for recreational purposes.

To meet their running costs, RWAs makes charges for the services they provide to their consumers. The RWAs collect all their charges directly from the consumers.

Under the Water Act, 1983, the Water Authorities Association was set up by the RWAs. This Association enables the RWAs to discuss among themselves and with the Government and other bodies, matters of common concern. The WAA also co-ordinates any necessary joint action by the RWAs and provides press and public relations services.

The Secretary of State for the Environment has the main responsibility to Parliament for promoting a national water policy. The Minister for Agriculture, Fisheries and Food is responsible, however, for land drainage and fisheries in inland and coastal waters.

The members of the RWAs are appointed. They are not elected.

The important role played by water companies must not be overlooked. There are 31 of them and they supply water to one quarter of the population of England and Wales (i.e. approximately 12 million people).

Assignment

In your local public or college library find out as much as possible about the National Health Service. Try and draw a diagram showing how the National Health Service is organised.

Local government

The structure of local government in England and Wales was fundamentally altered in April 1986. The government abolished the GLC (Greater London Council) and six Metropolitan County Councils. The network of local authorities is now as shown in Fig. 5.1.

With the abolition of the GLC and Metropolitan County Councils from April 1986, certain responsibilities have been taken over by the local Metropolitan Councils, e.g. Consumer Protection. Where services affect several councils, i.e. Police, Fire Service, Civil Defence, Transport, etc., joint authorities have been set up. In London there is an Inner London Education Authority. Residuary bodies have been set up to provide for the

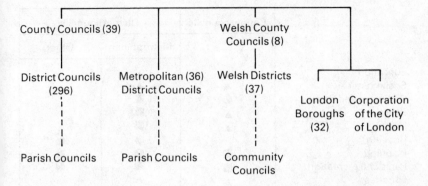

Fig. 5.1 The present structure of local government in England and Wales.

committed rights and liabilities of the GLC and Metropolitan County Councils.

The councils are elected. All persons over 18 years of age are entitled to a vote in local elections, provided they are:

(a) British subjects;

(b) Their names appear on the current register of electors. The register of electors is updated regularly by householders etc. completing a register of persons living at that address and returning it to the local election officer.

Certain individuals are not entitled to a vote in either local government or parliamentary elections, e.g. aliens, prisoners with sentences of more than one year, persons found guilty of corrupt election practices (e.g. bribing an elector). Electors vote in person or by post (e.g. the housebound, hospital patients, people working away) or by proxy, (members of the HM Forces, civilians working at sea or abroad). Voting by proxy means that you appoint somebody to vote for you.

It is anticipated that arrangements will soon be made for people who are absent on holiday at the time of an election, to have a vote.

Local councils usually have monthly meetings. Each councillor usually serves on two or three committees. Committee organisation differs to some extent from one authority to another. But the general pattern is that committees exist to deal either with matters concerned with a particular service (e.g. education) or groups of services (e.g. recreation and amenities) or are concerned with a function (e.g. finance or personnel) which affects all aspects of the activities of a local authority. A degree of specialisation is thus achieved.

The services provided by local councils are administered by the different types of local authorities as shown in Fig. 5.2.

	County councils	District councils	
		Metropolitan	Other
Education	▲	▲	
Social services	▲	▲	
Highways and transport	●	■	
Police	▲	■	
Fire	▲	■	
Housing		●	●
Planning	■	■	■
Parks and recreation	■	■	■
Libraries	▲	▲	
Environmental health		▲	▲
Refuse collection		▲	▲
Refuse disposal	▲	■	

▲ Sole responsibility ● Major responsibility
■ Shared responsibility with more than one local authority

Fig. 5.2 The functions of local authorities in England and Wales

Exercises

1 The Department of the Environment is responsible for ....?
2 Why is the Treasury so important?
3 Name three of the means of controlling and influencing public corporations.
4 Draw an outline map of your home town. (If you live in a large city do a map of the city centre/business area *and* of the area where you live). On it mark the situation of the various organisations controlled by your local Education Committee.

Central control over local councils operates in several ways. For example:
1 By legislation– local authorities have no powers other than those given to them by Parliament. Any act of a local authority which goes beyond these powers is Ultra Vires. Those responsible (i.e. councillors and officials) can be surcharged, i.e. made to pay back money illegally paid.

An Act of Parliament can compel local authorities to provide a service or give them powers to provide a service.

A local or private bill can be promoted by a local authority. This is to give it powers on its own. If Parliament disagrees with a local bill, it can reject it.

2 Inspection, e.g. for fire, police and education.

3 Grants given to encourage a local authority to spend money in a particular direction (e.g. police, coastal protection).
4 Advises councils of their capital allocations (*see* page 260).
5 'Rate capping' (*see* page 260).

Local government

Local government, like central government, has two main elements. In central government the elected element is the MPs who sit in the House of Commons. From their ranks come the Prime Minister, most of the Cabinet and Ministers not in the Cabinet. They are served by the second element – a permanent body of officials, i.e. the civil servants. Their job is to advise the Prime Minister, Cabinet and other Ministers. They see the policy of the government is carried out.

In local government the councillors are the elected element. The majority party in a local council nowadays often take all the leading positions – the chairmanships of the most important committees. Something like a cabinet system also operates in most authorities. This is often known as the Management Board. The local government service does roughly the same type of job as the civil service. It advises the elected councillors, carries out their policy decisions, and 'runs' the authority's services.

Contrast this set-up with that operating in public corporations and regional authorities where there is a *selected* element plus a body of full-time, permanent officials.

Remember too that elections are for ever changing the composition of the elected element. The permanent element carries on, irrespective of who has won a parliamentary or a local council election.

Why do we have a public sector at all? Some people believe that private enterprise could cater for all our needs. Other disagree. They believe that many facilities and benefits people now have, they would never have enjoyed if it had been left to the private sector. How many people could have provided their own education or swimming pool or have been able to buy all the books they now borrow from the public library? Would private enterprise have found it profitable to have supplied them on other than a limited scale?

Again, competition can be wasteful. Why have several different organisations digging up the same street to provide gas for those who live there? Because many public sector services are provided by monopolies (*mono* = one) some measure of control over them is needed. Many think this is best done through control via an elected element. If these people fail to do the job for which they were elected, they can easily be voted out at the next election.

Another argument for having a public sector is that some services *must* be provided, irrespective of their cost. Defence and law and order are examples which are often quoted to support this opinion. Some people believe certain facilities, because they meet an urgent need, should be provided even if at a loss, e.g. rural bus services. The government has recognised the importance of certain railway services by subsidising them.

Some people believe certain industries needed nationalising because their labour relations were poor (e.g. coal).

Arguments will continue to take place on this whole issue of public *v.* private sector. It is still, in many ways, a matter of opinion.

Assignments

1 Find out which and what type of local authority provides the following services in your area:
  (a) Refuse collection
  (b) Transport services (bus services)
  (c) Social services
  (d) Education
  (e) Police and Fire Service
2 Study your local newspaper for the past three weeks. What matters concerning your local council (including any decisions the council and its committees made) do you find mentioned there? Make a list of them showing very briefly what each item was about. Write a note of your opinion of any one of them.

Privatisation

'Privatisation' is a word you hear often and may hear more of in the future. It is a major part of Conservative government policy. The aims of privatisation are:
1 The transfer to private ownership of publicly owned assets, e.g. the sale to the public of Amersham International and of 51% of the shares in each of British Aerospace and Britoil.
2 The promotion of competition. Thus, the Telecommunications Act, 1981, permitted the connection of approved equipment (e.g. privately purchased telephones) to the British Telecom network. Other examples are the deregulation of express coach services and the provision of spectacles other than through registered opticians.
3 Encouraging the provision by private organisations and individuals of services at present provided by the public sector. Examples here include refuse collection, the cleaning of government offices, hospital laundries and catering.

Advantages

The arguments for privatisation include:

1 Where there are private shareholders there are likely to be stronger efforts made to cut costs, thus leading to greater efficiency.

2 One of the best known examples of privatisation has been the sale to their occupiers of council-owned houses. It is argued that this will lead to such properties being better maintained. Also the money received from the sales can be used to reduce public expenditure elsewhere or to cut taxes.

3 It gives consumers more choice, e.g. substituting private insurance provision for care under the National Health Service and the suggested voucher system in education. The owner occupier of the former council-owned house will have freedom from local authority restrictions, such as rules about the keeping of pets.

4 Privatisation means the removal of the not so efficient organisations. This is because competition will mean that services which used to be kept going by subsidies from the taxpayer, will now have to achieve commercial success – or depart.

5 Management and employees are more likely to regard the government as a 'soft touch' (i.e. to help the enterprise if it runs into difficulties) than a bank.

6 All governments have tended to interfere too much in the running of nationalised industries. Such interference was often neither desirable nor necessary.

Disadvantages

The arguments against privatisation include:

1 Cost cutting does not always mean greater efficiency. It can mean that an organisation is starved of funds, thus halting its development and successful operation.

2 In the case of public sector organisations, unprofitable activities which nevertheless may be very desirable socially (e.g. rural bus services), can be subsidised by profitable sections of the organisation. If privatisation operates, the private sector will 'cream off' the profitable activities – leaving the public sector and the taxpayer – to foot the bill for the unprofitable parts.

3 Many council-occupied houses are very well maintained because of the occupants' pride in their own homes. Examples of poor external maintenance, it is argued, are due to the cutbacks in funds provided by central government to the local authorities.

4 Privatisation will mean the duplication of services and the reintroduction of wasteful competition.

5 Valuable assets, bought over the years by public funds, have been sold off too cheaply to private investors. Furthermore, the benefits from public operation, which would otherwise go back to the public, will now be enjoyed by a relatively small number of people – the investors.

6 In certain instances, it is not evident that private sector organisations are providing an equally efficient (let alone better) service than was formerly provided.

The EEC

Membership of the EEC has had considerable consequences for the UK. Indeed, quite a number of people still think that we should never have joined and that it would be to our advantage to withdraw now.

The Community was created in 1958 by the Treaty of Rome. The six original members were Belgium, France, Germany, Italy, Luxembourg and the Netherlands. Britain was reluctant to join at that time, mainly because of the special ties with the Commonwealth. Any European nation can apply to join.

Britain, the Irish Republic and Denmark joined on 1 January, 1973. A referendum in Britain in June 1975, as to whether or not Britain should remain a member, showed two to one in favour of staying in. Greece joined in 1981, and Spain and Portugal joined in January 1986.

Objectives

The objectives of the EEC are numerous. The most important of them include the following:

1 The abolition between member states of obstacles to the free movement of capital, services and workers.

2 The establishment of common policies for agriculture and transport.

3 Ensuring that trade in the EEC is not harmed by monopolies and cartels (price rings).

4 Removing barriers to trade between EEC members.

To achieve all these objectives the European Community had to establish the means for making rules and regulations, issuing directives, making recommendations, giving opinions and taking decisions.

Fig. 5.3 shows the machinery which has been established to try and achieve these objectives.

The Council of Ministers

1 Each member state selects one of its Ministers to represent its national government on the Council of Ministers.

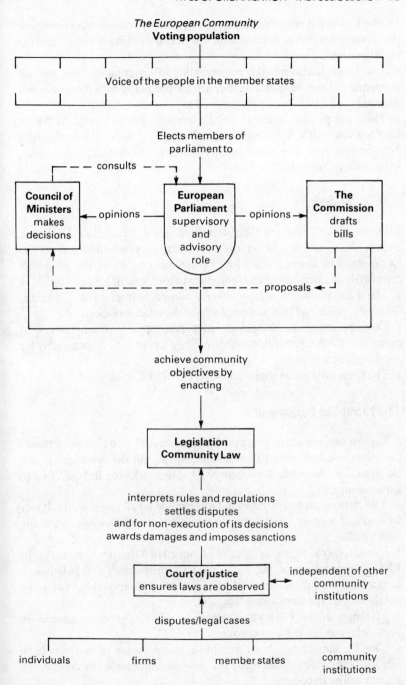

The European Community
Voting population

Voice of the people in the member states

Elects members of
parliament to

consults

| **Council of Ministers** makes decisions | opinions | **European Parliament** supervisory and advisory role | opinions | **The Commission** drafts bills |

proposals

achieve community
objectives by
enacting

Legislation Community Law

interprets rules and regulations
settles disputes
and for non-execution of its decisions
awards damages and imposes sanctions

| **Court of justice** ensures laws are observed | independent of other community institutions |

disputes/legal cases

individuals   firms   member states   community institutions

Fig. 5.3

2 The Council is responsible for making major decisions in carrying out the Treaty. But, it has to consult the European Parliament before making such decisions.

3 The Council also has the responsibility of ensuring that the general economic policies of each member are co-ordinated with those of other members.

4 There are 76 votes in the Council; Germany, France, Italy and Britain have ten votes each, Spain eight votes, Portugal, Greece, Belgium and the Netherlands have five votes each, Denmark and Ireland, three votes, Luxembourg, two votes.

The Commission

1 Drafts bills. These are then submitted to the Council of Ministers. Before the Council acts on the proposals, they submit them to the European Parliament for advice. Parliament can reject the proposals completely or amend them and send them to the Council for decision.

2 The Commission has 17 members, two each from Britain, France, Germany, Spain and Italy and one each for the other members.

3 Commissioners are pledged to independence of governments and of national and other particular interests. They accept joint responsibility for any decisions they make.

4 The Commission has considerable power in EEC affairs.

The European Parliament

1 Represents over 320 million people. There are 518 seats. Britain, France, Germany and Italy have 81 seats each; Spain, 60; the Netherlands, 25; Belgium, 24; Portugal, 24; Greece, 24; Denmark, 16; Ireland, 15 and Luxembourg, 6.

2 The Parliament has the right to be consulted on all major issues. It can, by a vote of censure dismiss the Commission, though this has not, so far, happened.

3 Its main task is that of advising the Council of Ministers (who make the EEC decisions) about the Commission's proposals for legislation. It questions the Commission and the Council of Ministers and has a measure of control over the Community's budget.

4 Members of the European Parliament (MEP's) serve on specialised committees and sit in political groups.

5 The Parliament has been described as the 'voice of the people of Europe'. The more it can bring the flow of funds unde·· its control, the greater will be its powers.

The European Court of Justice has ten judges – one appointed by each member state. Although it is independent, the Court is required to see that the aims of the EEC are achieved. The law of the Community is binding in the UK and has to be enforced, allowed and followed. This is an important development and raises the question of the power of our own Parliament to make laws and to have them enforced.

Summary

Our membership of the EEC has, so far, not been an unqualified success. In part, the unpopularity of the Community with many people in Britain is because it is largely blamed for the high level of unemployment. This is rather unfair, and it is largely untrue. The recession has been world wide and there are now over 12 million unemployed people in EEC countries.

It is possibly the size of the British contribution to the EEC which is the biggest bone of contention, for we are the biggest net contributor to EEC funds although we are not, by any means, the most economically prosperous member of the Community. The UK gets back less than 50 per cent of its contribution to the EEC. (70 per cent for Germany, 90 per cent for France.) All the other member countries get back more than they put in. The reason for this is that the other members of the EEC are large agricultural producers and get a large share of the EEC budget. 70 per cent of the total EEC budget is geared to the EEC's CAP (Common Agricultural Policy). This country has a relatively small agricultural sector.

Exercises

1 Why are you likely to hear more of privatisation in the future?
2 Give an example of how, so it is claimed, privatisation promotes competition.
3 State two arguments (with examples) against privatisation.
4 Name any two objectives of the EEC you care to select.
5 What functions are performed by the EEC's Council of Ministers?
6 Why are a considerable number of British people opposed to British membership of the EEC?

Assignments

1 What are the terms on which your local authority is willing to sell its own council houses to tenants?
2 What expenses will a person who buys a council house have to meet which he did not face before?
3 What advantages will he (and his successors) ultimately enjoy when he has finally finished paying for the house?
4 Investigate and list the services provided by your local authority to business organisations.

6 OTHER TYPES OF ORGANISATIONS

Objectives

At the end of this chapter you should be able to:

- Name five examples of organisations which belong neither to the public nor to the private sector.
- Explain briefly the functions of the examples you have chosen.
- In addition, explain briefly the functions of co-operative and building societies and of insurance companies.

In trying to understand the different organisations that now exist, we classify them (or 'put' them into groups) according to their interests and methods of working.

This chapter aims to tell you something of the very large number of organisations which do not 'fit' into either the public or private sector. In turn it would be nice, and convenient, if all these 'other' organisations fitted neatly into the third group – but they do not.

Some of them provide goods and/or services, e.g. co-operative and building societies and insurance companies. We can call these 'trading' organisations. Roughly they serve the same purpose as does a sole trader selling sweets and tobacco, a limited company making car components or an area electricity board selling electricity and appliances. They satisfy customers' wants.

Another group represent employers and workers. These aim to look after the interests of their members in the working situation, e.g. the Confederation of British Industry (CBI) – for employers, and its counterpart, the Trades Union Congress (TUC). The TUC is an amalgamation of individual trade unions such as the Transport and General Workers (TGWU), National Union of Mineworkers (NUM) and the National and Local Government Officers Association (NALGO). The TUC deals with matters which affect all their member unions including negotiations with the government.

Yet another set of organisations aim to protect the interests and professional standards of their members. Usually they hold examinations. Those with sufficient experience who have passed the examinations are admitted to membership. Members are entitled to use a distinctive set of letters behind their names (e.g. Association of Certified Chartered Accountants – ACCA). There are some 20 closely printed pages in Whitaker's Almanack listing the names and addresses of such organisations.

There are also groups which look after the interests of particular sets of people, e.g. Automobile Association (AA) and Royal Automobile Club (RAC) – for motorists.

Chambers of Commerce include manufacturers, distributors and professional men. They aim to help and protect the trading interests of their members. Chambers of Trade are similar to Chambers of Commerce but they cater especially for retail traders. Both Chambers have national bodies which co-ordinate the activities of the local branches. These national bodies are often in contact with government departments, e.g. when new legislation which is to pass through Parliament is being considered.

Most major industries have their own industrial research associations. They are usually registered as limited companies. Membership is open to any British firm in the particular industry. There are over 40 such associations and they are concerned with industries as far apart as food manufacture and leather.

There is a large number of organisations which can be classified as 'cause' groups. They represent people who hold similar opinions on some particular matter. They work together to achieve their aims, e.g. the Royal Society for the Prevention of Cruelty to Animals, Council for the Protection of Rural England, and Shelter (for the problems of the homeless).

Most towns and villages contain organisations catering for the leisure and personal interests of their members. They include clubs and societies of all sorts, ranging from dramatic societies to football, tennis, golf, badminton, bridge, squash, judo and swimming clubs (and many others!).

Other interests catered for include philately (stamp collecting), train and aircraft 'spotting', painting and drawing, model engineering, and gardening. In addition, there is a vast range of clubs where members can meet, talk, eat, drink and perhaps be entertained together. Often a sporting activity is their main aim (e.g. tennis, golf). Others however, exist purely as a meeting place for members, e.g. the network of Working Men's clubs which is found particularly in the North of England. Usually, these organisations rely on their members' subscriptions. Because these may be inadequate for their needs, they often organise social events. Invariably they have an elected committee with a chairman, secretary and treasurer. These officials, most of whom are unpaid, have responsibility for the club or association's affairs.

We shall now examine in some detail the most important of this 'third' group of organisations, which are neither public nor private.

Co-operative societies

They differ from the organisations already examined in various ways:

1 Retail co-operative societies are owned by and run for the benefit of their customers.

2 A member can attend general meetings of his society. The rule is 'one member – one vote'. Contrast this with a limited company where a shareholder's votes normally vary with the number of shares he holds (i.e. if his shares have voting rights at all).

3 A retail co-operative society is managed by a committee elected from and by its members. Some of these may be employees. Critics say that this principle does not lead to maximum efficiency. Some of the members have had no experience of managing a business before. The same criticism is also sometimes made about the members of other organisations.

4 Co-operative societies are responsible to the Registrar of Friendly Societies and not to the Registrar of Companies. This indicates the 'self-help' as opposed to the 'profit making' nature of a co-operative society.

5 Co-operative shares carry a fixed rate of interest. A member's holding is limited to £5000. It may be as low as £1. These shares are not sold or quoted on the Stock Exchange. If members want they can be repaid their share capital on demand. Note that it has now been made easier for a limited company to buy back its own shares from its shareholders.

6 Less than half a century ago co-operative 'divi' was many people's main source of saving. In the 1930s some societies paid dividends as high as 35p in the £1. Today blue trading stamps are used. Kept in books, they can be exchanged for cash, or as part payment for goods, or left in the society and earn interest.

7 Most co-operative societies have a department which provides educational and travel facilities.

8 Societies buy most of their requirements through the Co-operative Wholesale Society (formed in 1863). In effect this is an organisation with retail societies as members. The CWS engages in a number of manufacturing activities (e.g. margarine) and owns its own tea plantations, farms, and factories. The societies in turn, receive dividends on purchases from the CWS.

In order to amalgamate some of the societies and to save them from bankruptcy, the CWS and the societies formed Co-operative Retail Services Ltd. The CRS 'covers' the areas once served by some 150 societies.

9 The Co-operative Union, a national body like the CWS and the CRS, is financed by payments from societies based on the size of their membership. The Co-operative Union provides valuable advisory services to local societies on legal, labour relations, financial and educational matters.

10 Associated with the co-operative movement are organisations providing banking, insurance, building society, printing and publishing services. At Loughborough there is the Co-operative College which provides courses for employees and members.

Worker co-operatives

The worker co-operative movement in Britain is still, in terms of numbers, relatively small – but it is growing. Sizes range from two or three employees to as many as 500. The total turnover is about £200 million, spread among 700 enterprises and with a total exceeding 5500 employees.

This type of co-operative is usually established by employees of an organisation which has gone out of business. The workers take over the enterprise, and usually operate it on a limited scale. Often they put their redundancy money, and in many cases their personal savings, too, into the business. Sometimes they receive financial help from the Government funded Co-Operative Development Agency. Unicorn 1 (Taunton shirt production) and Unicorn 2 (Minehead shoes) were launched with the backing of the Transport and General Workers' Union. Some housing co-operatives have received funds from local authorities.

Directors are elected by the employee members of the co-operative. Meetings, which all employees are entitled to attend, are held, usually to discuss progress and problems.

Public attention in this country has tended to focus on high risk rescue co-operatives such as Meriden (motor bikes) and the Scottish Daily News – which collapsed. But, worker co-operatives are on the increase and their failure rates compare favourably with the collapse of small private businesses. One striking feature of the new, younger worker co-operatives is the move from traditional craft based activities into the new industries and services, particularly those with relatively advanced technology.

The first ever international Worker Co-Operative Trade Fair was held in London during February, 1984. One hundred co-operatives participated. They were from Great Britain, France, Ireland and Spain. This type of enterprise has recently received endorsement from the EEC. It is being supported by the Community in its efforts to reduce unemployment in Europe.

Exercises

1 What do the initials CBI stand for?
2 Where would you look for the name and address of an organisation dealing with the training and education of Works Managers?
3 If your soccer or tennis club is short of money after it has collected all the subscriptions due from members, how would it obtain extra cash?
4 How does a Chamber of Trade differ from a Chamber of Commerce?
5 How does membership of a co-operative society differ from being a shareholder in a limited company?
6 What are the differences between the Co-operative Wholesale Society and the Co-operative Union?

Insurance

Life would be easier if the unexpected and unforeseen never happened. Risks, however, always exist. If we do not guard against them in our personal and business lives, disaster can result. There are two main kinds of risks:

1 Personal risks include accidents of all sorts which can lead to injury or, at the worst, to death. They can occur on the way to and from work, at work, in the home or on holiday. They can happen to anyone, at any age, at any time.

2 In some cases commercial risks can be due to the same happenings as personal risks, e.g. a fire can damage a shop and result in the serious injury or death of employees and customers. Theft, the death of a partner, stock deterioration (e.g. due to rain coming in through a damaged roof) and damage to a plate glass window are all commercial risks.

Fidelity guarantee is concerned with the insurance an organisation may take out to guard against the dishonesty of an employee (e.g. a cashier stealing the firm's funds). The Export Credits Guarantee Department, which is responsible to the Secretary of State for Trade and Industry, insures exporters against the risk that the buyers abroad may not pay and against risks associated with revolution or disturbance. The ECGD is not a profit-making body but it has to cover its costs.

Insurance is based on pooling risks. A group of people pay regular sums (or premiums) into a 'pool'. This pool of money is held by an insurance company. If any of the risks insured against happens, the unfortunate person or organisation receives compensation from the pool. Nobody is allowed to profit from their misfortunes. Assume that a business has insured its stock against damage by fire. A fire breaks out and the stock is completely destroyed. The stock was insured up to a maximum of £100 000 but, when the fire occurred, there was only £80 000 of stock in the building. This means that only £80 000 will be paid to the business by the insurance company. Just because the stock was insured for £100 000 does not mean the business can collect £100 000. Otherwise, the business would be making £20 000 profit from losing its stock. If this were to happen, some unscrupulous individuals would be very busy starting fires!

Insurance, which is a form of contract, depends on the truth being told whenever a proposal form is completed. Assume a contract of insurance has been made and the insurance company has not been told the full facts. Nevertheless, all the premiums have been paid. If the risk insured against happens, and the insurance company in the meantime learns the truth, they will not pay out the sum of money originally agreed. For example, a man has a bad heart. He insures himself for £10 000 against his death occurring in the next five years. He does not tell the insurance company about his heart condition when he takes out the insurance policy. All the premiums are paid on time and he dies three years after the insurance started. Legally his wife (or other dependants) will not be entitled to collect the £10 000 from the insurance company.

There are many organisations associated with insurance. The large companies (e.g. Refuge, Prudential, Commercial Union) collect millions of pounds in premiums. They are amongst the largest of the institutional investors. The 1911 National Insurance Act introduced health insurance for all manual workers and for other workers earning under a certain wage. This Act also provided compulsory unemployment insurance for workers in certain types of occupation, which were particularly subject to the 'ups and downs' of trade. Since then a whole system of compulsory national (or state) insurance has been introduced to safeguard people against loss of income from sickness, old age, unemployment and the like. Many Friendly Societies were formed during the nineteenth century, to provide sickness and death benefits for working people. A number of them are still operating today – despite the existence of the system of national insurance.

Building societies

The building societies are supervised by the Registrar of Friendly Societies (not the Registrar of Companies). Many people save by putting their money in building societies and receiving interest in return. This money is then loaned out to others who use it to buy their own homes. The borrowers, in return, pay interest on their mortgages to the societies.

The rate of interest paid by borrowers is higher than that paid to people who entrust their savings to the building societies. The amount the societies can lend is governed by the funds they receive from depositors (and from time to time by government restrictions). This means their

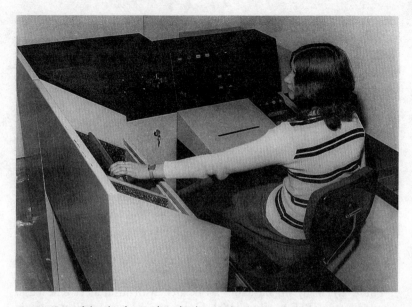

Fig. 6.1 One of the deed consoles, checking a deed wallet out of the system

interest rates have to be competitive, and tend to follow what was known as the Minimum Lending Rate (formerly known as the Bank Rate). The MLR has now been officially abolished as a means of controlling bank lending rates. Nevertheless, it is still, in effect, the rate the government charges for lending via the Bank of England to the discount market. Very few people can afford to buy their houses outright. The building societies thus bring together people with money to lend and those wishing to buy a house by instalments. When a borrower obtains a loan from a building society, the deeds of the house (or other property) are kept by the society (i.e. ownership remains with it) until the loan and interest are fully repaid. (*See* Figs. 6.1 and 6.2.) If repayments are not made, the society can then sell the house. This is rarely done, however.

There are over 400 building societies. Two of the biggest are the Abbey National and the Halifax. There is a national body – the Building Societies Association. Most societies belong to it. The Association insists that its members keep a proportion of their assets in 'liquid' (cash) form. It also recommends the rates of interest societies should pay to lenders and charge to borrowers. Commercial banks are now competing with building societies and vice versa, in many areas; for example, banks are now offering mortgage facilities to home buyers and building societies are offering cash cards and cash dispensing units amongst their services. The dividing line between the two types of institution and their services is becoming less distinct.

Fig. 6.2 A master column in its aisle of racking.
Photographs reproduced by permission of the Halifax Building Society.

Halifax Building Society

Deep underground, nearly 50 feet below the street, in a rock-cut vault, providing one million cubic feet of space, the Conserv-a-trieve installation performs the exacting task of storing the Society's ever-growing number of title deeds and files, so that they are secure, and speedily and conveniently retrieved whenever required.

Fifty-two machines form two separate systems for deeds and files. Each machine consists of an aisle of container filled racking serviced by a mobile master column carrying a selector head. Requests for documents, originating at third floor, are electronically transmitted, and the appropriate column delivers the required container, via conveyors, to the operating room at the centre. Operators at consoles check the documents in and out of the system and despatch them by a further conveyor to the upper office. An electronic memory records the whereabouts of documents until they are returned to the system.

Exercises

1 On what principle is insurance based?
2 Your sports car is a 1964 'banger'. When you insured it last year you told the insurance company that it was only a year old. You have an accident due to the failure of your brakes. Your car is badly damaged. Do you think the insurance company would pay you? If not, why not?
3 What is the principal service provided by building societies?

Assignments

1 *(a)* Make a list of all the clubs and societies you can trace in your town or area. Against each, state briefly the interest(s) it caters for (e.g. social, soccer).

(b) Describe briefly how any organisation of which you are a member (e.g. a Youth Club) is organised and managed. (e.g. How many officials and committee members are there? What business is conducted at the meetings of members?)

2 Compare and contrast the range of goods and services provided by your local co-operative society (or CRS branch) with those provided by any other organisation. A map may be drawn, if you wish, to help illustrate your answer.

7 THE INTERNAL STRUCTURE OF ORGANISATIONS

Objectives

At the end of this chapter you should be able to:

- Describe the structure and explain the functions of an organisation with which you are familiar.
- Produce an organisation chart of an organisation with which you are familiar.
- Describe the structure and explain the functions of an organisation with which you are unfamiliar.
- Give reasons for departmental structures.
- Explain the interrelationship between departments in at least two organisations of your choice.

In Chapter 4 you read about Roy Carroll and his unsuccessful venture into business as a sole trader. Five years later Carroll went into partnership with Brian Jones. They acquired a two shop business and were successful. The story of how Carroll and Jones managed their business and how it developed, continues.

At first, Carroll managed one shop (shop A). Jones managed the other (shop B). This arrangement worked quite well because they split the other jobs between them. Carroll did all the buying of stock and interviewing of representatives. Jones was more interested in keeping the accounts, attending to the correspondence, and making the necessary Income Tax and VAT returns. Obviously, the partners were not able to serve in the shops for all the time they were open. Carroll's wife helped in shop A. Jones was assisted by a retired shop assistant who liked to come in and help, but not for more than three days a week. These arrangements worked quite well. Carroll and Jones were agreed on all important matters. The business built up at a steady pace. Three years after they started, a very large housing estate was built. It was situated between the two shops, which were about five miles apart.

Not only did the sales of shops A and B grow, by leaps and bounds. There was now enough business for them to open a third shop (C) in the middle of the new estate. They employed an assistant to help Mrs Carroll run shop A. Carroll ran shop C, helped by a full-time assistant. Jones stayed at shop B, but a full-time assistant was employed there now in addition to the retired part-timer. Although their success delighted them, Carroll and Jones soon encountered problems they had not met before. Each of them now had to work much longer hours. Carroll had to divide his time between doing all the buying for the three shops, building up the trade done by shop C, and keeping an eye on shop A. Jones still managed shop B, but the amount of accounting and correspondence had expanded.

The business continued to get larger – and to prosper. Within seven years of forming their partnership, Carroll and Jones had nine shops but the work each of them now did was very different from when they had started operating together. Each of the shops now had a full-time manager with two assistants. Carroll spent the bulk of his time concentrating on the buying side. He travelled more than he had done before, looking at new products they hoped to sell. The partners had decided to keep on expanding the business. Jones now had two assistants to help him with the office work.

The two partners decided that the time had arrived to convert their business into a private limited company. They wanted more capital and they felt the need to enjoy the benefits of limited liability. Carjon and Co Ltd was formed with 20 shareholders in addition to the five director shareholders of the new organisation. These directors were Mr and Mrs Carroll, their son Frank, and Mr and Mrs Jones. With the extra capital introduced by the shareholders, most of whom were relatives or close friends of Carroll and Jones, they planned to build a new supermarket, a mile from the centre of the nearby city. In due course this was started and was a success.

Carroll and Jones were soon aware that their ways of managing the business would have to alter yet again. When the business had started, each partner had been able to supervise closely the shop for which he was responsible. He had been able to check waste, know most of the customers by name, and who to give credit to, as well. This was now impossible. There were too many shops and too many customers. A full-time buyer was engaged. Soon after, he had two assistants. A sales and credit manager, Ms Morrison, had also joined the organisation. Her function was to check daily the sales of all the shops and the supermarket, to promote the sales of new commodities, and to supervise the giving of credit to customers. The work of counting, checking and paying into the bank all the cash received, keeping the accounts and other office work, had proved far too much for Jones and his two assistants. An accounts and office manager was hired together with a full-time shorthand typist and two more assistants. This office manager soon had Carjon and Co Ltd linked to the facilities provided by a local computer service. Above all, Carroll, Jones and their fellow directors realised that new management skills were needed to co-ordinate (i.e. link together) the various activities. A general manager, Jim Davies was appointed. This, it was thought, would allow the directors, particularly Carroll and Jones, to devote more of their time to future development.

However, the new general manager was not as able as it had been thought when he was appointed. Davies was charming — but lazy. He spent far too little of his time supervising the shops. Indeed, one of them fared so badly that it was decided to close it. Davies left and a new general manager, Jim Barr took over. Carroll now spent more of his time, in co-operation with Barr, in supervising the shops. Future developments, were for the time being, left to his co-directors. The failure of the shop had been a nasty jolt to the old partners. In view of their steady progress till then, they had not anticipated setbacks.

However, progress returned. Extra employees were engaged because of the work load. Buying, Sales, and Stores Departments, each with its own manager now existed. Because of its success, Carjon and Co Ltd attracted the attention of a large public company — Hartley Delaney plc, who eventually took them over. The shareholders of Carjon were given shares in Hartley Delaney plc and Carroll and Jones both joined the main board of directors of the larger company. This new organisation was so large that it had Purchases, Sales, Stores, Accounts, Transport, Personnel and Public Relations Departments. Each department had its own manager and staff of assistants. All buying was done through the central office. The members of that department specialised so that any one buyer was engaged only in dealing with a limited range of goods. One member of the staff spent most of the time abroad, visiting manufacturers in various countries and deciding what goods to buy from them. The other departments were also organised on a specialised basis.

What can we learn from the story of Carroll and Jones?

1 While an organisation is small, one person can control it. He or she is able to do all the most important jobs and if any assistants are employed the manager can keep a fairly close eye on what they do.

As the business grows, the manager does not have the time to do all the jobs he or she used to do. The employees now perform many of the tasks. The manager/owner will spend more and more time supervising and making decisions (particularly if the organisation grows rapidly).

2 Again, as the organisation grows, and more staff are employed, the jobs of the assistants become more specialised. Thus, at one time Mr Jones and two assistants had attended to all the clerical and accounting work. This became impossible. Additional employees were engaged to do the work so that ultimately one clerk would spend the whole time dealing with the accounts, another would do nothing but tax and VAT matters and so on.

3 In the early days of the partnership, if you visited shop A, Mr or Mrs Carroll would serve you. If you wished to complain about anything they would attend to the matter. When the firm had its own supermarket if you had a complaint, you would ask to see the supervisor. If your complaint was a very serious one you might ask to see the supermarket manager. You would expect these people, each doing their own job, to be there. If a fire broke out while you were in the supermarket you would expect that there

would be somebody on the staff whose job it was to deal with such emergencies and to look after the customers' safety. It would also be obvious to the customer that there would be somebody, no doubt with their own staff of assistants, whose job it was to buy the many thousands of pounds worth of goods which the store, in its turn, sold to its customers.

At the same time you would expect that if you asked any member of the staff who was the boss (i.e. who was the person in immediate charge telling them what to do) they would be able to tell you.

Ultimately, you would find that there was a 'big boss' – the person in charge of the whole of the supermarket. But the big boss, in turn, was responsible to the directors at head office. They in turn had to answer to the shareholders, who were the owners of the business.

The set-up in any firm, so that each person knows who their immediate superior is and knows whose instructions they should carry out, is called the **structure** of the firm. The structure has to be such that there is always someone there to do all the necessary jobs. In the supermarket, for instance, if there had been nobody to attend to the recording of what goods were received and to their storage, how would they have reached the shelves in an orderly fashion? How would anyone have known exactly what had been received? How would it be known whether or not the firm was making a profit?

As a business develops and passes through different stages, new abilities and skills are needed. Some people whose talents were adequate when the business was smaller, possibly no longer have the necessary abilities. 'They are out of their depth' we say. New specialists have to be brought in to deal with the new situations and problems.

Notice too that every business does not just progress from the sole trader, to partnership, to private company and finally to public limited company. Many businesses remain as sole traders or partnerships. They may not grow at all but may just plod on with the same amount of business for a number of years. This doesn't mean that they will proceed on these lines all the time. Competition may force them out of business. A growing, thriving company may have serious setbacks. It may falter and have to be re-organised. The people at the top may have to be changed because they cannot deal with the new problems. In brief, businesses all differ. Some stand still, while others are expanding. At the same time some others are going downhill.

There is usually a small group of people who decide what the business should try to do and then try and ensure that their decisions are carried out. The ways different businesses set about these tasks will not be the same. But, in each case, having decided on their objectives, those in charge will try to make sure that they are achieved. At first, Carroll and Jones made all the decisions. When the business was made into a private company the board of directors of Carjon did this job. Ultimately, when the business was merged with Hartley Delaney plc, the board of that company decided on the objectives and tried to ensure that they were reached.

Remember also that in a large business, with the work specialised and carried out in departments, some departments do jobs which affect *all* aspects of the business. Thus, the Personnel Department will deal with the recruitment, training and welfare of *all* employees. The Finance Department will deal with any of the activities involving money. Other departments will not operate 'across the board' in this way. They will be concerned with one major activity. This does not mean they will be isolated from the other departments, but obviously they will not be involved with *all* aspects, as are the Personnel and Finance departments.

When you study other organisations, basically you will find the same features and problems as were noted in the example of Carroll and Jones.

Example 1

An organisation with which you are most likely to be familiar is a technical college or college of further education. Most of these colleges started, some of them over 100 years ago, in a very small way. At first there would be a Principal at the head, controlling four or five small sections, each with one or two lecturers in them. Possibly these sections would be Engineering, Science and Maths, Business Studies (or Commerce as it used to be called), and Building (or Construction as it is now known). At the beginning there would be one senior member of staff in each department, who would be responsible to the Principal for their section's activities. As the college grew, more teaching staff were employed. The sections became departments, and the person in charge, or somebody else, became the Head of that department. New courses and new subjects were added to what the college already provided. Initially, this new work would 'come under' an existing department. As it grew, it would be 'hived off' and a separate department to deal with it would be set up. This is what has happened in recent years to General Studies and Food and Fashion.

In very large colleges the expansion has been such that the work of the largest departments such as Engineering, and more recently Business Studies, has been split up, into separate departments. Thus, we can find colleges with separate departments of Mechanical, Electrical and Production Engineering. Co-ordinating their activities will be a Head or Dean of the Faculty of Engineering.

A Business Studies Department in a fairly large college will probably be organised with a Head of Department, Deputy Head, and senior members of staff, each with responsibility for one of the different categories of work such as Secretarial Studies, Professional Business Studies Courses, BTEC courses and Management Studies.

Some technical college departments 'service' others. Thus the General Studies department may provide courses of its own (e.g. GCSE and GCE A level courses in English, Government and Sociology). There will also be General Studies teachers whose work will include the teaching of General Studies to Engineering students.

At the head of the college is the Principal, who will probably be assisted by a Vice Principal whose job is to 'stand in' for the Principal when he or she is absent. The Vice Principal will deal with matters the Principal may delegate to him or her, e.g. supervising the introduction of some new courses, or linking up with the local authority's architects when some new additions to the college buildings are under consideration.

In a college, the body which is equivalent to a company's Board of Directors, is the Board of Governors. It usually consists of members of the local authority (i.e. councillors), representatives of commerce, industry, trade unions, staff and students. The Principal is responsible to the Government for the overall conduct of the college. The Heads of Department, in turn are responsible to the Principal.

In addition to the teaching staff, the college will have a range of administrative, clerical and other staff. This group will include all those who work in the college office, the technicians, maintenance and refectory staff and caretakers. In a number of colleges all these members of staff are responsible to the Registrar (in some colleges known as the Chief Administrative Officer), who in turn is accountable to the Principal. The Chief Librarian is usually responsible to the Principal directly.

A variety of committees exists in most colleges. The Academic Board, of which the Principal is usually chairman, has each departmental head as a member, plus representatives from each of the departments and from the student body. This Board discusses matters of an academic nature such as the content of courses and methods of examining and assessment. There may also be a Staff Student Consultative Committee, the aim of which is to allow student opinion to be brought to the notice of the staff and vice versa. The Students' Union is run very largely by the students themselves. Often a member of the staff will act as a link between the Union and the college authorities. (*See* Fig. 7.1).

Do not forget that it is unlikely that there are any two colleges in the country which are *exactly similar* in the way they are organised. Fig. 7.1, however, does show a type of framework which is found in many colleges.

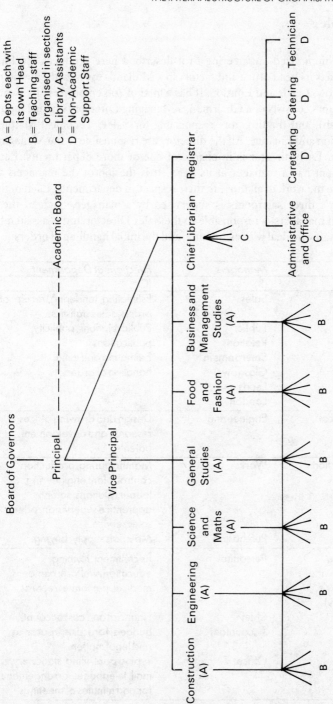

A = Depts, each with its own Head
B = Teaching staff organised in sections
C = Library Assistants
D = Non-Academic Support Staff

Board of Governors

Principal — — — — Academic Board

Vice Principal

Construction (A)   Engineering (A)   Science and Maths (A)   General Studies (A)   Food and Fashion (A)   Business and Management Studies (A)   Chief Librarian   Registrar

B   B   B   B   B   B   C   Administrative and Office C   Caretaking D   Catering D   Technician D

Fig. 7.1 Organisation chart of a Technical College or College of Further Education.

Example 2

The medium sized engineering firm described here produces machine tools. It has its head office and factory in a Midlands town, with salerooms in Glasgow, Leeds and London. It has a total of 400 employees. Its Board of Directors consists of a Chairman, a Managing Director (who is Deputy Chairman), and the directors responsible for Sales, Technical Matters, Production and Finance. All the directors are responsible to the Managing Director. Each director is in charge of one or more departments. Each department has a manager at its head. It is the job of the managers to supervise the work of all those in their respective departments. Each of the company's three salerooms is supervised by a manager. Each of these saleroom managers is responsible to the Sales Director and is assisted by a small staff who deal with estimating, and the initial handling of orders.

Director (A)	Managers (B)	Functions of Department (C)
1 Sales	Sales	Estimating, tendering, receipt of orders, sales statistics.
	Public Relations	Public relations, publicity, publications.
	Salerooms in Glasgow, Leeds and London	Estimating and initial handling of orders.
2 Technical	Engineering	Design and drawing offices; research and development; patents.
3 Production	Works	Manufacturing, production control, plant engineering, labour relations, safety, apprentice supervision, after sales service.
	Purchasing	Materials supply, buying.
4 Finance (He is also the Company's Secretary)	Personnel	Recruitment, training, education, welfare, canteens, medical, personnel records.
	Chief Accountant	Financial and cost accounts, budgets, forecasts, insurance and legal matters.
	Office	Typing pool, filing, stationery, mail, telephones, arrangements for and minutes of meetings.

The Chief Inspector and the team of inspectors are in a unique position. They are responsible for controlling the quality of the company's products. This can lead to disputes with, for instance, the Works Manager, who is mainly interested in reaching production targets. This does not mean that the Works Manager is not interested in quality. Far from it. But his or her main aim is to keep to dates when the production of certain ordered machine tools has been promised. Thus, the Chief Inspector has the right of access to, and is responsible to the Managing Director.

Page 94 shows a list of the managers, the directors to whom each is responsible, and the jobs allocated to each department.

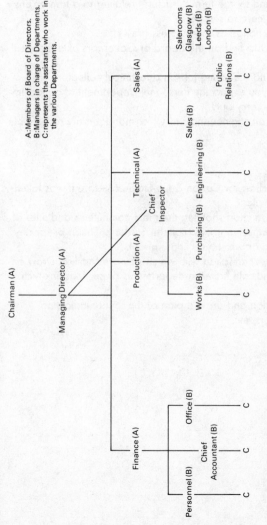

Fig. 7.2 Organisation chart of a medium sized engineering firm.

After studying the list of managers and their functions, on the previous page, write in your workbook, and from memory, as many of these different jobs as you can.

As pointed out in Example 1, referring to colleges, no two are ever exactly alike: the same applies to firms and their structural organisation.

Exercises

1 Why did Carroll and Jones open a third shop?
2 Why, as a business grows, does it become harder for one person to control it?
3 What do you understand by the term 'Structure' relating to a firm or any type of organisation you care to select?
4 How did Carroll's job change as the business grew?
5 Who would you expect to find on the Board of Governors of a technical college?
6 Name any two of the non-teaching jobs in a technical college.
7 What functions would you expect the Personnel Department of a medium-sized engineering firm to carry out?
8 In the example given of an engineering firm, which managers are responsible to the Sales Director?

Assignments

1 Draft an organisation chart for Carjon & Co Ltd, just before it was taken over by Hartley Delaney plc.
2 Produce an organisation chart showing the main committees and titles of the leading officials for *either* your own college Students' Union or for any club to which you belong or which you know about.
3 *(a)* Study any business organisation with which you are familiar. Draw an organisation chart and indicate how the departments or sections link with each other.
   (b) Select any one section and draw a plan of the layout indicating equipment, furniture, doors, etc.

8 THE OFFICE

Objectives

At the end of this chapter you should be able to:

- Explain the function of an office as a service.
- Explain the function of an office as a centre for the collection and processing of information in the running of a department.

Types of offices

Offices vary in nature and type. In manufacturing organisations the office supports the organisation in its main task of production. Other offices in commercial organisations such as banking, the law, and local government are concerned with supporting services rather than production. Individual organisations all have their own procedures. Nevertheless, many rules and systems are common to all. Some of these will be explained in the following chapters. It is difficult, for instance, to think of any organisation which does not become involved in buying and/or selling and receiving and/or making payments. Any organisation is involved at some point in buying something or having it bought on its behalf.

The function of an office

The office supports commerce, industry, and the public services by recording and providing information. Information is dealt with by an office in a variety of ways:

1 Providing information to other organisations. This can be in many varied forms, including price lists, quotations, and financial information.

2 Receiving and processing information from other organisations.

3 Keeping records of payments made and received, wages paid to employees and debts owed by and to the organisation.

4 The office will provide its own organisation with facts and figures for control purposes. It will also maintain records for future reference.

Office activities

The activities in an office include:

1 *Purchasing* which includes raw materials for production; services such as electricity and cleaning; items of equipment, e.g. machinery.

2 *Control activities* prevent loss of production by effective stock control; control costs and financial activities by accurate records; check records and documents for accuracy, and provide financial and statistical information through the use of computers.

3 *Sales.* Promotion of the organisation's products and services by advertising; arranging distribution to customers; maintaining customer records; checking on customer requirements and changes in requirements, i.e. market research.

4 *Processing of information* to and from the organisation, both written and spoken.

5 *Safe storage of papers and documents* through an efficient filing system.

6 *Presenting information* by duplicating, copying and typing. If we look at a sales invoice (*see* Fig. 8.1) this will lead us into contact with nearly every department in the organisation.

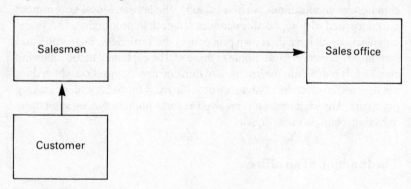

Fig. 8.1 Where does the order for goods come from?

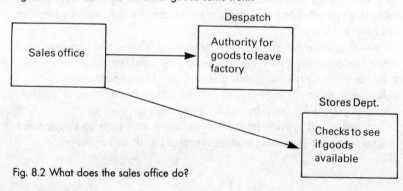

Fig. 8.2 What does the sales office do?

From this point let's look at a chart of the progress of an order through the departments in Fig. 8.3. This shows how the departments in an organisation have to co-operate with each other to meet the customer's order.

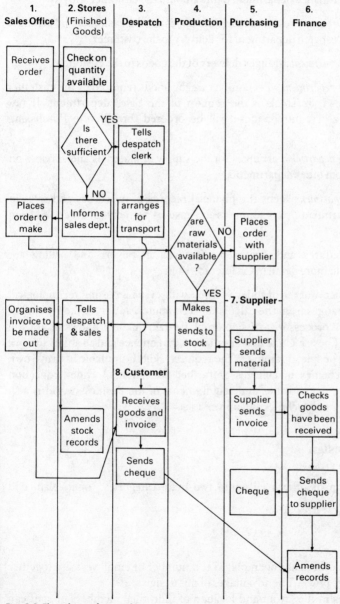

Fig. 8.3 Flowchart of an order.

Sales department requests Stores department to pack and label the goods ordered by the customer. If the goods are not available they request the Production department to make the goods. When the goods are finally delivered to the customer they arrange for an invoice to be issued and advise the Finance department of the amount the customer will pay.

Stores department packs and labels the goods for the customer and arranges with the Despatch department for delivery to the customer.

Despatch department arranges delivery of the goods to the customer.

Production department will manufacture the goods required by the customer if not already in stock at the request of the Sales department. If raw materials are required, these will be ordered through the Purchasing department.

Purchasing department arranges for the supply of materials and services on request from other departments.

Finance department keeps the financial records of purchases and sales of other departments, pays suppliers and ensures payments are received from customers.

The procedures and documents involved in buying and selling are explained in more detail in Chapter 10.

The office worker of today is faced with ever increasing technological aid. This ranges from the calculator to computer, and from the typewriter to the word processor (*see* Chapter 17). Certain qualities and skills are still required. These include neatness, accuracy, patience and an ability to work with other people. Training in the required skills is available in firms' own training schemes in colleges of further education. A wider education concerning the activities and requirements of the business world is also provided by polytechnics and universities.

Office design

The design of offices falls into two main categories: 'open plan' and 'corridor'.

Open plan

Most new offices are open plan, i.e. a number of employees are together in one large office. The advantages of this design are:
1 Changes in the layout and location of individual members of staff can be easily made.

2 Communication is easier than if a number of smaller offices exists. It is easy to see whether any individual is in or out of the office.

3 Efficient supervision and even distribution of work is made possible.

4 Machines and equipment can be used efficiently. For example, a calculator or typewriter can be used at different times by different employees. If each person is provided with a machine of his own it may be used for only an hour or so a day.

Disadvantages

There can be disadvantages to the open plan office unless efforts are made to overcome them.

1 Noise can be a problem, but with modern installation and fitted carpets this should be reduced.

2 Lack of privacy can be both annoying and the possible cause of lowering of efficiency. Many firms nowadays provide separate interview rooms where visitors can be received or personal matters involving staff can be dealt with privately.

3 The distractions caused by a number of people moving about can reduce work efficiency. After a time most employees tend to accept and ignore them.

4 Discussions between office employees – even if about the business of the organisation – can disturb employees working nearby.

Corridor offices

These exist where offices are separated by walls or other kinds of partition and lead from corridors. This type of office is often found in older buildings. Today, the offices of higher management (directors, managers, departmental heads and the like) are still usually self-contained. The major advantage of this arrangement is privacy and quietness. Whether an office be organised on the open plan or corridor design (or, as is often the case, a mixture of both), it is in the management's interest to provide good working conditions. Good work can be done under poor office conditions. A pleasant environment with adequate equipment, privacy and quiet is, however, more likely to lead to efficiency. Furthermore, the law has now taken a hand regarding the working conditions in offices. They are now governed by the Offices, Shops and Railway Premises Act 1963 which is a relevant statutory provision of the Health and Safety at Work Act 1974. Some of the main points of this Act are:

1 *Space.* 40 sq ft of floor space per person has to be provided. If the ceiling is lower than 10 ft, there must be 400 cubic ft of space per person.

2 *Temperature.* The temperature of the office must not be less than 16°C (60.8°F) after the first hour of working.

3 *Drinking water.* An adequate supply of drinking water, at places accessible to the staff, must be provided and maintained at all times. Unless water is supplied in the form of a jet from which people can drink, there must be a supply of disposable cups or beakers, or non-disposable cups or beakers with adequate facilities for rinsing them.

4 *First Aid.* Adequate first aid facilities must be provided. This means there must be one first aid box for the first 150 employees, and a further box for every additional 150 employees or part thereof.

5 *Fire precautions.* If more than 20 persons are employed or if more than 10 persons are employed elsewhere than on the ground floor, a fire certificate must be obtained from the local fire authority. This means that officers of the authority have visited the premises, inspected them and have decided that they reach the required standards regarding fire precautions, e.g. fire alarms have been provided and reach to every part of the premises, fire safety doors have been installed.

6 *Reporting of accidents.* Any accidents causing the death or absence from work for more than three days of any employee must be notified by the occupier of the premises to the local council.

These are only a few example of regulations in the 1963 Act. Local councils are responsible for the enforcement of the Act. They have to appoint inspectors to carry out this duty. The enforcement of those sections of the Act relating to fire precautions is, however, usually the responsibility of the local fire authority (*see* Fig. 5.2).

Computer based systems in the office

The introduction of computers into the office is not a recent event but with the development of micro-computers the use of the computer is no longer confined to very large commercial or public organisations. There are many different kinds of computers. The very large ones, called 'mainframes', can cost several millions of pounds. Large companies, banks and government organisations have mainframes. These organisations have specialised staff called Data Processing Staff who work the computer.

Medium size firms have minicomputers which can cost from £20 000 upwards. Minicomputers are not as powerful as mainframes but they are more than adequate for the work of most companies. There are two main categories of microcomputer. The home computer is usually the cheapest and is used by the home enthusiast. The business microcomputer which can cost as little as £400 to £5000 is being introduced in large numbers into smaller firms – often where only two or three people are employed in the office.

Many people feel we are only at the beginning of the 'Computer Revolution'. Although computers have been in use in business for many years the developments now taking place in microtechnology will allow for more and more jobs to be carried out in the office by the computer. Fortunately, much of the work done by computers is boring and repetitive. It is the sort of work most people do not like to do anyway.

The introduction of the computer has not changed the basic functions of the office. But the computer can search through files of information much more quickly than people can, and it can handle calculations more quickly than people. Thus it can process, store, retrieve and communicate information more rapidly. It gives business much greater access to large amounts of information than even manual methods could.

Some of the applications of new technology in the office include:

1 word processing;
2 accounting, including purchasing and stock records;
3 databases – customer records, electronic filing systems;
4 wages calculations;
5 retail sales records – computer linked tills in retail stores;
6 costing information and forecasting;
7 information transmission from department to department and from firm to firm.

Since the use of modern computer based systems operates throughout the office, information is given in the relevant chapters of the application of computer systems as they apply.

The electronic office

The growth of the electronic office has implications for an organisation. The variety and types of jobs are changing and this brings with it the need to examine working areas to ensure that staff are able to carry out their duties effectively. This involves a study of the design of furniture, keyboards for computers, VDU screens, soundproofing, and many other areas to ensure that staff are able to work efficiently and in comfort. It is in the interest of all organisations to pay attention to the working environment of their staff.

Safety first

All employees should be aware of the safety regulations. A few simple points to remember are:

1 Read the instructions on what to do in case of fire or other emergencies.
2 Familiarise yourself with the nearest fire exit.

3 Do not block or obstruct fire exit doors.
4 Keep gangways clear.
5 Keep firedoors closed.
6 Take care with waste paper. Never use a waste paper bin as an ash tray.
Always have the safety of yourself and colleagues in mind. If you see a
potential safety hazard report it to your superior.

Assignments

1 *(a)* Draw an outline plan of an 'open plan' office for the following sections
in an office:

Wages   3 staff
Personnel   2 staff
Filing/Mail   2 staff
Sales   4 staff
Accounts   2 staff
Office Manager

(b) Draw an outline plan of a 'corridor office' for the sections and staff in
(a).
2 *(a)* Name the three major types of computers.
(b) Select an appropriate type of computer for the following firms:
(i) Bank
(ii) Small builders
(iii) Medium size engineering firm
(iv) College administration
(v) A newsagents.
3 If you are in a job or on a training course investigate your organisation
and list the details of the safety rules and instructions displayed. If you are
at college investigate the area mainly used by your department. Your tutor
will identify the area if in doubt.
4 Draw an outline of your office and indicate the sections and staffing.

9 DEALING WITH CLIENTS AND VISITORS

Objectives

At the end of this chapter you should be able to:

- Identify the main types of visitors.
- List the main rules of good practice in reception.
- Understand the basic procedures for communicating by telephone and letter.
- Explain how you would deal with a customer with a complaint.

Dealing with clients/customers and visitors to any organisation is extremely important whether by letter, telephone or personal visit. Think of any occasion when you have to contact an organisation, how important it is on a personal visit to be greeted pleasantly and courteously and to feel welcome, and how unpleasant it can be if you are treated in an offhand manner. If you have to telephone, to be greeted in a pleasant and helpful way overcomes many fears and creates a good impression of an organisation. Even today with the growth of telephones in our homes, many people are still unsure when contacting an organisation for the first time.

Reception

A reception area in the organisation should be clean and tidy and often firms place plants and flowers in reception to make it attractive to the visitor. If you have to work in a reception area there are a few simple but important points to remember.

1 There are many different types of visitors to an organisation:

   (a) Regular visitors – such as maintenance people to service and repair equipment.

   (b) Salesmen – wishing to see staff in different departments.

   (c) Visitors from other departments or firms in the same organisation.

   (d) Existing and new customers/clients making a personal visit.

2 A register of visitors is usually kept giving their names, who they are visiting, the time of arrival and departure and, if there is a car park and they have arrived by car, the registration number of their car.

3 Never keep a visitor waiting if it can be avoided. Do not hold private conversations with other members of staff while a visitor waits for attention.

4 Make visitors feel welcome with a smile and a pleasant greeting even if you do not feel like it.

5 If contacting another office by internal telephone to see if someone will see a visitor without an appointment, be tactful. Even if that particular person answers, say 'Is Mr. Smith available? There is a Mr. Jones in reception who would like to see him'. If Mr. Smith is too busy and suggests Mr. Jones should make an appointment, you can suggest this to Mr. Jones without causing offence. These are only a few examples of the points to bear in mind; most important of all is to consider how you would like to be received if you were the visitor.

The telephone

Chapter 15 deals with the services offered by British Telecom. Many of them are designed to help the existing or potential customer/client contact the organisation. It is important to create the right impression on the telephone. If you are dealing with calls on the switchboard announce clearly the name of the firm and ask how you can assist the caller. Do not ignore the telephone call while doing something else or keep the caller waiting any longer than necessary after answering. Remember, they are paying for the call. If you answer an extension in an office announce the department and your name to avoid possible confusion. If you have to take a message for a colleague (*see* page 189) write it down to make sure you have all the details and do not forget.

The letter

The style of the business letter has changed over the years but it is still an important means of communication. With the development of electronic mail, many communications will pass from organisation to organisation in this way. In contacting clients/customers by letter it is important to ensure that the content is clear, it is well set out and any enclosures mentioned in the letter are included. The letter is an ambassador of your organisation; it creates an impression and it should be a good one.

Customers' complaints and grievances

In any organisation, however efficient, there will be occasions when complaints and grievances arise. Complaints usually fall into two categories:

1 service;
2 goods.

Most complaints are genuine; they should be treated as such until proved otherwise. Never be rude or aggressive to a customer even if they are rude and aggressive to you. Try to calm them down and obtain the facts to get a clear picture of the complaint. Beware of apologising before you know the facts. This can give the impression that your organisation is always wrong which is not necessarily the case.

Where it is necessary, seek help and advice from senior staff. There are legal obligations on organisations to remedy faults but many organisations go beyond their legal obligations to create goodwill and to ensure the customer returns in future. Many organisations accept and remedy unjustified complaints to avoid bad publicity.

Overcoming complaints

The most successful way of dealing with complaints is to try to prevent them happening.

1 Do not become involved in arguments. This only irritates the customer and makes the situation worse.
2 Never make promises you cannot keep or give information when you are not sure – find out.
3 Do not ignore the customer's complaint but put them in touch with the right person or department if you cannot help.
4 Do not put complaints aside and forget them. This only makes the situation worse.

Assignments

1 Draw up a page of a visitors' book suitable for your own organisation or the college. Indicate by titles the use of each column and enter details of three different types of visitor.

2 A customer has enquired by telephone for details of your products and a price list. Draft a suitable letter in reply indicating the enclosure of the information required.

3 *(a)* You answer the telephone extension in an office and you find there is a customer calling your firm with a complaint. Unfortunately, the call is for the sales office and would mean transferring the caller. When you explain this the customer becomes annoyed and points out in forceful terms that you

are the third person they have spoken to. List what action you would now take to help the customer.

(b) On investigation you find this kind of incident occurs frequently. Your office manager asks you to draft for him a memo to the switchboard operator and one to departmental staff to alleviate this problem. Draw up suitable memos.

4 State what happens to an order received from a customer indicating which departments in the firm may be involved and for what reason.

5 *(a)* List the qualities an employer would look for in a newly-appointed office worker.

(b) Give the qualities an employer would look for in staff for the following jobs:

(i) Wages clerk
(ii) Sales office clerk
(iii) Receptionist/switchboard operator
(iv) Filing clerk
(v) Purchasing department clerk
(vi) Shorthand typist

6 *(a)* Obtain advertisements for three computer systems from newspapers or magazines and give details of possible applications in the office.

(b) Explain the meaning of the terms 'hardware' and 'software'.

10 BUYING AND SELLING

Objectives

At the end of this chapter you should be able to:

- Complete business documents necessary for buying and selling.
- Explain the purpose of the documents involved.
- Describe the sequence in buying and selling.

Buying and selling goods or services is part of our lives. We all buy and sell whether for our employers or ourselves. The producer buys raw materials and sells the finished product. For instance, the production of bars of chocolate involves a series of transactions resulting in the finished chocolate being sold in the shop to the customer. The final purchase by the customer in the shop would be for cash. Most of the transactions, however, before the chocolate reached the shopkeeper, would be on credit – when payment is made later. This means that records will have to be kept of money owed by and money owed to a business. Although the design of forms and records varies from firm to firm, the basic information given remains the same.

Just as you have to decide what to buy and where the best bargain is, so does a business. To help it, a business often has a person responsible for buying called a Buyer or Purchasing Officer. It is his job to place orders with suppliers for goods required by his firm. To help him he keeps records known as his 'sources of information'. These give details of present and possible future suppliers, prices, and delivery dates, together with details of discounts, if any, offered on purchase prices. This information is obtained from journals published about his particular trade, e.g. Office Equipment News, and Yellow Pages, from publications such as Kelly's Trade Directory, by attending trade exhibitions and meeting visiting sales representatives. Before any purchase is made someone in his firm will have to ask him to buy something they require. This is the beginning of a business transaction. We will take as our example the firm of Anyfirm plc, 16 The Place, Leeds L52 6TS who require two new office desks. The sales

---

PURCHASE REQUISITION

No. *16*
Date *1st July 19 —*

From *Sales* Dept.
To *Purchasing* Dept.

Reference/Code	Description	Quantity
	Office Desks	*Two*

Date for delivery	Signature
August 19 —	*P Hewitt*

FOR PURCHASING DEPT. USE		
ORDERED FROM	ORDER NO.	DATE

Fig. 10.1

department of Anyfirm plc ask the Purchasing department for the two desks by completing an internal purchase requisition. This is shown as Fig. 10.1.

This document gives the name of the department ordering the desks, the goods required and any special conditions such as the date by which the goods are required. It must be signed by the head of that department.

Letter of enquiry

When the Purchasing Officer receives this requisition he will check his sources of information and select possible suppliers. It may be necessary to make enquiries of several firms to ensure that good terms are obtained. This may be done by letter (*see* Fig. 10.2), as some firms do, or by a pre-printed form where only blank spaces have to be completed. (*see* Fig. 10.3). In the case of goods needed at regular intervals (e.g. stationery) a regular

Exhibit 13.04

ANYFIRM plc
16 The Place
Leeds LS2 6TS

TELEPHONE: 42631
TELEX: 62143

DATE 3rd July 19 –

OUR REF. WG/AS
YOUR REF.

Messrs. K. Smith & Co.
The Parade
Sheffield.

Dear Sirs,

Enquiry No :1620

Please advise me of the cost of two standard office
desks. We would require delivery to the above address
within one month of order date.

Yours faithfully,
ANYFIRM plc

W. Gledhill

W. Gledhill
Purchasing Officer

Fig. 10.2

supplier will be used so there will be no need to make enquiries for each order.

Quotation

The possible suppliers will reply in the form of a quotation. They may also include catalogues of the goods they sell together with price lists and terms of sale (i.e. any discounts and how soon payment is required after the goods have been delivered). In our example the Purchasing Officer receives three replies, each with a very similar price but with the following delivery conditions on receipt of an order.

K Smith & Co, The Parade, Sheffield   – Delivery immediately
                                                 from stock

A Jones Ltd, City Street, Sheffield   – Delivery 2 months

A Price, High Street, Sheffield   – Delivery 6 weeks

In view of the original enquiry sent out, which quotation do you think the firm should accept?

As the firm required delivery within one month then the quotation of K Smith & Co would be the most suitable one. It meets the delivery requirements, and the prices of the three suppliers are similar. If the price

---

ANYFIRM plc
16 The Place
Leeds LS2 6TS

OUR REF.   YOUR REF.

Telephone: 42631
Telex: 62143

Messrs. K. Smith & Co.
 The Parade
  Sheffield

Date _____ 3rd July _____ 19 –

Dear Sirs,

ENQUIRY No : 1620

We should be pleased if you would let us have a quotation for the following items:-

        Two office desks (standard)

Delivery to above address within one month of order.

Would you please advise us of any special conditions or terms of sale.

Yours faithfully,
ANYFIRM plc

W. Gledhill

W. GLEDHILL
Purchasing Officer

Fig. 10.3

had been much higher, then the Purchasing Officer would have had to decide which was most important – cost or a longer delivery time.

Having chosen a supplier the firm will place an order.

Purchase order

The order is an offer to buy or, as in this case, an acceptance of a quotation. It is usually on a pre-printed form. Firms will not normally accept delivery of goods unless an official order has previously been sent to the supplier. The order will have the following information on it:

1 The name and address of both firms concerned;
2 A reference number;
3 The date the order is made out;
4 The description and quantity of goods required;
5 Any instructions regarding delivery times and dates.

<table>
<tr><td colspan="3">ANYFIRM plc
16 THE PLACE
LEEDS LS2 6TS</td><td colspan="2">Order No. 48231
This number to be quoted
in full on all correspondence</td></tr>
<tr><td colspan="3">To:
K. Smith & Co.
The Parade,
Sheffield.</td><td colspan="2">Date 14th. July 19-</td></tr>
<tr><td colspan="5">Dear Sirs
Please supply and deliver the following goods to the above address on or before the specified date: as soon as possible</td></tr>
<tr><td>Quantity</td><td>Size</td><td>Description</td><td>£</td><td>p</td></tr>
<tr><td>2</td><td>Standard</td><td>Office Desks</td><td>75
Each</td><td>00</td></tr>
</table>

Yours faithfully
for and on behalf of
ANYFIRM plc

W. Gladhill

Purchasing Officer

Fig. 10.4

The top copy is sent to the supplier and will be signed by the Purchasing Officer. A copy of the order may be sent to the department requiring the goods and a further copy may be sent to Stores to check the goods on delivery. The Purchasing Department will keep a copy in their files for reference.

Discounts

The Purchasing Officer will, when looking at the quotations, have considered any possible discounts offered. The discounts usually offered are:

1 *Trade discount.* This is a discount allowed to firms in the same trade, or by a manufacturer to a wholesaler, or by a wholesaler to a retailer. The amount of discount can vary from customer to customer. It usually alters according to the quantity ordered to encourage customers to buy in bulk. The price before discount is deducted is called the 'gross price', and after discount the 'net price' or 'trade price'.

2 *Cash discount.* This is a discount given to customers to encourage them to pay their bills on time and may be in addition to the trade discount. If payment for the goods is made within a specified time then the allowance is deducted from the net price or trade price and the reduced amount is paid, i.e. '2½ per cent 28 days' means two and a half per cent can be deducted from the net invoice total if payment is made within 28 days of date of invoice. The entry is shown in the terms column of an invoice. The entry of the word 'net' means 'no cash discount is allowed'.

Delivery and packing

The Purchasing Officer must be familiar with certain terms and conditions used by a supplier affecting delivery and packing costs. These can include:

1 *Ex works.* The price does not include delivery and the purchaser must arrange and pay for transport and delivery.

2 *Carriage paid.* The price includes delivery of the goods to the customer's premises.

3 *Carriage forward.* The price of the goods quoted does not include delivery. The goods will be delivered but an extra charge for delivery is made.

4 *Returnable empties.* Many firms who supply goods in expensive packing, such as wooden crates and drums, make a charge on the containers. This is refunded when the containers are returned to the supplier in good condition.

5 *Value Added Tax.* VAT is a tax on sales turnover. It is raised at every level of activity starting with the first supplier and ends with the final customer. At each stage VAT is charged to the buyer on the selling price. The government department responsible for collection of VAT is HM Customs and Excise. Every firm or individual whose turnover in taxable supplies of goods and/or services exceeds an amount set by the Chancellor of the Exchequer, must register with HM Customs and Excise and keep records of all purchases known as inputs and all sales known as outputs. At the end of each tax period (normally three months) a firm completes a return (VAT 100) showing all input tax and total output tax. It is important to firms that detailed records are kept for completion of the VAT return and to enable checks to be made by officials of the Customs and Excise. The actual rate of tax varies from one type of goods to another according to government policy (*see* note attached to Fig. 10.5).

Exercises

1 Name two sources of information available to a purchasing department.
2 Trade discount is given for prompt payment. TRUE/FALSE
3 Who pays the delivery and transport costs on goods purchased 'Ex Works'? PURCHASER/SUPPLIER
4 After a quotation has been accepted what document will a Purchasing Officer send to a supplier of goods as confirmation?
5 What is received by a purchaser in reply to a letter of enquiry?
6 Who normally signs an internal requisition?
7 Why do firms allow cash discounts?
8 Who receives the top copy of a Purchase Order?

Sales

Let us now look at the order for the two desks from the point of view of the supplier, K Smith & Co, The Parade, Sheffield. When the original enquiry was received by K Smith & Co it would have been sent to their Sales Department who would send a quotation and probably a catalogue and price list as well. When the quotation was accepted by Anyfirm plc and the order received by K Smith & Co the transaction became a legally binding contract between the purchaser and supplier. The purchase order received from Anyfirm plc must be checked very carefully to ensure that all details are correct. Any queries must be dealt with immediately.

Credit control

K Smith & Co will probably have to check Anyfirm plc's credit worthiness, i.e. their ability to pay, if this is the first time they have ordered goods. This is usually done in two ways: (1) by obtaining a banker's reference or (2) by a reference from some other trades with whom Anyfirm plc have credit. Having obtained credit references, a limit of credit (i.e. the maximum amount Anyfirm plc is allowed to owe at any one time) is usually set on a customer.

It is then the responsibility of the Accounts Department to keep a strict control on payments and to 'follow up' overdue accounts to prevent bad debts.

Invoice

When K Smith & Co have accepted the order from Anyfirm plc they will make out an invoice. This is a business document prepared whenever one

---

Exhibit 13.06

INVOICE

K. SMITH & CO.
THE PARADE,
SHEFFIELD
S15 2RS

No. _A 6036_

To:

Anyfirm plc
The Place
Leeds LS2 6TS

V.A.T. Reg. No. 126 4210 08

Date .... 21st July 19-

Order No.	Date	Despatch Per	Date Despatch	Terms	
48231	14/7/19-	Own transport	20/7/19-	2½% 28 days	
				Goods Value	V.A.T.

Quantity	Description		Price	£	p	£	p
2	Standard Office Desks A 4/S2		£75	150	00		
	Less 10% Trade Discount			15	00		
							*
		AMOUNT EXCL. TAX		135	00	13	16
		10% V.A.T.		13	16		
E. & E.O.		TOTAL		148	16		

Fig. 10.5

person sells to another on credit. The invoice lists the goods purchased and tells the purchaser how much he owes the supplier.

*VAT is 'strictly net' and has been calculated at ten per cent on the sum of £135 less two and a half per cent cash discount. Customs and Excise VAT Notice 700 Page 41 states VAT must be calculated on amount less cash discount whether the discount is taken or not.

	£
Cost of desks	135.00
less 2½ per cent discount	3.38
	131.62
∴ 10 per cent VAT =	£13.16

It also tells the purchaser:

1 Invoice number and date;
2 VAT Registration Number;
3 Original order number and date;
4 Method of delivery – firm's own transport or other carrier;
5 Terms of payment – cash discount if any offered;
6 Quantity and description of goods supplied;
7 The letters E & O E are printed on the invoice meaning 'errors and omissions excepted'. This allows for any errors in calculation or omissions from the invoice.

The invoice is a printed form, usually in a 'document set', i.e. a number of copies fastened together. The number of copies varies from firm to firm. Copies used as delivery notes and advice notes will not show the price of the goods. The copies of the invoice are usually dealt with as follows:

Top copy. This is sent to the person buying the goods, (i.e. Fig. 10.5, Anyfirm plc).

Second copy. This copy is usually sent to the Accounts Department of the seller and entered in the Sales Day Book. It is then filed for future reference.

Third copy. This may be used as an advice note and sent to the buyer. It advises him that the goods have been despatched and by what means (seller's own transport or other delivery firm such as British Rail or Roadline).

Fourth copy. This will be sent to the seller's Stores to instruct them what goods to pack and to whom the packages are labelled.

Fifth copy. This copy is sent to the Transport Department. In effect it tells that department to arrange delivery. If the seller's own transport is used a copy of the invoice may be used as the delivery note. Alternatively, a separate delivery note may be made out in duplicate, one copy being signed by the purchaser on delivery and retained on file by the seller in case of any query on delivery. The other copy is left with the purchaser. If the goods are delivered by a private transport company a consignment note is completed and signed by the seller. It shows the number of packages and weight consigned, the name and address of the person sending the goods (the consignor), and the name and address of the person who is to receive the goods (the consignee). The consignment note is supplied by the transport firm and shows whether goods are carried at the seller's risk or at the transporting firm's risk.

Pro-forma invoice

A pro-forma invoice is similar to a quotation and is used as follows:
1 When goods are sent on approval. If a quotation has to show a number of items with discounts, it will probably be more convenient to make it out in the form of an invoice showing the purchaser how the invoice will be made out if they decide to purchase the goods.
2 When goods are sent on a Sale or Return basis, i.e. only goods sold are paid for. It is necessary to show the person receiving the goods the price that will eventually be charged.
3 Where payment is required before the goods can be sent or goods are sold cash on delivery.

Debit note

This is similar to the invoice and is used to make adjustments to an invoice. Some firms use a further invoice instead of a separate debit note. If, for instance, a supplier has made an undercharge on the original invoice he will use the debit note for the difference. In the supplier's Accounts Department the debit note will be treated in the same way as an invoice.

Credit note

As its name implies, the credit note is issued to the purchaser by the seller when money is owed to the purchaser. This can occur when there is an overcharge for goods delivered or as the refund of a deposit on packing materials returned. A credit note is also used when, for any reason, goods are returned to the supplier, e.g. too many goods delivered. The credit note is usually printed and typed in red. It should, whenever possible, show the original invoice number and date. It is usually issued before payment of an invoice is made so that the purchaser can deduct the amount of credit from the invoice total. Some firms use an invoice form typed in red instead of a separate document but practice varies from firm to firm.

Anyfirm plc The Place Leeds LS2 6TS From *K. Smith & Co.*	**GOODS RECEIVED NOTE**		No. *416* Date *21st July 19—* Order No. *48231*
Quantity	Description		No. of Packages
Two	*Desks*		*Two*
Condition on Delivery *Good* Accepted/~~Refused~~	Stock Reference *A/15/5*		Received by *G. Wheelhouse*

Fig. 10.6

Goods received note

When the goods are delivered at the purchaser's premises the Stores Department, who were sent a copy of the original order, will complete a goods received note or an entry in a goods received book.

They will record the name of the supplier, details of the goods received, the condition of the goods on delivery (in case of damage), and the original order number. This information will then be checked against the original order. This ensures that what was ordered has been received. Details will then be passed to the Purchasing Department.

Statement of account

Sales made to each customer are recorded in their personal ledger account. At regular intervals, usually the end of the month, these entries are transferred to a statement of account which is then sent to the customers concerned. With the greater use of accounting machines, many firms make entries in the ledgers and on the statements of account at the same time.
The Statement of Account shows:
1 The balance brought forward from the previous period;
2 Details of net amount on each invoice issued during the current period;
3 Any payments made by the customer or credit notes issued to the customer during the period;
4 The balance owing at the end of the month.

The Statement of Account is not only a record of goods supplied but a reminder to the purchaser of the amount owing. The sum of all final balances on the Statements of Account will be the same figure as the total debtors in the seller's accounts.

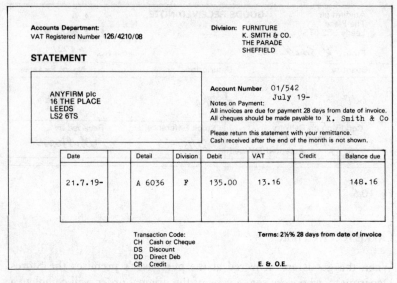

Accounts Department:
VAT Registered Number 126/4210/08

STATEMENT

Division: FURNITURE
K. SMITH & CO.
THE PARADE
SHEFFIELD

ANYFIRM plc
16 THE PLACE
LEEDS
LS2 6TS

Account Number 01/542
July 19-
Notes on Payment:
All invoices are due for payment 28 days from date of invoice.
All cheques should be made payable to K. Smith & Co

Please return this statement with your remittance.
Cash received after the end of the month is not shown.

Date	Detail	Division	Debit	VAT	Credit	Balance due
21.7.19-	A 6036	F	135.00	13.16		148.16

Transaction Code:
CH   Cash or Cheque
DS   Discount
DD   Direct Deb
CR   Credit

Terms: 2½% 28 days from date of invoice

E. & O.E.

Fig. 10.7

Payment

The final stage of the transaction is payment by the purchaser to the seller after the invoice has been checked against the order.

Exercises

Write the answers in your workbook.
1 Explain what is meant in the terms column of an invoice by '2½ per cent 28 days'.
2 What do the letters E & O E printed on an invoice mean?
3 What document is issued if an overcharge is made on an invoice?
4 What document is issued when goods are sent on sale or return?
5 Give the name of two departments in a seller's firm who may receive a copy of an invoice and state why.
6 Give two reasons why a credit note may be issued.
7 Who issues a debit note, the seller or the purchaser?
8 What is meant by a document set?
9 What is the name of the document sent to the purchaser recording invoices issued, usually at the end of a month?
10 What will be the net amount payable if goods are purchased at a gross cost of £120 and are subject to a trade discount of 25 per cent?

Documents

The business transaction involves a number of documents, some issued by the purchaser and some by the seller. Each document is a response to action requested. Although the design and layout of the forms varies from firm to firm the basic information given or requested is common to all. The sequence can be summarised as shown.

Document	Completed by	Purpose
Internal purchase requisition	A department in a firm	To request goods
Letter of enquiry	Purchasing Department of firm wishing to buy goods	For information from possible suppliers
Quotation	Sales Department of firm wishing to sell goods	Giving information of prices, terms of sale and delivery dates
Purchase Order	Purchasing Department of firm buying goods	Forms a legal contract for supply of goods
Invoice	Sales Department of seller	To advise buyer of cost of goods and amount to be paid. Copies can be used as advice note, packing note, delivery note
Debit Note	Sales Department of seller	To make adjustments to an invoice. It increases amount owed
Credit Note	Sales Department of seller	To make adjustments to an invoice. It decreases amount owed
Statement of Account	Accounts Department of seller	A record of all transactions between seller and a customer for a certain period. Acts as a reminder to pay and shows final balance owing.

Computer based systems

The use of the computer in the procedures involved in buying and selling can provide the firm with a fast and efficient service for customers and provide information (data) for use by different departments. Let us look at a simple example.

Orders are received by the firm's sales department which inputs the orders daily by using VDUs (visual display units). Each customer is given a code number and when the operator types in the code the customer's record appears on the screen. The operator types in the details of the order including the catalogue numbers, the quantities ordered and other relevant details including the price and any discounts. When all the orders have been entered the computer program (a list of instructions to the computer) takes over and carries out a sequence of activities;

1 Updates each customer record.
2 Prepares requests for the warehouse to pack the goods for delivery (packing notes).
3 Updates the stock records for each item ordered. If the re-order level has been reached for a particular item it prepares instructions for the production of more or prepares a re-order to an outside supplier.
4 Prepares the invoice for issue to customers. When required the documents are printed and passed to the departments concerned. At the end of the month, each customer's statement of account can be printed showing all the month's transactions and the final balance owing.

In addition the computer can be programmed to provide information for management concerning sales of particular items by individual sales representatives and sales by areas. When a payment is received or a credit note issued, the customer's account can be amended accordingly. The integration of all this information provides a data base (information bank) for all kinds of facts and figures. The sequence of documents in the business transaction is exactly the same as when the manual method is used but all documents now originate from the original entry of the order.

In a similar manner, the handling of purchases can be computerised. The order will be issued and stock records adjusted when the goods have been received and checked against the order.

Assignments

1 You work in the Purchasing Department of J Smith & Co Ltd. The Purchasing Officer asks you to find the names and addresses of three possible suppliers of office equipment. Select one of the suppliers and write a letter of enquiry for two typists' chairs. Supply your own address for J Smith & Co Ltd.
2 On 6 June, G Ruston & Co, Eastgate, Whitby, Yorkshire sent their enquiry

note No 674 asking the price, terms and delivery date for the following:
2 × 4 drawer filing cabinets (lockable)
1 × typist's desk and chair.

   Make out a suitable quotation as a reply supplying any further details required including your firm's name and address, price, etc.
3 You are employed by W Brown & Co, High Street, Burnley, Lancs. By referring to the price list in Assignment 4 complete an order form for the following items:
10 reams A4 typewriting paper (bond)
20 reams A4 typewriting paper (bank)
6 packs correcting fluid
1 pack of A4 Divider cards (100)
100 shorthand notebooks (160 pages)

4 Goods Supplies Ltd.
Townend,
Huddersfield.

Price list as at 1 January, 198X

Ref No	Description	Price
P/1	Reams A4 Bond typewriting paper	£2.10 per ream
P/6B	Reams A4 bank typewriting paper	£1.60 per ream
C/3	A4 Divider cards (blank)	£2.00 per pack of 100
192	Correcting fluid	£1.50 per pack
134	Desk pen sets	£1.69 each
29/B	Desk tidiers	£2.11 each
P/6	Drawing pins	60p per box
P/19	Rulers	£1.20 per 10
621	Shorthand notebooks	15p each

Trade discount 20% − Terms of payment 2½% − 30 days VAT @ 10%
   Complete the invoice to be sent to W Brown & Co on the 10 February, 198X in respect of the items supplied in Assignment 3.
   On the 15 February, W Brown & Co returns the 100 shorthand notebooks as unsuitable. Make out the credit note in respect of this returned item.
5 You receive a telephone call from the purchasing department of W Brown & Co (see assignment 3) complaining that instead of the 20 reams of A4 typewriting paper ordered your firm has sent A5. They are annoyed and complain that this type of mistake has occurred several times recently. List what action you would take to remedy the problem.
6 You are secretary of your local youth club committee. At a recent committee meeting it has been decided to purchase some new equipment. The committee have asked you to obtain details and prices of (i) 22″ colour television set and (ii) a table tennis table.
   (a) Obtain the names and addresses of two suitable suppliers for each of these indicating the reference source(s) used.

(b) Write a suitable letter of enquiry for each of these items to one of your possible suppliers. Supply a name and address for the youth club.

7 You are employed in the purchasing department of Anyfirm plc. On 5 June, 19.. A Smith & Co Ltd, Atlas Works, London delivered the following goods to your firm by their own vehicle:

2-4-drawer filing cabinets @ £110 each

4 tables @ £54 each

Subject to 20 per cent Trade Discount

Cash discount: 2½ per cent allowed if payment is made by 10th of the month following delivery.

On 15 June you returned two tables as defective for which you received a credit note on 25 June.

The goods were supplied to your order A/694 dated 26 May, 19..

Complete the following:

(a) The invoice you receive from A Smith & Co Ltd dated 6 June 19..

(b) Make out the credit note you receive on 25 June, 19..

(c) If payment is made to A Smith & Co on 2 July what would be the amount paid?

8 You are employed in the purchasing department of J Ashley & Co Ltd, Globe Works, Notown. Mr J Jones in the accounts department requires an order placing for the following goods:

1 8″ × 5″ Card Index Cabinet

3 Waste bins, plastic

100 Wallet folders

Carry out the following tasks making up any additional information such as order number, dates, etc.

(a) Design and draw a suitable document for Mr Jones to use to indicate his requirements to your department (purchasing). Indicate on the document its correct name. Complete the document by entering the details shown above.

(b) The purchasing department has to find a suitable supplier. List details of the different sources of information whereby such suppliers may be found, and from any one of these sources choose the name and address of one supplier. Make out one copy of the order placed with the chosen supplier for the items required by Mr Jones. Normally more than one copy of the order will be prepared. How many copies would you prepare and what use would be made of them?

(c) You receive a letter from the supplier you have chosen referring to your order and indicating that waste bins are supplied in three sizes – large, medium and small. The supplier asks what size you require. You are also asked if you require index cards for the cabinet. Write a letter informing the supplier that you require small waste bins and do not require any index cards.

(d) Two weeks after the date of the order the goods were delivered by the supplier's own transport and on the same date an invoice was sent by post. Make out the invoice using the following information:

1 8″ × 5″ Card index cabinet   £56

3 Small waste bins (plastic)   £2 each

100 Wallet folders   £18 per 100
  All the prices are to have 15 per cent VAT added.
  The whole order is subject to 15 per cent Trade Discount and the terms
of payment are 2½ per cent if paid within 30 days of the invoice.
  (e) When checking the invoice prices you find that the amount charged
for the waste bins is the price of the large bins. Obtain the correct price for
the small waste bins from your teacher. Make out the credit note from the
supplier to correct this error. Date the credit note one week after the date
of the invoice.
  (f) One week after the date of the credit note J Ashley & Co Ltd pay the
amount due in respect of this order. Calculate the amount to be paid to the
supplier.
9 Design a statement of account for a customer A James plc (use a suitable
local address). You are the supplier and the following transactions took place
during the month of April 198..

April 1	Balance	£126.50
April 6	Sold goods invoice 1678	£96.00
April 10	Received a cheque for the balance at 1 April less 5 per cent cash discount	
April 16	Sold goods invoice 2067	£124.00
April 23	Sold goods invoice 2732	£210.00
April 27	A James plc returned some goods purchased on 16 April value £10 and was allowed credit on credit note 26.	
April 29	Received a cheque for £100.	

Complete the statement of account and calculate the new balance on 30
April.
10 Your company has just been awarded the agency to sell a new microcomputer called the Oracle. This micro has software capable of keeping
customer accounts, issuing invoices and statements of accounts at the end
of the month. The price including a printer is £1400 and is particularly useful
for the smaller company.
  (a) Draft a suitable letter to your potential customers advising them of the
availability of the new micro-computer.
  (b) Design a suitable advertisement to appear in the local press. Use a
suitable name and address for your company.

11 STOCK CONTROL

Objectives

At the end of this chapter you should be able to:

- State the need for stock control.
- Explain the purposes and advantages of stock records.
- Complete stock records from given details.

Fig. 11.1

The purchasing procedure we have seen in Chapter 10 results in firms holding various types of stock. These are reserves, not only of raw materials for production, but of finished goods for sale. The types of stock held by firms vary according to the firm's business. A retail store or a wholesaler will hold large stocks of best-selling finished goods. They will hold relatively few stocks of the more exotic but slower selling goods such as expensive furniture, but will order for a customer on request. Equally, the question of the type of goods will affect stock levels. More durable goods such as paper can be kept for a reasonable length of time. Perishable goods such as fresh fruit will have a more limited storage time.

As there are various types of stock, firms vary their systems of stock control to maintain adequate stock levels. It is important, however, to a firm that it should have an effective stock control system for:

1 The holding of stock means a firm is using its capital. Large amounts of stock means investing a large amount of cash which cannot be used elsewhere in the business.

2 If too little stock is held then production may be halted with consequent delay in the supply of goods to customers. Disappointed customers can mean a loss in sales. As you know yourself, if you want a particular item when shopping, if one shop is out of stock you will more than likely go to another shop rather than wait.

3 Without good stock control stocks may be lost through damage, deterioration or pilfering.

4 The Purchasing department rely on effective stock control supplying up-to-date information on stock levels so that goods can be re-ordered. Otherwise, the firm will 'run out' of certain items.

Stock valuation

As stock held represents part of the firm's capital, accurate records are necessary to enable correct valuation to be made. The value of stock at the beginning and end of a financial period affects the profit level recorded for a business. Too high or too low a value put on stock will affect the profits shown for a business. There are several different methods of stock valuation, the generally accepted basis being: 'cost price or net realisable value, whichever is the lower'. This means that if goods have fallen in value since they were purchased then they will be valued at the reduced amount. If they have increased in value they will be valued at purchase price value.

The most widely used methods of valuation are:

1 *Cost price.* Goods are valued at the invoiced price charged for them when they were purchased from the supplier.

2 *LIFO* The 'last in first out' assumes that stock will be used from the last lot of goods received previous to the date of issue. If that lot of goods is not sufficient, the balance will be taken from the previous lot unissued and so on.

3 *Current selling price.* i.e. on the basis of value at the time of sale. Goods which have deteriorated in stock will probably be sold at less than purchase price.

4 *Average price.* Several purchases during the year may have been bought at different prices. An average cost is calculated for the different purchases. With each new purchase the average price is re-calculated.

5 *FIFO* The 'first in first out' method assumes that stock will be used in the order of 'first stock in first out', i.e. the oldest stock is always used before the newer stock. The remaining stock is valued at the last price. This method is very similar to the cost price method.

The tables below give three examples of calculating the value of stock issues. Different figures result from the three methods:

1 Last in first out (LIFO)

Date	Received	Issue Price	Stock after each transaction
January	10@£15 each		10@£15 each = £150
March	10@£17 each		10@£15 each = £150
			10@£17 each = £170
			= £320
May		8@£17 each = £136	10@£15 each = £150
			2@£17 each = £34
			= £184
July	20@£20 each		10@£15 each = £150
			2@£17 each = £34
			20@£20 each = £400
			= £584
November		20@£20 each = £400	8@£15 each = £120
		2@£17 each = £34	
		2@£15 each = £30	
		= £464	

In this case the cost of goods issued is stated to be £136 + 464 = £600.

2 Average cost method Each time there is a receipt of goods the average cost of the goods held in stock is recalculated. Any issues are made at that price until another receipt of goods when the price is recalculated and so on.

Date	Received	Issued	Average cost per unit of stock held £	No. of units in stock	Total value of stock £
January	10@£15 each		15	10	150
March	10@£17 each		16	20	320
May		8@£16 each = £128		12	192
July	20@£20 each		18.5	32	592
November		24@£18.5 = £444	18.5	8	148

In this case the cost of goods issued is stated to be £128 + £444 = £572.

3 First in first out (FIFO)   The goods received first are issued first. In this case the cost of goods issued is stated to be £120 + £440 = £560.

Date	Received	Issue Price	Stock after each transaction
January	10@£15 each		10@£15 each = £150
March	10@£17 each		10@£15 each = £150
			10@£17 each = £170
			= £320
May		8@£15 each = £120	2@£15 each = £30
			10@£17 each = £170
			= £200
July	20@£20 each		2@£15 each = £30
			10@£17 each = £170
			20@£20 each = £400
			= £600
November		2@£15 each = £30	
		10@£17 each = £170	
		12@£20 each = £240	8@£20 each = £160
		= £440	

Documents

You will remember that in Chapter 10 when the Purchasing Officer of Anyfirm plc made out the order, a copy was sent to the stores so they were aware of deliveries due.

On receipt of the desks from K Smith & Co a goods received note was made out recording delivery of the desks. The whole transaction started, however, with an internal purchase requisition from the Sales Department of Anyfirm plc. Had the desks been in stock in Anyfirm plc's stores, they would have been issued direct. The authority, then, for withdrawals from stock is the internal requisition. Any receipts or issues are recorded in a stock book or index of stock record cards.

This record card forms the basis for stock checks. All receipts and issues are recorded and a balance is calculated which should agree with any physical check that may be made. There are three important stock levels recorded on the card in addition to a description and stock reference code. They are maximum stock level, minimum stock level and re-order level.

1 *Maximum stock level.* This is an agreed maximum stock level to prevent overstocking. It will take into account cost, space available, and usage.

2 *Minimum stock level.* Stock should not be allowed to fall below this level. This acts as a safeguard against delays or disruption of deliveries from suppliers.

STOCK RECORD CARD

Location   Row ....
               Bin ....

Item ....
Units ....
Reference ....

Max. stock ....
Reorder level ....
Min. stock ....

Receipts					Issues				Balance	
Date	From	Order No.	Units	£	Dept	Ref	Units	£	Units	£

Fig. 11.2 Stock record card

3 *Re-order level.* When this level is reached the store-keeper will issue an internal purchase requisition to the Purchasing Department for a further supply. This level is usually calculated by multiplying the daily usage by the number of days for delivery from the supplier, plus the minimum stock level. If we take as an example the following:

A4 Bond paper (Reams)
Daily usage – 2 reams
Normal delivery – 10 days
Minimum stock – 12 reams
Then the re-order level will be – 2 reams
(daily usage) × 10 (number of days delivery) = 20 reams + 12 reams (minimum stock) = 32 reams

When the balance on the stock record card is 32 reams further supplies will be ordered.

In addition to maintaining stock records a physical stock check will still have to be made to check for pilferage, deterioration, clerical errors and out-of-date or out-of-fashion stock. The latter is particularly important in retail shops where fashions change and sales of old stock are held regularly.

There are three main methods of checking stock.
1 Perpetual stocktaking where small sections of stock are checked at regular intervals throughout the year ensuring all stock is checked by the end of the year.
2 Periodic stocktaking – This is of particular value in large stores where a stock check is made at regular intervals.
3 Annual stocktaking which takes place at the end of a company's financial

year. A valuation is taken of stock in hand for the firm's balance sheet and calculation of profit.

If a physical check reveals a discrepancy with the record card then an investigation may be necessary to establish the reason for the difference. It may be because of:

1 Failure to enter goods received or issued on the stock record card.
2 Goods may have been issued without the authority of a requisition.
3 Goods may have been stolen.
4 Goods may have been entered on another record card in error.

If the difference is found to be an error the corrections can be made. If, however, the discrepancy cannot be traced a report will have to be made to higher management.

Exercises

Write the answers in your workbook
1 Give two reasons why a firm should have a stock control system.
2 What is regarded as the correct basis for valuing stock?
3 Explain what is meant by 'minimum stock level'.
4 What would be the re-order level if daily usage was 10 units, it took 12 days for delivery and minimum stock was 80 units?
5 Name the two documents used to record receipts and issues of stock.
6 What does the figure in the 'balance' column on the stock record card mean?

Fig. 11.3 Stocktaking by micro computer.
Reproduced by permission of Triumph Adler (UK) Ltd.

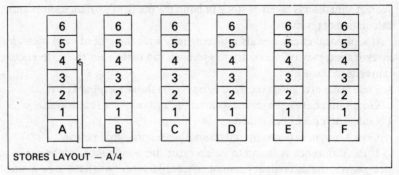

Fig. 11.4 Stores layout to assist location of stock.

Stock location

One of the problems that must be solved in many firms' stores is the location of particular items of stock. This is overcome by giving each item of stock a location reference, usually alphabetical or alphabetical and numerical.

By looking at an index of goods in stock, the code could be indicated by, say, A/4, this would mean row A, section 4. The articles would then be easily located and issues made quickly and efficiently. In very large firms specialist stores may be located in more than one place, each serving a particular area of the firm with a central stores keeping control.

Computerised stock control

As you already know, it is important for organisations to keep correct stock records. The computer enables an organisation to maintain effective stock levels. What should be in stock at any time can also be checked. If a VDU is available in the stores, by entering the stock code number the quantity and location of the particular item in stock can be shown on the screen. Customer queries can be handled quickly and deliveries promised ex stock if the item is available. It may be that the firm has depots throughout the country, the firm's computers or terminals at each depot can be linked by telephone lines (using a piece of equipment called a MODEM). Thus, if an item is not in stock at the depot receiving the enquiry the assistant can quickly check if another depot has the item in stock. This can all be done whilst the customer is still on the telephone. Delivery can then be arranged. This ensures that orders are not lost. More effective use of other depots' stock is also made.

Mail order firms now provide a service whereby their agents can telephone an order into a regional office. By using a computer the staff receiving the call can check that the item is in stock; they then place the agent's order immediately. This speeds up delivery and avoids long delays and disappointment if the item is out of stock.

By the use of effective stock control retail organisations can avoid *(a)* being out of stock (meaning lost customers) *(b)* having too much stock (spoiled stock or changes in fashion (can mean losses)); thus, the shop is better able to meet customer requirements. If the firm uses tills linked to a computer, stock management becomes much more simple. As each sale is recorded the stock levels are adjusted. As goods are received into stock details are fed into the computer.

Assignments

1 Calculate the minimum, maximum and re-order stock levels from the following information:
Total stock should never exceed 35 days usage.
Daily usage — 3 units
Normal delivery — 10 days
An average of 12 days stock should always be kept.
2 Draw up and complete a stock record card for the following:

A4 Bond paper	Minimum Stock	40 units
Units — Reams	Maximum Stock	200 units
Stock Code — A4/B1	Re-order level	80 units

1st July Balance 94 units
2nd July Requisition 162 Sales Department 14 units
3rd July Requisition 202 Typing Pool 20 units
10th July Requisition 321 Accounts Department 5 units
16th July Requisition 394 Typing Pool 20 units
Order stock from Office Supplies Ltd, Hull to maximum level when re-order level is reached. Delivery time one week from date of order.
3 *(a)* Using the FIFO method calculate the value of stock issued and the value of closing stock from the following information.

Month	Receipts	Issues
January	10@£30	
February	10@£34	
May		8
July	20@£40	
November		24

(b) Using the figures above calculate the value of stock issued and the value of closing stock on the basis of the average cost method.
4 You are employed as a stock clerk with J Woods & Co Ltd and part of your duties is to be responsible for the stationery stock within your company. On 1 April 19.. the company receives 50 reams of offset duplicating paper

(A4 – white) which had been ordered on 17 March, order number 8162.

(a) Design and draw a suitable record card to allow for at least 16 entries. Make the entry for the 50 reams. Ignore money values. Show receipts, issues and balance in units (reams) only. The maximum stock level is 60 reams, re-order level 24 reams, and minimum stock 16 reams.

(b) Enter the following issues for the month of April on the record card:

Date	Requisition no.	Reams
April 4	201	4
9	207	6
12	226	3
17	248	8
19	253	3
25	271	2
30	290	5

(c) On 19 April you order a further 40 reams. They were received on 3 May. The following issues were made during May. Continue with the entries on your record card and do not forget to enter the quantity received on your latest order.

Date	Requisition no.	Reams
May 1	321	5
6	326	3
10	332	7
15	340	4
21	345	8
24	352	3
30	360	2

(d) On 31 May you take stock and find that you have three reams more in stock than the balance shown on your record card. Explain how this might have happened. What checks would you make to discover any error?

(e) The original supply of 50 reams received on 1 April was invoiced at £3.20 per ream, and the second order received on 3 May at £3.50 per ream. Make out a second stock record card with monetary values and enter the issues for April and May showing the value of the stock on hand at 31 May. The FIFO method of valuing issues should be used.

(f) There are three general methods of taking stock, i.e. stocktaking at the end of the financial year, perpetual stocktaking, or periodic stocktaking. Your Chief Financial Accountant has suggested that the year-end method be adopted and has asked you for a memo outlining the advantages and disadvantages of the three systems.

5 Describe the advantages that might be gained by an organisation using a computer for stock control.

6 A large retail organisation with 120 shops is considering installing a computer to handle orders for stock from its various branches. The stock is supplied from a central depot. Explain what advantages you consider might be obtained over the present manual system and what additional equipment might be necessary in each shop.

12 METHODS OF PAYMENT

Objectives

At the end of this chapter you should be able to:

- Identify a suitable method of payment for a business transaction.
- Explain the different banking services available to an individual or a firm.
- Explain the different methods of payment available through the Post Office.
- Distinguish between different types of bank accounts.
- Complete bank documents for the transfer of money.
- Complete Post Office documents involved in the transfer of money.

What do we mean when we say 'methods of payment'? We all know that it is easy to make a payment. We do this whenever we buy anything. In exchange for what we want – a bar of chocolate, clothes, records – all we do is hand over the necessary bank notes and coins. This is payment by cash and many of our purchases are made this way. Consider what you bought or paid cash for today. It probably includes a number of payments for small amounts. The advantage cash has, of being easy to transfer and acceptable to all, can also be its drawback, for to lose money is easy. How can you tell one coin from another? It is possible to identify notes as each has a serial number, but how many of us record the numbers of the £5 notes we may have from time to time? Imagine the problems arising if all firms had to buy and sell everything for cash! Because of these difficulties many alternative methods of payment have been developed by the banks and the Post Office. Individuals and businesses can open accounts and use the many services provided both to 'hold' money and to make payments.

Bank accounts

The banks operate two main types of accounts – a current account and a deposit or savings account. They also offer special services which involve

the creation of, for example, a budget account, a revolving credit account
or a personal loan.

1 *Current account.* The current account could be called the 'cheque
account'. It is on this account that cheques are made out and cash is
withdrawn for payment of bills. This account does not earn any interest
but is used to settle debts.

2 *Deposit account.* This account is for money not immediately required and
interest is paid on the money deposited in it.

3 *Budget account.* As an additional facility banks offer a budget account
where the bank assists a customer to budget. The account holder totals
his expected annual bills for certain items, e.g. electricity, clothes, rates,
holiday accommodation, and mortgage repayments. To this total is added
a charge for operating the account. This final total is then divided by twelve
and each month this amount is transferred from the current account to the

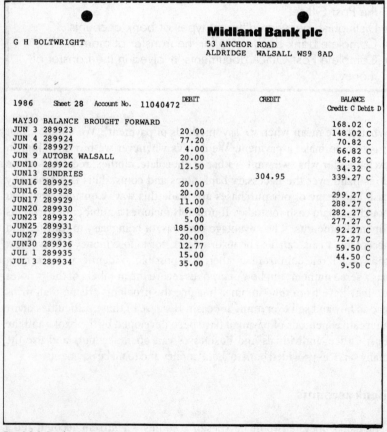

Midland Bank plc

G H BOLTWRIGHT

53 ANCHOR ROAD
ALDRIDGE   WALSALL WS9 8AD

1986 Sheet 28 Account No. 11040472	DEBIT	CREDIT	BALANCE Credit C Debit D
MAY30 BALANCE BROUGHT FORWARD			168.02 C
JUN 3 289923	20.00		148.02 C
JUN 4 289924	77.20		70.82 C
JUN 6 289927	4.00		66.82 C
JUN 9 AUTOBK WALSALL	20.00		46.82 C
JUN10 289926	12.50		34.32 C
JUN13 SUNDRIES		304.95	339.27 C
JUN16 289925	20.00		299.27 C
JUN16 289928	20.00		
JUN17 289929	11.00		288.27 C
JUN20 289930	6.00		282.27 C
JUN23 289932	5.00		277.27 C
JUN25 289931	185.00		92.27 C
JUN27 289933	20.00		72.27 C
JUN30 289936	12.77		59.50 C
JUL 1 289935	15.00		44.50 C
JUL 3 289934	35.00		9.50 C

Fig. 12.1 Bank statement.

budget account. Any bills can be paid by cheque as they arise and at the end of the year any under or over-payment is adjusted.

Bank statement

At regular intervals each customer receives a statement from the bank showing all payments and withdrawals which have gone through the customer's account together with any bank charges during a particular period.

The date shown is the date the transaction took place at the bank, *not* the date any cheque was made out. The three columns show the type of transaction, thus credits are amounts paid into the account, debits are withdrawals or charges, and the balance is the amount in the account after each transaction. It is possible to obtain on request details of the amount in your account by completion of an enquiry form at your bank branch.

Midland Balance Request

Please provide me with the balance of my/our account(s).

Name(s) of Account   G H BOLTWRIGHT
(*Block Capitals*)

Current
Account Number   1 1 0 4 0 4 7 2

Other Accounts   DEPOSIT   4 6 0 2 7 7 3 1
                                  Account Number

Signature   GH Boltwright   Date 11 May 1987
                                        Account Number

FOR BANK USE ONLY	Signature Checked	Return To

Midland Balance Information

As at the close of business last night the balances of your accounts were . . .

Cheques you have issued recently may not have been debited to your account and are therefore not included in the balance.

You can now obtain Current Account and Saver Plus Account balances from Midland AutoBanking machines. Please ask for details.

Current Account £ _____ Cr/Dr
_____ Account £ _____ Cr/Dr
_____ Account £ _____ Cr/Dr

The Listening Bank

Fig. 12.2 Balance enquiry.

Opening a bank account

As you probably know from some of the television advertisements, it is very easy to open a bank account. Having selected a bank, you call in at one of their branches. In addition to a deposit of money (as little as £1) the bank will ask you for a specimen signature. This enables them to check the way your cheques will be signed, thus guarding against fraud. The name of at least one referee (someone who knows you and will vouch as to your honesty and integrity) but usually two must also be supplied. One of these could be your employer. When the references have been checked and are satisfactory, a cheque book will be sent to you. You are then a customer of that bank.

Bank Giro Credit

Paying in to a bank account is a very simple process for both individuals or firms. Separate paying-in slips are provided by banks for deposit and current accounts. Many firms have their own paying-in book similar in form to the Bank Giro Credit slip (for current accounts) together with a copy of the slip which is retained in the book. Having completed the form, this together with the money is handed to the cashier who will check the money and stamp and initial the counterfoil. A non-account holder can pay an account holder by completing a Bank Giro Credit giving details of the payee's account. Some banks now include paying-in slips at the back of the customers' cheque book.

A cheque as a method of payment

Although banks have accepted instructions to pay money in many unusual ways, they prefer the instruction on a bank cheque form.

These are printed and supplied by the bank and many are now personalised in that they have the name of the customer printed on them.

Each part of the cheque has a purpose and must be completed correctly for the cheque to be valid.

1 *Date*. The date is usually the date on which the cheque is made out and the cheque is valid for six months from that date. If a cheque is not presented to the bank in six months it will have to be returned to the person who issued it for re-dating. If required a cheque can be post-dated, i.e. it can be made out for some future date and the cheque cannot be presented until that date.

2 *Payee and drawer*. The person to whom the money is to be paid is called

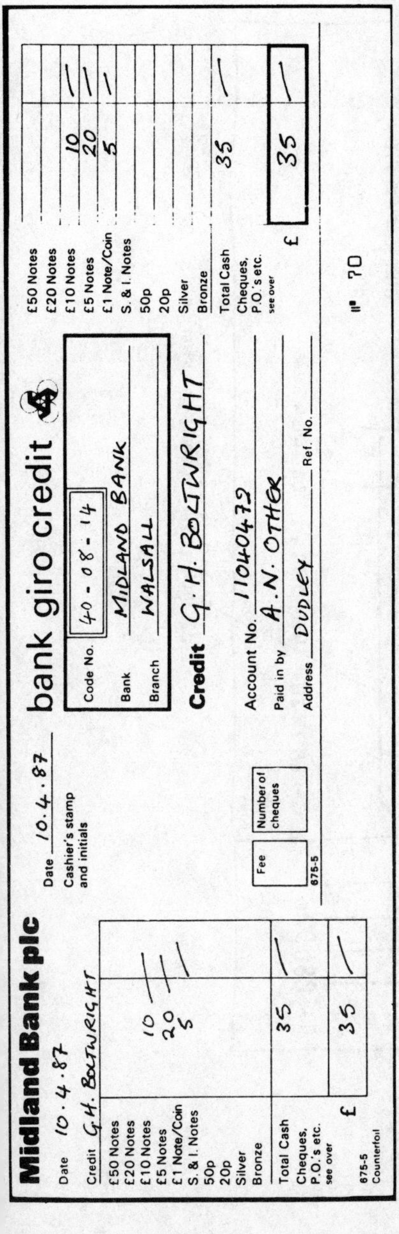

Fig. 12.3
Bank Giro Credit.

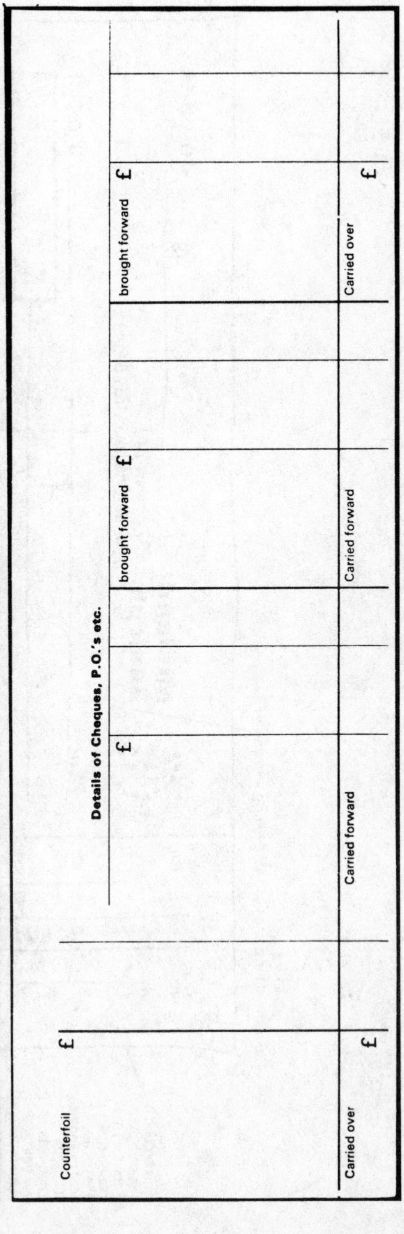

Reverse of
Bank giro credit.

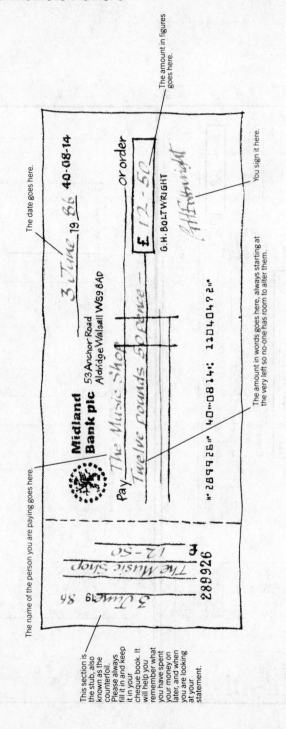

The date goes here.

The amount in figures goes here.

Midland Bank plc

53 Anchor Road
Aldridge Walsall WS9 8AD

3 June 19 86   40-08-14

Pay The Music Shop _____ or order

Twelve pounds 50 pence ———

£ 12-50

G.H. BOLTWRIGHT

GHBoltwright

ⅱ•289926•ⅱ 40ⅱ•08ⅱ14ⅱ: 1104072 2ⅱ•

The name of the person you are paying goes here.

The amount in words goes here, always starting at the very left so no-one has room to alter them.

You sign it here.

This section is the stub, also known as the counterfoil. Please always fill it in and keep it in your cheque book. It will help you remember what you have spent your money on later, and when you are looking at your statement.

3 June 19 86

The Music Shop

£ 12-50

289926

Fig. 12.4

the payee and the name is written in after the word 'PAY'. The drawer is the person making out the cheque authorising the bank to make payment and must sign the cheque. The bank on which the cheque is drawn is known as the drawee.

3 *The amount.* The amount is written in figures in the box provided. The number of pounds is written in letters after the name of the payee on the second and third lines, any pence being in figures. Again, this is to guard against fraud.

4 *The counterfoil.* This should be completed to record details of the cheque issued. In some cheque books a front page is provided to record details in list form.

If a cheque needs any alteration this can only be done by the drawer who will cross out the part to be amended, write in the amendment, and initial it. It is much safer, however, for the drawer to destroy such a cheque and issue a new one. Safeguarding cheques is very important to prevent loss or misuse since the cheque represents money. Cheques can be pre-printed as crossed cheques (*see* Fig. 12.5) or the drawer can draw two vertical lines on an open cheque making it a crossed cheque. A crossed cheque cannot be cashed but *must* be paid into a bank account, Post Office Giro bank or Savings Bank. This means that if a thief gets hold of it he cannot cash the cheque at a bank. Cheques can be further safeguarded by using specific crossing, i.e. writing a form of instruction within the crossing on the cheque, as shown in Fig. 12.6.

This is a specific instruction to the banks about the use of the cheque. The use of 'Account Payee only' means the cheques should be paid only into the account of the payee named. If cheques are lost or stolen the drawer must advise his bank immediately and confirm by letter. These

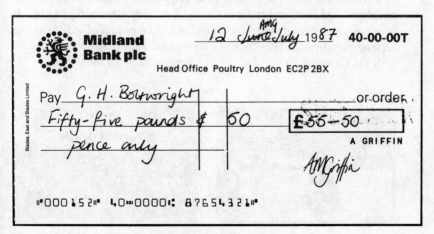

Fig. 12.5 Cheque amended and initialled by drawer.

Fig. 12.6

cheques will be 'stopped', i.e. payment will not be made on these cheques, provided you act swiftly. The safest crossing is that of 'A/c Payee only, Not Negotiable'. If the cheque is lost or stolen it will be of no use to the thief or finder. This is because it is impossible for this cheque to be paid into any bank account other than that of the named payee.

Firms find it convenient to pay suppliers' accounts and employees' wages, and individuals find it convenient to pay for shopping, meals, etc. without the risk of carrying large sums of money. If you have little cash but you have your cheque book with you it would not be necessary to miss a bargain when out shopping as payment can be made by cheque.

Cheque card

A Bank cheque card is an assurance that the bank will pay anyone accepting any cheque you sign (up to £50). It means you can pay by cheque anywhere with no questions or delays. It can also be used to withdraw cash up to £50 at any of the branches of the banks taking part in the scheme. In addition, through the Eurocheque scheme a holder can cash two cheques per day up to £50 each at banks in most European countries. The ready acceptance of cheques backed by a cheque card considerably improves the use of payment by cheque and reduces the need to carry large sums of cash. It is necessary, however, for the cheque card to be produced at the time of signing the cheque. The signature on the cheque card must correspond with the signature on the cheque. The person receiving the cheque writes

Fig. 12.7

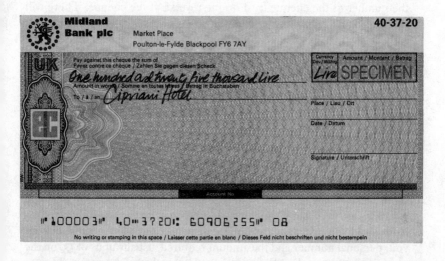

Fig. 12.8

the number of the cheque card on the reverse of the cheque. There will be no difficulty in making payment in shops or restaurants with a cheque card as payment is ensured providing the conditions on the back of the cheque card are observed.

Bank cash card

The number of cash dispensers being installed at bank branches in towns is increasing rapidly. This enables a bank customer to obtain cash outside normal banking hours. When the bank issues the customer with a cash card the customer is given a personal number. These numbers are not printed on the card in any readable form as it is for the customer's own personal use. This ensures that if the card is lost no one else can use it. When cash is required you insert the card in the dispenser outside the bank, tap out your personal number and the amount required, usually units of £5, on the machine buttons and you will receive cash together with your card to use again. The amount of cash obtained will be debited to your personal account. Additionally, many of the dispensers offer other facilities on request, e.g. bank statements, or your bank balance. These cash cards are particularly useful if on holiday or travelling on business as they can be used at any time at any branch of the bank concerned, that has a cash dispenser. The use of the card is limited, however, to once in any one day. (*see* Fig. 12.9.)

The development of autobanks or cash points is proving more and more popular with bank customers. Such facilities are a further example of the use of micro technology. By linking the cash points to the bank's computer it is possible to include new services. Thus a customer can be given an immediate balance figure on his account. Also the bank is able to use the display screen in order to advertise new services for the customer. Some banks use the cheque card (*see* Fig. 12.7) to enable customers to withdraw money from the cash dispenser.

Fig. 12.9

Bank Giro system

By this method of payment many different accounts can be paid by issuing one cheque. It is widely used to pay employees' wages. All the amounts are listed on a credit transfer summary sheet (*see* Fig. 12.10) showing the name of the person or firm to be paid, their bank branch and code, and their account number. A credit slip is completed for each payee or firm. The payer then writes one cheque for the total amount. The lists of payments to be made, the slips and cheque are then sent or handed into the payer's bank who then distribute the credits to the bank to which they are addressed. A non-customer, that is a person without a bank account, can also pay money through the inter-bank credit clearing system, simply by completing a form, paying in the amount concerned together with a small fee. Many organisations such as mail order companies, the Electricity Board and British Gas have arrangements with the banks where accounts can be paid in and the payee is responsible for any charges incurred.

Standing orders and direct debits

These two banking services are of particular value to firms and individuals where regular payments are to be made. With a standing order for fixed amounts you complete a form (Fig. 12.11) giving the bank details of the amount to be paid, to whom, and when such payments have to be made. The bank then makes the payments as and when they are due and debits the account concerned. Direct debit is slightly different, however. Instead of instructing the bank to make payment, the person or organisation who is to receive payment advises the bank of the amount due. The bank deducts it from the payer's account and makes payment. Using either method payments will not be overlooked. It is important to remember that money will be taken out of the payer's account. Many firms now prefer the direct debit method where payments can increase. This method prevents the problem of writing to every customer requesting that the standing order be increased, finding that some have failed to do so, and having to repeat the request together with the collections of under-payments. Safeguards are provided by the banks to prevent money being withdrawn from an account without the payer's knowledge. Payments by either method can be stopped by advising the bank branch. These services are widely used for subscriptions to magazines and clubs, rental payments and mortgage repayments. Firms such as television rental companies encourage customers to use these services.

TO **Midland Bank plc**   bank giro credit summary form

Branch _____ Date _____

Please distribute the bank giro credits attached as arranged with the recipients.

Number of Items

Our cheque for £ _____ is enclosed.

Customer _____

Address _____

Signature/s _____ _____

Bank sorting code number	For account of and account number	Amount	Total amount for each bank
	Totals carried forward £		

2121-4

Fig. 12.10

Other banking services

1 *Credit cards.* Providing the organisation concerned will accept credit cards they can be used for payments instead of cash. The holder of a credit

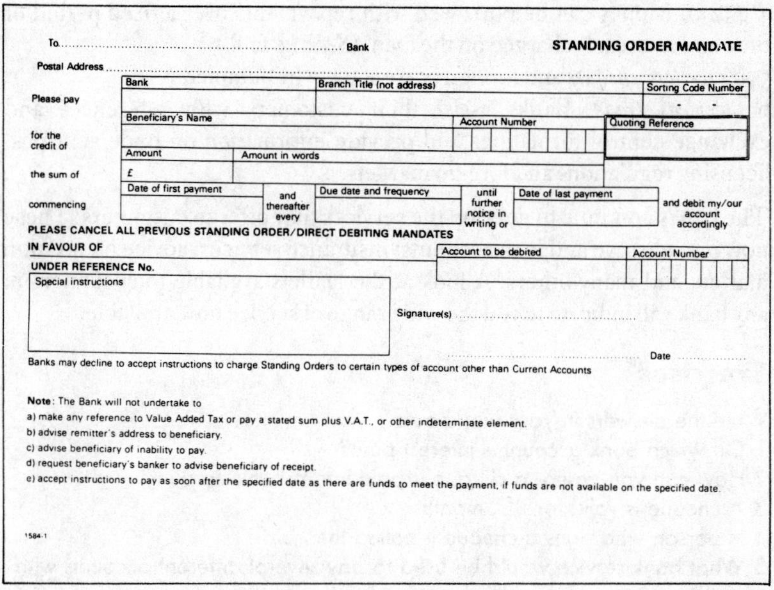

To .... Bank   **STANDING ORDER MANDATE**

Postal Address ....

Please pay — Bank | Branch Title (not address) | Sorting Code Number

for the credit of — Beneficiary's Name | Account Number | Quoting Reference

the sum of — Amount £ | Amount in words

commencing — Date of first payment | and thereafter every | Due date and frequency | until further notice in writing or | Date of last payment | and debit my/our account accordingly

PLEASE CANCEL ALL PREVIOUS STANDING ORDER/DIRECT DEBITING MANDATES

IN FAVOUR OF

UNDER REFERENCE No. — Account to be debited | Account Number

Special instructions

Signature(s) ....

.... Date ....

Banks may decline to accept instructions to charge Standing Orders to certain types of account other than Current Accounts

Note: The Bank will not undertake to

a) make any reference to Value Added Tax or pay a stated sum plus V.A.T., or other indeterminate element.

b) advise remitter's address to beneficiary.

c) advise beneficiary of inability to pay.

d) request beneficiary's banker to advise beneficiary of receipt.

e) accept instructions to pay as soon after the specified date as there are funds to meet the payment, if funds are not available on the specified date.

1584-1

Fig. 12.11

card hands it, say, to the assistant in a shop for a purchase and the assistant records all details. The top copy is signed by the customer and given to him. Copies are then sent to the organisation who issued the card who send a statement, usually monthly, to each customer showing what is owed. The customer then pays the credit card issuing firm. Interest is charged on sums not paid within a limited period (14–21 days). Barclaycard (operated by Barclays Bank), Visa (operated by the Co-operative Bank) and Access (operated by Midland, Lloyd's and National Westminster) are examples of credit cards.

2 *Overdrafts.* Firms and individuals can, by prior arrangement with their bank, obtain an overdraft. This means the bank will make payments on cheques up to an agreed amount in excess of what is in their account. They are, in effect, borrowing from the bank and are charged interest on the amount overdrawn. Any payment into the account will reduce the overdraft and any payment out will increase it.

3 *Night safes.* This facility enables customers to place money in the custody of the bank after the bank has closed. It is a very useful service for retail stores who can lodge the money after they have closed. A normal paying in slip is completed and the money is placed in a locked pouch provided by the bank. The pouch is then placed in the night safe which is built into the outside wall of the bank. Next day the customer goes to the bank, collects the pouch and pays the money into his account.

4 *Loans.* Money can be borrowed with repayments over a fixed period of time and interest is charged on the loan. (*See* Fig. 12.8.)
5 *Travellers' cheques* and foreign currency can be obtained.
6 *Overseas trade.* Banks assist their customers with references and exchange control formalities and provide information on trade statistics, licensing regulations and foreign markets.

The banks continue to develop the services they offer to customers. These now include save and loan accounts; insurance services; advice on taxation matters and many others. A look at the leaflets available to customers in any bank will indicate to you the wide range of service now available.

Exercises

Write the answers in your workbook
1 On which bank account is interest paid?
2 How can you ensure a cheque is paid into a bank account?
3 A cheque is valid for .... months.
4 A person who signs a cheque is called the ....
5 What bank service would be used to pay several different accounts with one cheque?
6 Name one of the two services offered by banks for payment of regular payments.
7 What bank service is available for retail shops to deposit money after normal banking hours?
8 How would you endorse a cheque to be paid into the payee's account only?

Payments through the Post Office

The Post Office, in addition to the mail and telecommunications services, provides a variety of services enabling money to be transferred from one person or firm to another through postal orders, and the Girobank.

Postal orders

These are available in various denominations from 25p to £10. The value of any postal order can be increased by affixing not more than two stamps with a total value of no more than 9p. A postal order can be, in some ways, compared with a cheque. The name of the payee (the person receiving the postal order) should be shown, and the post office of payment. The counterfoil should be completed and retained as this is proof of payment and would be needed in case of any query. Postal orders may be crossed like cheques and then can only be paid into a bank account. An uncrossed postal order can be cashed at a post office. This is a very useful method of payment to anyone without a bank account and is often used for small purchases by mail order, or small gifts. In addition to the value of the postal order an additional fee, called 'poundage', is charged. A postal order is valid up to six months after the last day of the month in which it is issued. Therefore a postal order purchased in February can be presented for payment up to the end of the following August.

National Girobank

National Girobank, a wholly-owned subsidiary of the Post Office, is an established part of the banking system of this country and offers a wide range of services to both business and personal account customers. The bank uses as its branches the national network of 20 000 post offices.

Girobank's operational centre is at Bootle, Merseyside, where all account records are held and customer transactions processed, using advanced computer equipment. Its head office is in Milk Street in the City of London.

The British Giro Service was introduced in 1968 as a basic money transmission service. It rapidly developed into a major banking institution with a wide range of facilities and, as Girobank, is now a clearing bank, a member of the London Bankers' Clearing House and a participant in many of the committees which direct much of British banking. It is a sponsoring bank in the Bankers' Automated Clearing Service (BACS), a settlement bank in the Clearing House Automated Payment System (CHAPS), a member of the Society for Worldwide Interbank Financial Telecommunications (SWIFT), a principal member of the VISA International Service Association and a founder member of the Association for Payment Clearing Services (APACS), the organisation responsible for the operation and development of inter-bank payment systems.

Girobank was a prime mover in the formation and development in 1985 of LINK – the UK's first fully shared, branded, network of ATMs (automated teller machines). The partners in LINK are: Girobank, Abbey National Building Society, Co-operative Bank, Nationwide Building Society and Funds Transfer Sharing Ltd – a consortium of financial institutions.

Initially providing balance enquiries and cash withdrawals for LINK and most VISA card holders, the ATMs will eventually offer a whole range of electronic banking services available 24 hours a day, seven days a week, with customers of all the participating organisations being able to use other members' machines.

Services

Services to personal account customers include: current (chequebook) account, with free banking while the account is in credit (charges are made for debit transactions only while the account is actually overdrawn); a cheque card which conforms to the standard design and style adopted by the Clearing Banks' Cheque Card Committee and which guarantees cheques or transfers up to £50; a transfer service for paying other Girobank account holders; standing orders and direct debits for automatic regular payments; free postage-paid envelopes to send transactions direct to the bank; regular detailed statements; automated banking through the LINK network of ATMs; VISA credit card allowing instant credit to a maximum set by the bank; a deposit account for savings; a higher interest savings account; personal loans; revolving credit facility; mortgages; bridging loans to assist with house purchases; Postcheques which, with a Postcheque card, can be used when travelling abroad; travellers' cheques and foreign currency; facilities for making and receiving payments worldwide; and a range of insurance services through leading UK insurance companies. New services are being developed continually by the bank to keep pace with changes in the financial services market.

Withdrawals
With a Girobank cheque card up to £50 can be drawn in cash every day at any post office by completing a Girobank cheque made out to 'Self'. Up to £100 can be drawn at the post office named on the card.

Deposits
Deposit into a Girobank account can be at a post office (for cash) or by

Fig. 12.12 Girobank cheque

Fig. 12.13 Girobank cheque card

post direct to Girobank (cheques etc). A transfer/deposit slip (contained
in the chequebook) is completed, made out to 'Self' and either handed over
the post office counter with cash or enclosed with the cheques or other
items in a pre-addressed, postage paid envelope provided. Wages, salary
or pension can be credited direct to a personal account.

Transfers
When paying another account holder a transfer/deposit slip is completed,
showing the account number of the person to be paid. The slip is then
sent to the Girobank Centre where the payer's account is debited and the
account of the payee credited.

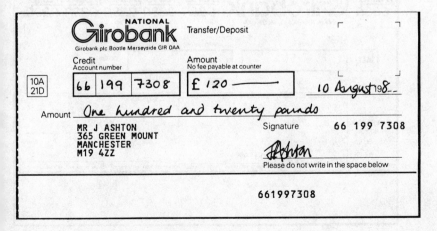

Fig. 12.14 Girobank transfer/deposit form

Non-Girobank account holders can make payments into Girobank accounts using the Transcash service at post offices. The form, available at the counter, is completed and handed with the cash to the counter clerk. Most household bills such as gas, electricity, telephone, rates and water rates can be paid in this way using the detachable Transcash slip provided.

THE ANDY WAY TO PAY AT THE POST OFFICE

Trans cash

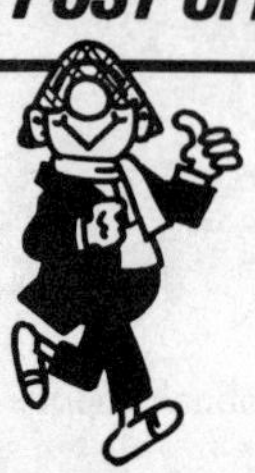

Transcash cuts out the need to spend time and money trailing all over the place to pay bills. And with Transcash there is no need for envelopes or stamps when you are shopping by post. All you need to know is the name of the organisation you are paying and their Girobank or Freepay account number. And then you just fill in a Transcash slip and hand it over the post office counter with your money (and Transcash fee if applicable). We will give you a receipt and make sure your payment details and money arrive safely.

Date

19

Credit
ACCOUNT NUMBER

Amount
STANDARD FEE PAYABLE AT PO COUNTER

£

Trans cash — NATIONAL Girobank — Trans cash Trans cash Trans cash Trans cash Trans cash

Girobank plc Bootle Merseyside GIR OAA

14D

Credit
ACCOUNT NUMBER

Amount
STANDARD FEE PAYABLE AT PO COUNTER

£

This is not a cheque

PAY Name of organisation

Signature

YOUR full name and address
BLOCK CAPITALS PLEASE

POSTCODE

Date

19

Please do not write or mark below this line Please do not write or mark below this line Please do not write or mark below this line Please do not write or mark below this line

Fig. 12.15 Girobank Transcash form

Any person over the age of 15 can open an account by completing an application form (available at post offices) and sending it, with an initial deposit of £10, to Girobank.

Services to business customers include: full current account banking; a service for the deposit of branch or agent takings at post offices during long weekday hours and Saturday mornings; a change-giving service at local post offices; rapid marshalling of funds into central accounts to facilitate efficient cash management; payment and collection services, including cheque, credit transfer, standing order and direct debit (Girobank is a sponsoring bank in BACS – Bankers' Automated Clearing Services); money market deposits for short-, medium- or long-term investments; specialist investment services including wholesale deposits and Certificates of Deposit; foreign exchange payments; cash transfer through CHAPS and Town Clearing; full international money transmission for payments and receipts, foreign currency and travel facilities; credit facilities, including overdrafts, short- and medium-term loans, acceptance credits and leasing finance, advanced payment and deferred purchase schemes and financing for the purchase of local authority mortgages; credit of pay, allowances and expenses to employees and pensioners (payment instructions can be in paper list format or on computer tape or via BACS; dividend payments; Transcash; collection services for local authorities and housing associations to have rent, rates and mortgages paid at convenient post offices; a service for building societies whereby investors can make deposits to and withdrawals from their building society accounts at post offices. Business customers can

STATEMENT OF ACCOUNT			NATIONAL Girobank		G70►
Number	66 199 7308	29SEP86	Girobank plc Bootle Merseyside GIR 0AA		Serial 622
			VAT registration number 243 1700 02		
Summary			Transactions		£
previous balance	23SEP86	£334.06		DEBITS	
total debits		254.79	25SEP C 003545	SELF	50.00
total credits		762.32	25SEP S 6013102	ALLIANCE BS	130.00
current balance	29SEP86	841.59	25SEP T 6202007	NORWEB	49.80
			29SEP C 003544		
				CREDITS	
			29SEP T 6130003		762.32
	MR J ASHTON 365 GREEN MOUNT MANCHESTER M19 4ZZ				

D Deposit S Standing Order OD Overdrawn
C Cheque DD Direct Debit
T Transfer TC Transcash

Enquiries: Please address any enquiry to the Manager, Customer Account Services quoting your account number.

Fig. 12.16 Girobank statement

arrange to receive a statement on each day there is a movement – debit or credit – on their account.

Building societies

In the past, building societies have been associated with private house purchase and savings facilities. An increasing number of societies are beginning to offer services similar to those provided by banks, e.g. the payment and transfer of money.

Exercises

Write the answers in your workbook
1 How can the face value of a postal order be increased?
2 Which reference book gives details of overseas money payments?
3 What do you call the additional fee for a postal order?
4 In addition to Europe what country operates International Giro Services?
5 Where is the National Girobank Centre?
6 Give two occasions when an individual may receive a Girobank statement.
7 Name the Girobank form completed when one account holder pays another account holder.
8 Explain briefly how a Girobank account holder could pay a non-account holder.

Assignments

1 Obtain a blank cheque form and complete from the following particulars:
Payee: J Smith & Co
Drawer: A N Other
Amount: £110.96
Use current date
2 Obtain a blank paying-in form and complete for the following:
96 – 1p coins
24 – 2p coins
26 – 5p coins
10 – 10p coins
 5 – 20p coins
56 – £1 coins
22 – £5 notes
10 – £10 notes
 2 – £20 notes
 1 – £5 Scottish bank note
Cheque from A N Other for £10.20
Cheque from Anyfirm Ltd for £15.10

3 *(a)* Complete the bank statement which would be received by Anyfirm Ltd at the end of the current month using the following details:

Date		£
1st	Balance b/f	250.20
6th	Payment made by cheque	7.40
10th	Standing Order paid by bank	6.00
16th	Paying-in slip total	36.20
20th	Payment made by cheque	20.00
24th	Wages withdrawn by cheque	126.00

(b) What is the amount left in Anyfirm Ltd's account at the end of the month?

4 You are employed in the accounts department of Anyfirm Ltd, High Street, Longton. Having received an invoice from J Smith & Co, The Grange, Yorktown, you are asked to pay their account by credit transfer. Complete the necessary documents from the following information:

Your bank: Midland Bank plc, Longton
Bank Code: 06-40-06
Account No: 620731
J Smith & Co bank at Midland Bank plc, Yorktown
Bank Code: 09-49-09
Account No: 125267
Amount of Invoice: £152.90

5 *(a)* As an employee of Anyfirm Ltd you are asked to complete the standing order instructions to your bank as in Assignment 4 for the following:

Payee: Office News Ltd
Amount: £26.00
Bank: National Westminster Bank plc, High Street, Anytown.
    Code: 40-18-40
    Account No: 620671
Payable quarterly commencing 1 January, 19..

(b) Explain briefly the difference between 'standing order' and 'direct debit'. Give reasons why many firms prefer direct debit to standing order.

6 *(a)* Give three reasons why payment by cash may not be suitable for modern business transactions.

(b) State the steps necessary in opening a bank account.

7 How would you make the following payments through the National Girobank system?

(a) £25 to a non-account holder with a bank account;
(b) £15 regular monthly payments to a building society;
(c) A bill for £40 in a retail store.

8 List and describe three services offered by a bank. Illustrate each of these services with a pamphlet from a bank, drawings, and cuttings from newspapers.

9 Anyfirm Ltd, High Street, Yorktown has a number of accounts to pay. Their bank is the Midland Bank, Yorktown, Code Number 07-49-60, Account Number 167432. These accounts are settled on 8 April via payments made by Bank Giro system (credit transfer):

(a) G Wheelhouse & Co, Midland Bank, Newtown
   Code 06-14-64   Account No. 82746   £72.00
   A Franklin Ltd, Barclays Bank, Longton
   Code 14-00-64   Account No. 642713   £110.20
   J Ashley & Sons, Lloyds Bank, Newtown
   Code 08-00-72   Account No. 132167   £19.80

Make out the appropriate documents to effect these payments. Write a brief account of what happens to these documents from the time you have completed them.

(b) The following payments are to be made by cheque:

3 April, 19..	A Jones Ltd	£6.25
11 April, 19..	D Green & Co	£15.40
16 April, 19..	W Briggs & Sons	£4.20
23 April, 19..	D Bagshaw & Co	£16.40

Make out the cheques using a general crossing for the first two, and a specific crossing for the others.

(c) On 30 April, 19.. a payment is to be made by standing order of £60.40 to Nationwide Insurance Co. Their bank is Lloyds of Branton, Code 09-00-46 and their account number is 467432. Complete the standing order form.

(d) On 5 April, 19.. Anyfirm Ltd has the following notes, coins, etc. to pay into the company's account:

30 – £5 notes   18 – 5p pieces
17 – £1 coins   40 – 2p pieces
15 – 50p pieces   10 – 1p pieces
32 – 10p pieces

plus cheques: £16.20, £8.95, £4.95

Complete the paying-in slip and then answer the following questions:

(i) Who provides the paying-in slips?
(ii) How many copies are needed?
(iii) Who keeps the copies?
(iv) Is it necessary for the cheques to be endorsed before paying them in? All three show Anyfirm Ltd as the payee.

(e) In addition to the paying-in slip on 5 April, the following amounts were also paid into Anyfirm Ltd's account.

12 April – £52.20
19 April – £26.40
26 April – £72.30
29 April – £57.40

On 1 April, 19.. Anyfirm Ltd's bank account balance was £560.90. Taking into account all the transactions in *(a)* to *(e)* of this assignment, make out the bank statement as at 30 April, 19.. showing clearly the balance at that date.

13 THE MAIL ROOM

Objectives

At the end of this chapter you should be able to:

- Explain the procedure for dealing with incoming and outgoing mail.
- Explain the procedure for dealing with mail received to be seen by more than one person.
- Describe the use and value of mail room machinery and equipment.
- State the regulations involved in using a franking machine.
- Complete a postage book and franking machine control card.

It is important to any organisation that their mail is dealt with efficiently and quickly. Incoming mail should be available for staff at the start of work. All outgoing mail should be despatched whenever possible on the day it is prepared. Failure to deal with mail currently can mean missed opportunities. If you consider the importance of purchasing and sales documents, and remittances such as cheques and postal orders, then you will realise how serious inefficiency can be.

The mail room staff have a very important part to play and they should feel that looking after the post is a responsible and important job. Many firms appoint a responsible member of staff as the mail room supervisor who will be in control of its organisation. New junior staff often start in the mail room. It provides a training ground and an awareness of the activities of the firm.

For convenience we will divide our examination of the general rules and equipment for dealing with the mail into inward mail (letters and parcels received) and outward mail (letters and parcels sent out). The type of equipment required will vary from firm to firm depending upon the quantity of mail to be dealt with. Ideally the postroom should be situated on the ground floor. The room should be of a reasonable size to allow for handling positions for incoming mail, outgoing mail and parcels, with suitable benches and tables.

Incoming mail

1 Mail room staff should attend earlier than the remaining members of staff, so that mail can be distributed before they arrive or be available for collection on their arrival. Some firms hire private boxes from the Post Office enabling them to call at the Post Office and collect their mail early in a morning without waiting for normal delivery. They are given a box number which is included in their postal address.

2 Mail is sorted into three groups:

(a) Registered mail is recorded in a book and usually dealt with by the supervisor.

(b) Mail marked 'private' and/or 'personal' is not opened. It is passed unopened to the person to whom it is addressed.

(c) Other mail is opened and the contents removed. All letters and enclosures should be stamped with the date and in some cases firms use a combined date and time stamp. A careful check is made that all enclosures are included and they are attached to the letter.

3 Any remittances (cheques, postal orders, etc.) must be checked with any advices, monthly statements or remittance slips and initialled and entered in a remittance book. Any discrepancy should be reported immediately to the supervisor who will decide what action should be taken.

4 Having opened the mail it is then sorted by reference, subject or department address. Any queries should be handed to the supervisor to save time. All empty envelopes are re-checked to ensure the contents have been removed.

5 Any letters or documents for distribution, i.e. those to be seen by more than one person, will have a mailing list or routing slip attached (Fig. 13.1). If urgent, they will be endorsed with the name of the people concerned and photocopied indicating each person's copy and delivered to them.

Name	Department	Date
A Jones	Sales	
R Rogers	Accounts	
H Cassidy	Personnel	
Return to A Wright for Filing		

Fig. 13.1 Routing slip

6 Mail will then be distributed to the offices concerned by messenger service. In some organisations a member of staff from each department calls at the mail room and collects the department's mail. The messenger delivery service is preferable. It avoids any confusion and ensures mailroom staff are not delayed in completing their work. All remittances, having been checked, are taken to the cashier's department.

Machines and equipment for incoming mail

The type and variety of equipment will vary from firm to firm but usually includes:

1 Letter opening machine. The envelope is fed into the machine which can handle envelopes of varying sizes and a narrow strip is sliced off the envelope. The envelopes can be fed through again in reverse when checking that the envelopes are empty after mail has been removed and distributed. This machine will save a considerable amount of time and will speed up the handling of the mail. The machines are easily stored when not in use.

2 Date and time stamp.

3 Sorting equipment, i.e. wire, wood, plastic or metal trays, pigeon hole shelving or even basket trolleys.

4 A photocopying machine.

Outgoing mail

1 Regular collections of mail from departments when the mail has been signed will prevent congestion at the end of the day. A definite time should be set for the last collection of the day to ensure that all mail is dealt with and despatched that day.

2 Departments should be asked to mark in pencil any letters requiring special services such as recorded delivery or registered post so that the attention of mailroom staff is drawn to them. Other mail has to be sorted into first and second class.

3 Where large quantities of mail, e.g. invoices, statements of account, price lists and advertising materials, are posted on a regular basis, then special equipment such as folding, inserting and sealing machines (Fig. 13.5) should be used.

4 To avoid letters being sent to the wrong address, window envelopes should be used wherever possible. This type of envelope has a cellophane window on the front. When the letter is folded and inserted the address on the letter shows through the window.

5 Check all enclosures are with the letter. Where necessary use a stapler

Postage Book				
Date	Addressee	Type	Amount	
			£	p
Nov 1	W Chapman	Letter		18
1	W H Hill	Parcel	1	52
2	P E Barrow	Letter		13
2	M Booth	Letter		18
2				

Fig. 13.2

or paper clip to fix them together. Never use pins to fasten documents together. These can be a serious safety hazard, projecting through the envelope.

6 Sort letters into groups of first and second class mail. Check the weight of any bulky envelopes and parcels and calculate the amount of postage required.

7 Enter details of outgoing mail in the post book.

The post book is a record of the amount of postage used and provides a record for reference purposes in case of any query. With the use of franking machines many firms have discontinued the use of post books. The stamps in hand should always be the difference between stamps received and stamps used. Any discrepancies should be reported to the supervisor.

8 Deliver all mail and parcels to the Post Office. In the case of very large quantities of mail the Post Office will make collections from the firm at agreed times.

Methods of stamping mail

For small quantities of mail stamps can be used. Where larger quantities of mail are involved a postal franking machine can be used. The franking machine franks an impression of a stamp on the envelope. The machine is hired or purchased from a Post Office authorised supplier and the following conditions apply:

1 A licence is issued to the user of a franking machine.

2 Payment for postage must be made in advance. A credit meter on the machine is set for the pre-paid amount in 1p units. The meter is removed from the machine and taken to the post office named on the licence for setting of the units pre-paid. It is then sealed by the Post Office.

3 A franking machine control card (see Fig. 13.3) is completed each day with

the reading of the meter. At the end of the week, the card is posted to the post office which deals with the postage pre-payment.

4 All franked mail must be handed into the post office, not placed in a post box. If special arrangements are made the franked mail can be placed in a special envelope and put in the post box. The machine is locked when not in use and kept in a secure place to prevent misuse. When franking the mail, the franking machine is set for the required postage (up to 99p according to the type of machine). The envelope is fed into the machine. The postage used is then recorded on an ascending meter. This meter records the total postage used. The total shown increases as each letter is franked. A descending meter records the amount of postage left in credit. This will decrease as each letter is franked. If required, an advertising slogan can be printed in addition to the stamp. The use of a franking

---

FRANKING MACHINE CONTROL CARD

User ....

Machine (or Meter No.) .... Setting or Recording Unit ....

Meter Office (as shown on Record Card)...

I certify that the following entries for the above machine for the week ended... are correct

and that the correct date has been shown on each day's posting

CHECK DATE DAILY

Put initials in column below to show date has been changed		ALL MACHINES Reading of Ascending Register (Totalisator)	LOCKING MACHINES Reading of Descending Register (Credit Meter)	ALL MACHINES Last entry in col. "Total Deposits" or "Total Settings" on Record Card
	Mon.			
	Tue.			
	Wed.			
	Thur.			
	Fri.			
	Sat.			

NOTE 1. Whether or not the machine has been used, this card must be posted on Saturday, or on Friday if no postings are made on Saturday.

Signed...

.... 19...........

NOTE 2. The daily entry must be made on completion of each day's postings.

Post Office Examining Officer's initials...

Fig. 13.3

Fig. 13.4 Franking mark

Fig. 13.5 The ASI AKB Folder/Inserter.
Reproduced by permission of Addressing Systems International Limited.

machine eliminates the need to keep a large number of stamps. A postage book is not really necessary unless a few loose stamps are kept for late posting of mail. For larger firms the modern franking machine can have attachments for sealing and stacking envelopes. A gummed label is used for parcels and bulky packets.

Additional machinery

In larger firms with a considerable quantity of mail such as invoices and advertising material, a wide range of equipment for sealing envelopes and folding and inserting documents into the envelopes can be used. These machines can be linked to give an automatic operation where the paper is folded, inserted into the envelope, and sealed and franked with the required postage.

Addressing machines

Although there are still addressing machines using metal stencil or spirit plates, the development of micro technology has overtaken this type of

Fig. 13.6 The ASI Sprinter
Addressing machine. Reproduced by permission of Addressing Systems International
Ltd.

machine. The modern addressing machines are in fact micro addressing systems. They have their own software, keyboard, display, disc drives and printers. The ASI Sprinter in Fig. 13.6 is capable of accessing 2000 entries at any one time and can print 1500 addresses per hour. It is possible to access only the addresses required and to select by post code or alphabet. This machine is particularly useful for repetitive printing of information on labels for all kinds of applications, i.e. addressing, labelling for bottles and packages, files, special messages on letters, despatch labels, etc.

Exercises

Write the answers in your workbook
1 What is the purpose of employing new juniors in the mail room?
2 Why should mail room staff attend earlier than other office staff?
3 Why is it necessary to separate mail marked 'personal' and/or 'private' from other mail?
4 What do we call the book in which we enter money, cheques, and postal orders received?
5 State the two ways of dealing with letters and documents received which have to be seen by more than one person.
6 Name two machines or pieces of equipment used for dealing with mail.
7 Why should you set a last collecting time for outwards mail?

8 How can you avoid letters being sent to the wrong address?
9 Give two conditions necessary for the use of a franking machine.
10 Name two pieces of equipment used for outgoing mail.

Parcels

Because of the problem of bulk and packing it is useful to have a separate working area in the mail room with a good strong working surface to hold parcels scales. A shelf or cupboard for storage of equipment such as brown paper, string, scissors and labels should also be available.

Reference books and leaflets

A notice board is useful to exhibit leaflets obtainable from the Post Office on postal rates and services. A small bookshelf should also be provided for reference books such as the Post Office Guide and Postcode Directories.

Mail room furniture and equipment

There is a wide range of furniture and equipment available for the mail room including sorting trays, workbenches, trolleys and mail sack holders. The choice of equipment will depend on each individual firm's needs. The use of suitable furniture, equipment and machinery will increase both efficiency and speed in dealing with the mail.

Electronic mail

It is possible to send mail by electronic means. Information can now be transmitted by British Telecom's Prestel system. Messages can be passed from one Prestel user to another providing the sender knows the other person's or firm's access code. With the development of Viewdata systems both within companies (in-house) and via public systems, it will be possible to transmit and give access to a great deal of information without the need for a lot of paper.

In addition British Telecom now offer their Teletex service. This is an automatic transmission service which is thirty times quicker than telex. A variety of types of equipment will be able to use this service. It will enable terminals to be connected to other terminals.

Business correspondence, documents, and a variety of data and messages can now be transmitted between terminals, from city to city in approximately 10 seconds per page. Any information which can be produced on a conventional typewriter can be accurately reproduced.

Letters can be typed and sent automatically at the touch of a few keys. Unlike telex, the terminals are able to carry out other functions than transmitting communications. The standard texts can be drawn from a file (like word processing) and held in the memory. After adding such variables as the name, address and date the letter can be transmitted. Whilst such a letter is being sent the terminal can be used to type another message. Incoming messages will be indicated to the operator, but will only interrupt other work if the memory is nearly full.

Teletex subscribers will be able to communicate with all telex subscribers (over 1½ million worldwide). The system is to be gradually extended throughout Europe, Canada and the USA. Many of the countries are committed to adopt such systems.

Copies of text received through Teletex can be stored electronically or printed for normal filing. Paper work is thus reduced to a minimum, and office productivity increased.

Assignments

1 Give the steps to be followed in opening incoming mail in an office to ensure no mistakes are made and that the mail is available for commencement of work.
2 An important part of the work of an office junior is dealing with outgoing post. How would you ensure that this work is carried out efficiently, and what aids may be available?
3 List and describe the use of three pieces of equipment or machines in the mail room, illustrating your answer with drawings and/or cuttings from magazines, etc.
4 You are responsible for the franking machine in the mail room of J R King & Co Ltd. Complete a franking machine control card from the following details for the week ended 8 March, 19..

The meter office is Chesterfield P O, and the machine number is D8572 and operates on 1p units.

At the commencement of business on Monday, 4 March, the number of units used was 78 508 (ascending register) and the number of units purchased 80 000.

Monday   – used 1320 units.
Tuesday   – purchased units to the value of £60.00. Used 1780 units.
Wednesday – used 1076 units.
Thursday   – used 1408 units.
Friday   – used 1250 units.
5 From the franking machine control card in (4), calculate:
    (a) the total value of postage used in the week, and
    (b) the balance of credit at the end of the week.
6 (a) Select any organisation with which you are familiar and investigate how they deal with incoming and outgoing mail. List the equipment and its purpose.

(b) Is there any other item you consider would be useful? Give your reasons.

7 Draw a plan of a mail room that you would consider necessary for a large office block employing 200+ staff. Indicate the layout for dealing with both incoming and outgoing mail and the necessary equipment.

8 You are in charge of your firm's mail room. Supply your own name and address for the firm. Both inward and outward mail are handled.

(a) £50 in cash has been handed to you with which you have to purchase stamps. The following is a summary of the mail going out from your company over a period of one week:

Monday
Jones Bros, York, one letter, first class, 40 gms.
Brown and Harrison, Swansea, one letter, second class 80 gms.
A Millar, London, one parcel 3 kg.
Evans & Wright, Brighton, one registered letter, value £150, 45 gms.
E Jennings & Co, Sheffield, one letter, first class, 50 gms.
R Smith, Wolverhampton, one letter, second class, 42 gms.

Tuesday
N Smith, Croydon, one letter, first class, 72 gms.
Six sales representatives, one letter each, second class, 40 gms.
T Simpson, Glasgow, one letter, first class, 40 gms.
A Brown, Manchester, one parcel, 5 kg.

Wednesday
J Wood & Co, Nottingham, one letter, second class, 30 gms.
D Myers & Co, Brighton, one letter, first class, 40 gms.
C Black, Bermuda, one letter (air mail), 20 gms.
Hotel Majestic, Torquay, one letter, first class, 60 gms.

Thursday
A Wilks, Birmingham, one letter, first class, 26 gms.
A Millar, London, one parcel, 3 kg.
Six circular letters to sales representatives, second class, 45 gms.
J Smith, Carlisle, one letter, first class, 50 gms.
A Brown, Manchester, one letter, first class, 46 gms.

Friday
F Wood & Co, Workington, one parcel, 5 kg.
Wilkinson & Co, Newcastle, one letter, second class, 46 gms.
Anyfirm Ltd, Leeds, one letter, first class, 70 gms.
L Smith, Sheffield, one letter, first class, 40 gms.

Draft the rulings for a postage book. Enter the above mail in this book as you would have done in the office, i.e. on a daily basis, balancing and carrying down the balance each day.

(b) Explain the procedure for dealing with a registered letter. Give some possible reasons why a letter may be registered.

(c) Assume that instead of using a postage book as in *(a)*, you have a franking machine. Supply the machine number, meter office. The machine operates on 1p units. At the commencement of duty on Monday the ascending meter was 8015 units and the number of units purchased (total column) was 25 000

units. Complete the franking machine control card for the week for the postage in *(a)*.

(d) In handling the incoming mail, you have eight departments to which mail is normally distributed. The average daily mail received is 100 (letters or packages), with the occasional registered letter. Quite frequently the letters contain cheques, postal orders, etc. Sometimes a few letters are received for the attention of two or three different departments.

Draft a memorandum from yourself to the Office Manager (use your teacher's name) outlining in detail the procedures you use for dealing with inward mail. Conclude by suggesting any item of equipment or machinery which the company does not have at present but which you think it would be an advantage to purchase.

14 POSTAL SERVICES

Objectives

At the end of this chapter you should be able to:

- Identify a suitable postal service for a business need.
- Explain different postal services available to an individual or firm.
- Complete the appropriate documents for postal services.

We have dealt with the flow of documents between firms in buying and selling. In our everyday life we are concerned with writing or receiving letters or greetings cards, and we have come to accept the postal delivery service to our home and place of work as a part of everyday life.

The Post Office delivers two categories of letter mail – first class and second class and charges two rates. A higher rate is charged for first class letters. As most letters are posted late in the day, first class letters are sorted the same night and less urgent letters (second class) are sorted during the next day. Every working day the postal service delivers over 11 million first class letters, 22 million second class letters and 0.5 million parcels. Collections are made from 100 000 posting boxes as well as from post offices and thousands of large postal users' premises. The Post Office have almost 23 000 post offices. In addition to the many varied postal services and Girobank service, post offices deal with many other services such as the payment of pensions and family allowances. They also issue licences for guns, television sets and cars, sell premium bonds and national saving certificates and accept payment of telephone accounts. In addition, many claim forms and leaflets for welfare services are available at local post offices. In this chapter we shall be concerned with the major postal services. Full details of all services and conditions are shown in the Post Office Guide.

Post Office Guide

The Post Office Guide is an important reference book giving a comprehensive guide to all the services provided by the Post Office. This

What a Postcode represents

The postcode is a combination of up to seven letters and numbers which define different levels of geographic unit.

The largest geographical unit is known as a Postcode Area. Each area is represented by the first one or two letter characters of the postcode.

There are 120 Postcode Areas.

Each postcode area is itself divided into carefully chosen smaller geographical units called Districts, which are represented by the number in the first half of the postcode.

There are 2,700 Postcode Districts.

Postcode districts are divided into smaller geographical units called Sectors. These are designated by the figure which begins the second part of the postcode.

There are 8,900 Postcode Sectors.

Finally, the complete postcode pinpoints one street, or part of a street, with the last two alpha characters.

There are 1.5 million postcodes in the country.

There are 22 million addresses in the UK. Some addresses (around 170,000) have their own unique postcode because they receive large quantities of mail per day. They're called Large User Postcodes. The remaining addresses are covered by Smaller User Postcodes, and on average there are 15 addresses to each small user postcode.

Fig. 14.1

guide is published annually and contains information on all inland and foreign postal and telecommunications services. In addition, major items, such as methods of payment, savings, licensing and insurance and pension facilities at post offices are included. Supplements are issued regularly giving details of any amendments to the Guide. These can be obtained by filling in a postage prepaid card at the time of purchase of a Guide and sending it to the local Head Postmaster. The supplements are numbered 1 onwards and it is possible to check that each supplement is received.

Postcode

In addition to continuing to provide new services to meet the requirements of individuals and firms, the Post Office has mechanised the sorting of mail to reduce costs and improve services. Postcodes are the key to mechanical letter sorting and this country has the world's most sophisticated postcode system. All 21¾ million addresses in the United Kingdom are now postcoded. It is important to use the postcode in addressing letters and parcels.

The postcode is a combination of alphabetical and numerical characters divided into two groups. The first group represents an area in the country and a district within it, and the second group represents a sector within the district, and a street or part of a street within the sector.

Recorded delivery

This is a useful service for sending documents such as birth certificates and examination certificates which have considerable personal but little money value and where it is important that delivery is made. Firms can use this service for important quotations and contracts, and returning birth certificates or examination certificates to applicants for jobs. Any inland postal packet except parcels, railway letters and parcels, airway letters and COD packets can be sent by this service. A recorded delivery fee must be pre-paid in addition to normal postage. The address of the packet must be written on a special recorded delivery receipt form (*see* Fig. 14.2). The gummed label at the end of the receipt form is detached and stuck on the packet in the top left hand corner. The recorded delivery packet is then signed for on delivery. The sender can ask for proof of delivery at the time of handing in the packet at the post office or at a later date, on payment of a small fee. Certain items, such as notes, coins, and jewellery should not be sent by recorded delivery.

P 835088 **Recorded Delivery**

Certificate of Posting
for Recorded Delivery
How to post
1 Enter below in ink the name and full address as written on the letter or packet.
2 Affix the numbered adhesive label in the top left-hand corner of the letter (or close to the address on a packet).
3 Affix postage stamps to the letter for the correct postage and Recorded Delivery fee.
4 Hand this certificate, together with the letter, to an officer of The Post Office.
5 This certificate will be date-stamped and initialled as a receipt. Please keep it safely, and produce it in the event of a claim

Name

Address

Postcode

Recorded Delivery should not be used for sending money or valuable items.

For
Post Office
use

Recorded Delivery no
P 835088

Accepting
Officer's initials

Date Stamp

P2297Aug 85

Fig. 14.2 Certificate of Posting for Recorded Delivery (orange)

Registered post (registration)

This is available for any first class letter except an airway or railway letter. A fee for registration is paid in addition to the normal postage charge. In the event of loss or damage compensation is paid by the Post Office. This

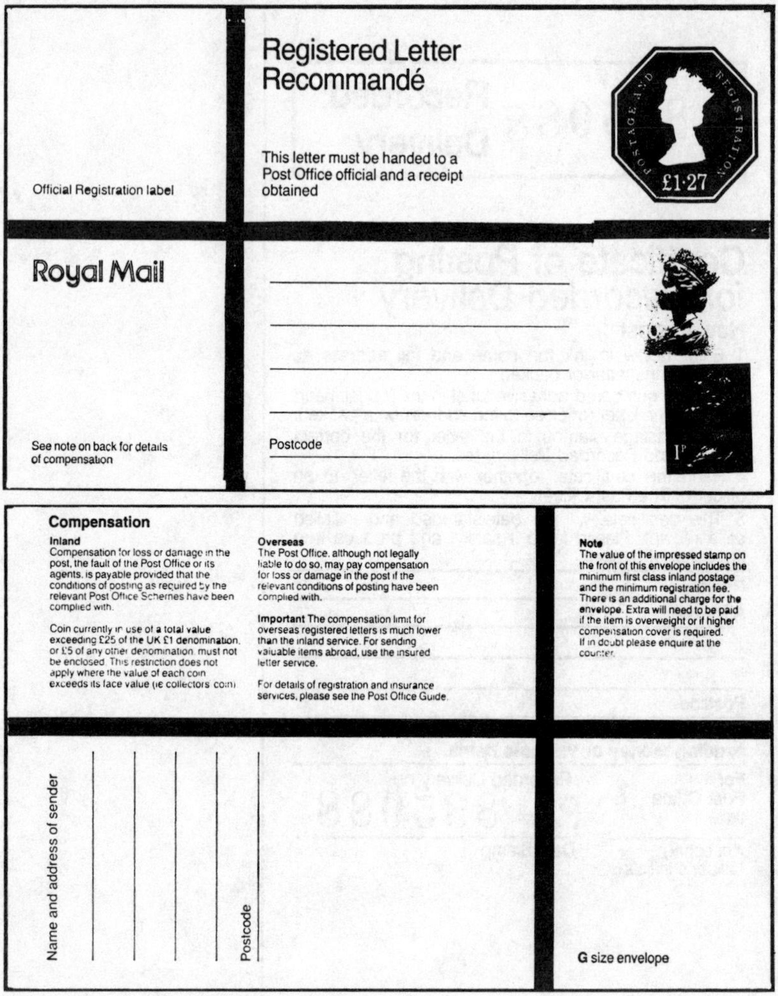

Official Registration label

Registered Letter
Recommandé

This letter must be handed to a
Post Office official and a receipt
obtained

POSTAGE AND REGISTRATION £1·27

Royal Mail

See note on back for details
of compensation

Postcode

1ᵖ

Compensation

Inland
Compensation for loss or damage in the post, the fault of the Post Office or its agents, is payable provided that the conditions of posting as required by the relevant Post Office Schemes have been complied with.

Coin currently in use of a total value exceeding £25 of the UK £1 denomination, or £5 of any other denomination, must not be enclosed. This restriction does not apply where the value of each coin exceeds its face value (ie collectors' coin).

Overseas
The Post Office, although not legally liable to do so, may pay compensation for loss or damage in the post if the relevant conditions of posting have been complied with.

Important The compensation limit for overseas registered letters is much lower than the inland service. For sending valuable items abroad, use the insured letter service.

For details of registration and insurance services, please see the Post Office Guide.

Note
The value of the impressed stamp on the front of this envelope includes the minimum first class inland postage and the minimum registration fee. There is an additional charge for the envelope. Extra will need to be paid if the item is overweight or if higher compensation cover is required. If in doubt please enquire at the counter.

Name and address of sender

Postcode

G size envelope

Fig. 14.3 Registered envelope (blue and white)

compensation, which is limited, varies with the amount of registration fee paid by the sender. This service is used for valuable articles. All letters containing coins, bank notes, and jewellery must be registered. Anything intended for registration must be handed in at a post office and a certificate of posting (*see* Fig. 14.4) confirming payment of a registration fee must be obtained.

A receipt is obtained for a registered delivery. Special secure envelopes can be purchased from the Post Office for registered mail (*see* Fig. 14.3). Alternatively, any ordinary envelope must be marked with a vertical and

The Post Office
Certificate of Posting
for inland ordinary letters and parcels
and overseas ordinary letters

Received	items as listed	Accepting Officer's initials	Date stamp

Enter below in ink the name and full address as written on each item, and present them in the order listed. (For Cash on Delivery parcels, enter also the reference number of the Despatch/Inpayment Document.)
No compensation will be paid in respect of money or jewellery sent in the ordinary post.

Name	Address	Postcode
1		
2		
3		
4		
5		
6		
7		
8		

P326 Dec 83 (continue overleaf if necessary)

Fig. 14.4 Certificate of Posting (pink)

horizontal blue line on the back and front of the envelope, and must be secured with wax, gum or other adhesive substance. This service is often used by firms who have to pay the wages in cash of employees who are working away from the normal pay location.

Certificate of posting

This may be obtained from a post office when a letter or parcel is posted. A certificate of posting for a compensation fee parcel is issued free and a certificate of posting for a letter, packet or ordinary parcel costs 1p.

Business reply service

This service enables firms to enclose an unstamped reply card, letter card, envelope, folder or gummed label of the special design (Fig. 14.5) in any magazine, book or correspondence. Their customers can then reply without having to pay any postage. The postage charges are paid by the firm and are based on replies received. It is a particularly useful service frequently used by firms when they are advertising. It encourages people

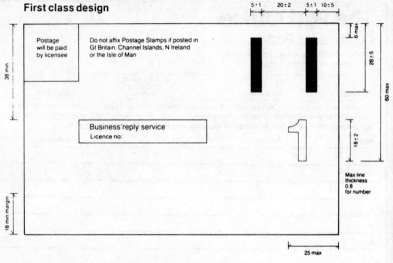

Fig. 14.5 Business Reply Service envelope design

to reply without having to pay any postage. The following conditions apply:

1 A licence must be obtained from the local Head Postmaster and a licence number will be issued.

2 A sum of money sufficient to cover expected charges for approximately one month must be paid in advance. When the sum is nearly exhausted, a further sum is paid to renew credit.

3 The design must be submitted to the local Head Postmaster for approval. Printing cannot be done until the design has been approved.

4 Delivery is normally once daily on the second delivery whenever there is more than one delivery of ordinary correspondence.

5 In addition to the licence fee, a small surcharge is made as well as the normal postage charge for each reply delivered.

Freepost

This is a further service enabling firms' clients to reply without the expense of postage. Unlike the Business Reply Service where a special card or label, etc. is required, the firm include a special address in their communications or advertisements. The reply bearing this address can be posted in the usual way, but without a stamp. The addressee pays postage on all replies received (replies may only be sent second class). The service may be extended under one licence to cover several branches of the same firm or subsidiary companies at different addresses. The obvious advantage of this service is that the firm's customers do not have to obtain a special card, envelope or label. Firms mention this service in their advertising on television and posters, and in newspapers, magazines and journals. The following conditions apply:

1 A licence must be obtained from the local Head Postmaster.

2 A sum of money sufficient to cover expected charges for approximately one month must be paid in advance. When the sum is nearly exhausted a further sum is paid to renew credit.

Where a firm operates both Business Reply and Freepost Services the sum paid has to be sufficient to cover both services.

3 The Head Postmaster will specify on the licence the precise terms of each address to which Freepost items may be posted. This address only must be used in any communications or advertisements.

4 Delivery is normally once daily on the second delivery where there is more than one delivery of normal correspondence.

5 In addition to the licence fee a small surcharge is made as well as the second class postage charge for each reply delivered.

Admail

This is a facility for direct response advertiser selling off the television screen. Admail provides the advertiser with a local address to which replies can be posted. In certain circumstances Admail is available to press, radio and direct mail advertisers.

Poste Restante

Letters and parcels to be called for may, as a rule, be addressed to any post office except a town sub-office. The words 'To Be Called For' or 'Poste Restante' should appear in the address, i.e.

Mr A Brown,
Poste Restante, (*or* To Be Called For)
Post Office,
BARNSLEY,
South Yorkshire.
S70 1AA

This service is for the convenience of travellers and may not be used in the same town for more than three months. It can be used by firms to send correspondence when staff, including salesmen, are to be away from home for a period of time.

Express Services

1 *Royal Mail Special Delivery.* Under this service the Post Office undertakes to deliver first class letter packets specially, where appropriate, to enable next working day delivery to be achieved. Special Delivery does not give full courier service but reduces the possibility of a day's delay. The packet is despatched by the next ordinary mail from the office of posting and is picked out from other mail and delivered in the usual way. If they arrive late for normal delivery they will be delivered during working hours subject to availability of staff. If this is not possible it will be delivered by normal mail the next day and the Royal Mail Special Delivery fee will be refunded. This service is available to places in Great Britain and Northern Ireland except certain remote places where such delivery would not be possible. All letter packets intended for this service must be handed in at post offices only. The delivery address must be written on a Royal Mail Special Delivery certificate of posting and the gummed label at the end of the certificate of posting must be detached and stuck on the packet. A Royal Mail Special Delivery fee, in addition to the normal postage, is payable.

2 *Airways letters.* The Post Office has an agreement with British Airways for acceptance of first class letters from the public at certain airport offices for conveyance on the next available direct air service to the destination, to be called for either at the airport or town terminal or to be transferred to the ordinary post by the airline. This applies to certain routes only.

3 *Intelpost.* This is a high speed facsimile service for the transmission of urgent copies of documents between Intelpost centres in the UK and certain towns and cities in the USA, Canada and the Netherlands. Documents up to A4 size may be handed in at post offices displaying 'Intelpost Here'. For an additional fee they can be collected by messenger. At the destination the copies can be either collected or delivered. This is a very fast and useful service for copies of drawings, designs and contracts. Customers with compatible equipment can also transmit to Intelpost centres for counter pick-up.

4 *Datapost.* This service provides a fast, secure and highly reliable courier service for urgent packages. There is no limit to the weight of a consignment but individual items must not exceed 27.5 kgs. There are two services:

   (a) Datapost Sameday: provides same day collection and delivery both locally and intercity.

   (b) Datapost Overnight: provides next day delivery. Items should be taken to any post office displaying 'Datapost Here' or ring the operator for Freefone Datapost to arrange collection.

Royal Mail
Special Delivery

Date and time of posting _____

Date rec'd in Delivery Office _____

A 979478

Certificate of Posting for Royal Mail Special Delivery

How to post

1 Enter below in ink the name and full address as written on the letter or packet.

2 Affix the numbered adhesive label in the top left hand corner of the letter (or close to the address on a packet).

3 Affix postage stamps to the letter for the first class postage and Special Delivery fee, and write the sender's name and address on the back of the letter.

4 Hand this certificate, together with the letter, to an officer of the Post Office.

5 This certificate will be date-stamped and initialled as a receipt. Please keep it safely, and produce it in the event of a claim.

Name _____

Address _____

_____

_____

Postcode _____

The unregistered post should not be used for sending money or valuable items.

For Post Office use

Special Delivery No

A 979478

Accepting Officer's initials

Date stamp

P3453 May 85

Fig. 14.6 Certificate of posting for Royal Mail Special Delivery

If the Post Office fail to meet the delivery time on both services payment is refunded to the sender.

Railway letters

The Post Office have agreements with British Rail and some private railway companies for acceptance of first class letters at certain stations for transmission to another station. At the destination station the letter can be collected or placed in the post for normal delivery. In addition to first class postage the railway concerned will make their own charge. Details of this service and express services can be obtained from the local Head Postmaster.

Late posted packets

This service is for letters by first class service only. Posting boxes for first class letters are provided on all Travelling Post Offices, i.e. mail trains to which sorting carriages are attached. Registered letters and recorded delivery are accepted up to five minutes before departure, but a small additional fee is charged for this service. Details of times can be obtained from the local Head Postmaster. It can be a very useful service when items such as quotations and bills are completed late and are urgently required by the addressee. Stamps must be stuck on to the value of all charges before the packet is presented.

Cash on delivery

This service enables firms to have the cost of the goods requested by a customer paid for on delivery. The cash on delivery service can only be used where the goods have been ordered and not for goods sent without request. This is to prevent firms using this service as a means of selling goods without orders. The service is useful to firms selling by mail order where the credit worthiness of the customer is not known. It also protects the customer as goods do not have to be paid for until delivered. The sender of any goods by this service must sign a declaration form that the contents of the packet have been requested by the addressee. The Post Office provides an adhesive address label on which the sender must write in ink:

1 The name and address of the addressee;
2 The sender's name and address;

3 The amount of the trade charge (i.e. the amount to be paid on delivery). Tie on labels cannot be used.

The amount to be collected on delivery must not exceed £100. A COD fee is charged to the sender in addition to normal postage and registration charges. Normally the COD packet is delivered by the postman and the amount collected. If, however, the trade charge exceeds £50 the packet is kept at the post office and advice is sent to the addressee who must call and collect it after paying the trade charge.

Exercises

Write the answers in your workbook
1 Name the most important reference book giving details of postal services available.
2 What Post Office service would you use to send your birth certificate to a future employer?
3 By what service should you send £50 in £5 notes?
4 Your employer is away on holiday in Torquay and he has asked you to forward an urgent letter he is expecting while he is away. Show the address you would write on the envelope. His name is W. Anderson. Include a Torquay postcode if you know one.
5 Name the two services which enable a firm to pay the cost of postage of letters on customers' replies.
6 Name a Post Office express mail service.
7 Give three conditions imposed by the Post Office relating to the use of the Freepost service.
8 Name the service available to a mail order company who wish the cost of goods to be paid on delivery.

Collection from private boxes

An individual or a firm can rent a private box at a post office so that they can collect mail instead of waiting for delivery by the postman. Usually, the mail will be handed to a caller but at some offices the mail is placed in a locked box and the renter has a key. This service can be very useful to a firm. It enables mail to be collected before the normal delivery is made. This allows the firm's mailroom staff to deal with the opening and distribution of mail before the normal office day starts. The box number is included in the full address, i.e.

Anyfirm Ltd.
P O Box No.....
6 The Place,
LEEDS.
LS2 6TS.

In certain cases the Post Office may agree to dispense with the street name and number. The address is then:

Anyfirm Ltd.
P O Box No.....
LEEDS.
LS2 6TS.

Selectapost

Where arrangements can be made, the Post Office will deliver mail separately to different departments or branches of a firm, provided they are in the same delivery area as the main office to which the communications are addressed. This can be useful to very large firms where departments may be some distance apart. Thus, the firm may ask those who write to it to include, for example, 'Sales Office' in the address. Post Office sorters then route such letters to the Sales Office which may be in an office away from the main office.

Re-direction

Where an individual or firm moves address, on payment of a fee, arrangements can be made to re-direct mail to the new address for an agreed period of time.

Household deliveries

The Post Office will deliver unaddressed items to every address in a specified area from just one postman's round or a specific postcode area up to the whole country. There are certain regulations on size and weight and the sender should be clearly identified. Any such items must conform to the British Code of Advertising Practice. A specimen is required before distribution is agreed. Items are required one week before the delivery is to commence and is usually completed within two weeks, except during December. This is a very useful service for advertising products and no doubt you have received such literature at home.

Parcels services

The rate charged for parcels is based on weight. Reductions in the national rates apply where parcels are posted and delivered in certain local or country areas. Full details are available in the Post Office Guide. The maximum weight for parcels is 25 kg and the maximum dimensions are – length 1.5 m, length and circumference combined 3 m.

Compensation fee parcels

This provides compensation if a parcel is lost or damaged in the post, subject to Post Office conditions such as adequate packing. A certificate of posting is completed.

After payment of the compensation parcels fee, the post office clerk will initial and date stamp the top portion of the certificate of posting and this is retained by the sender. The amount of compensation depends on the fee paid.

Postage forward parcel service

This service is similar to Business Reply and Freepost in letter mail. It is intended for use where a firm wishes to obtain a parcel from a client without putting him to the expense of paying postage. The parcel is posted in the normal way, using a special label, but without a stamp. The firm to which the parcel is addressed pays the postage. This service is very useful to a firm which uses agents for the sale of goods by mail order and for goods sent on approval. The conditions which apply are:

1 A licence must be obtained from the firm's local Head Postmaster.
2 A sum of money to cover expected postage costs for approximately one month must be paid in advance.
3 The label design must be approved by the local Head Postmaster.

Overseas postal services

The Post Office operates very comprehensive letter and parcel services to all parts of the world. Full details are included in the Post Office Guide and leaflets of rates applicable are published by the Post Office.

Electronic mail

With the growth of computers in business it is now possible to transmit mail by electronic means. There are many different systems in operation in this country, including private viewdata systems (those for use between

The Post Office
Certificate of Posting for
Compensation Fee Parcel

How to Post

1 Enter below in ink the name and full address as written on the parcel.
2 Tick the appropriate box at the bottom of the form to indicate the compensation cover required.

Name

Address

Postcode

Stamps for Compensation Fee
(to be cancelled by accepting officer)

For Post Office use

COD Deposit/
Inpayment Document No

Compensation Fee Paid

p

Accepting Officer's initials

Date Stamp

Tick compensation cover required

Up to £60 ☐

Up to £125 ☐

Up to £225 ☐

Up to £350 ☐

PP89 Feb 84

Fig. 14.7 Certificate of posting Compensation Fee parcels

offices and branches of one company at home and abroad) and public viewdata systems such as Prestel and Telecom Gold. If we examine one system – British Telecom's 'Telecom Gold' – you will quickly see the advantages over the normal postal system.

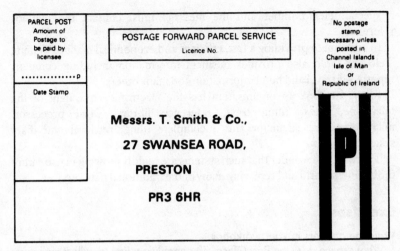

Fig. 14.8 Postage forward parcels label

Telecom Gold

The Telecom Gold Electronic Mail Service operates from a large computer centre in London. When an organisation subscribes to the service many of its existing terminals – microcomputers, word processors, VDU's – may be able to connect to the Telecom Gold computer by simply dialling a number on the telephone. This connects the telephone receiver to the terminal via a modem (a special item of equipment for converting electronic impulses on telephone lines to be understood by the computer) by keying in the private password. In order to use Telecom Gold an organisation needs a standard telephone line, a terminal and a modem. It is possible to transmit information from a simple telex to a circular for up to 500 business correspondents.

Through a service called 'Dialcom' it is possible to transmit and receive information to and from the United States and many other rapidly expanding international business centres. It is possible to contact Telecom Gold users via a Telecom Radiopager when an urgent message or telex arrives in their mailbox. They can then retrieve their mail from the nearest linked terminal – at home, at a client's office, or in their own company building. Service engineers or representatives with portable terminals can use the nearest telephone.

Through Telecom Gold an organisation can contact any telex subscriber on the UK and International networks. An organisation's business contacts can send telexes direct to its mailbox. Telecom Gold has a special telex number and the message must contain the mailbox reference.

In addition to providing a fast, efficient and economical mailbox system, Telecom Gold also provides business information including company reports, air travel and hotel information and many others.

In the mailbox an organisation has the electronic equivalent of the telephone, telex, filing trays, reference library, word processor, microcomputer, calculator and a complete filing, retrieval and diary system.

There is little wonder that such systems are rapidly growing in use within the business world and replacing many of the traditional mail services.

Exercises

Write the answers in your workbook

1 What service does the Post Office offer enabling a firm to collect mail early in the morning before normal delivery by the postman?

2 State the overnight service available for sending computer material through the mail.

3 If I move address what have I to do to get my mail re-directed to my new address?

4 What Post Office service enables me to cover the value of a parcel against loss?

5 If I am in doubt about a postal service where can I find details of it?

Assignments

1 Obtain the current postal rates leaflet issued by the Post Office and calculate the cost of each of the following:

(a) A second class letter, weight 40 g to Glasgow.

(b) A first class letter, weight 310 g to Jersey.

(c) A first class letter, weight 200 g to Dublin.

(d) A registered letter, £450 value, weight 45 g to London.

(e) A second class recorded delivery letter, weight 70 g to Leeds. Advice of delivery requested at time of posting.

(f) A parcel weighing 6 kg addressed to Bradford.

(g) A compensation fee parcel to Birmingham weighing 8 kg, value £70.

2 Your employer has been considering an advertising campaign by post to the firm's customers. He wishes to receive replies without the customer having to pay postage. You are asked to investigate how this may be done. Give your employer a written report on any possible services and any conditions which may apply, including any examples of the use of such services by other firms.

3 Your employer is considering launching a new product by mail order. It is anticipated that a large number of parcels will be despatched daily. You are asked to check (i) if a collection can be made from your firm's premises by

the Post Office; *(ii)* if arrangements can be made to allow some customers to return parcels without charge at the time of posting. Advise the Office Manager via a memorandum as to what can be done.

4 Select three postal services and explain their value to firms.

5 Indicate the appropriate postal service for the following:

(a) Examination certificates to be sent to a prospective employer.

(b) A gold watch to be sent for repair.

(c) A letter to be collected by your firm's sales representative in Glasgow.

(d) A parcel to London — contents value £200.

(e) A parcel value £45, charges to be paid on delivery.

(f) A very urgent quotation to a customer which cannot be mailed before 8 pm.

(g) A service to allow prospective customers to reply without cost, following a television advertising campaign.

(h) An important contract to a customer where you want to have confirmation of delivery.

15
TELECOMMUNICATIONS

Objectives

At the end of this chapter you should be able to:

- Choose a telephone service for a given situation.
- State which method of telecommunication should be used in a given situation.
- State the advantages of the telex service.
- Describe System X.

In Chapter 14 we examined the need to deal efficiently with written communications. In business, situations arise where the most appropriate method of communication is the spoken word. If a query arises often a telephone call will clear up the query with a minimum of delay. One snag is that there is no written evidence of any agreements or conversations made by telephone, although quite obviously in the relatively near future many business phones will have a tape recorder attached to them. However, in both personal and business life the telephone service is being used more and more. It is a convenient and effective method of communication. Often the first contact many people have with a firm is by telephone. It is important that they are dealt with pleasantly and efficiently. Using the telephone effectively is a skill we must develop (*see* Chapter 9).

Switchboards

Most firms have a switchboard. This is a control point where all calls are received. They are then transferred to individuals' telephones which are called 'extensions'. The switchboard operator should have a pleasant voice and manner and a good knowledge of the work done in different departments. A list of all personnel in the firm and their extension numbers should be available. If the caller does not know the extension number of the person to whom they wish to speak, the operator can look it up and connect the caller to the right extension. Switchboards can be divided into two main types.

1 *Private Manual Branch Exchange (PMBX)*. With this type of switchboard all incoming and outgoing calls are usually made through the switchboard operator. But outside telephone numbers may be dialled from extensions after asking the switchboard operator for a line. Internal calls (i.e. calls from department to department) are usually made on a separate system with a separate telephone.

2 *Private Automatic Branch Exchange (PABX)*. With this type of switchboard all incoming calls are received by the switchboard operator. Outgoing calls can be made direct from an extension. The operator is not involved when such calls are made. The extension user can obtain an outside line by dialling a single number (usually 9). An additional internal call system is not necessary as each extension user can call another extension without contacting the switchboard operator.

The new generation of call-connect systems available from British Telecom uses microprocessors and other electronic components. One example is the Monarch call-connect range. The range of models vary but they have many common facilities that transform the telephone into a flexible business tool. These include:

1 *Call diversion*. To overcome the problem of incoming callers getting the engaged tone or no reply it is possible to divert calls. An extension user can instruct the system to divert incoming calls to another extension. This is particularly useful if an important meeting is not to be interrupted by the telephone. The diversion can be applied to all calls, or calls that arrive while the extension is engaged, or just calls that are unanswered within a given period of time. Both internal and external calls are diverted and a special ringing signal announces the diverted call at the receiving extension.

2 *Call back*. If an extension user cannot contact a colleague a 'call back' code can be used. The system monitors the colleague's extension and when he next completes a call it automatically connects him to the caller who gave the code.

3 *Enquiry callers*. Extension users can 'hold' a caller while they make an enquiry call to a third party. The enquiry call can be to another extension or an external call, and the extension user can alternate between the two parties or return to the held call.

4 *Call transfer*. Transferring calls to other extensions is simple and foolproof. If the transfer of an incoming exchange line call fails the call is not cut off but is automatically reconnected to the operator.

5 *Extension group hunting*. Extensions in one area such as a sales department can be organised into groups. The incoming calls for that area will 'hunt' amongst the extensions in the group until they find one that is free.

6 *Conference calls*. An optional 'conference' facility where up to four parties

can speak and listen to each other simultaneously. One of the parties to the conference can be a caller on a public exchange line.

7 *Call barring*. The system provides for an unobtrusive way of keeping expensive unofficial calls to a minimum. The system can be instructed to prevent individual extensions from making certain types of calls.

8 It is possible to link the call connect system with the organisation's computer to record outside numbers called and duration of calls/costs to each extension. This information can then be printed to check costs and allocate these costs to each department.

These facilities together with many others give the operator very effective control. Indications are given to the operator of calls 'queuing'. If a caller is waiting for an extension to answer and there is no reply after 30 seconds the call is automatically returned to the operator. If the appropriate security code is entered the console becomes a terminal connected to Monarch's central processing unit. Some parts of the data stored in the system can then be altered as required: extension numbers can be changed, the composition of extension groups altered, and the facilities applied to extensions changed.

Reference sources

The major reference sources for telephone users are the telephone directories published by British Telecom. They are:

1 Alphabetical directories.
2 Classified business directories (Yellow Pages).
3 Local directories.
4 Commercial directories.
5 Telephone dialling codes lists.

In addition to published directories, switchboard operators and individual telephone users keep personal directories of telephone numbers in alphabetical order. To help in the dialling of regular numbers a call maker can be used. It can be operated by tape, card or key. All the user has to do is to insert a card and set the tape or press a key on a special attachment. The call will then be dialled automatically.

Telecom services

British Telecom offer a wide range of telephone services to subscribers. These include:

STD

Subscriber trunk dialling enables a subscriber to dial directly to many parts

```
┌─────────────────────────────────────────────────────┐
│                 TELEPHONE MESSAGE                     │
│  Date    10.08.198--                                  │
│  Time    12.45                                        │
│  From    Mike Robertson                               │
│  Tel. No.  0449 238618        Ext. 219                │
│  Message for. Karen Hayes                             │
├─────────────────────────────────────────────────────┤
│  Message:  Sorry but unable to make the               │
│            Friday meeting. Please call                │
│            to rearrange for next week.                │
│                                                       │
│                                                       │
├─────────────────────────────────────────────────────┤
│  TAKEN BY    John Ringle                              │
└─────────────────────────────────────────────────────┘
```

Fig. 15.1

of the country and abroad without going via the British Telecom operator. Local, national and international dialling codes are given in your local directory. By dialling the required code, then the number of the person called, a connection is made. For example, if I wished to dial Barnsley 0755 from Huddersfield I would dial 97 (the Barnsley code number) followed by 0755.

Telephone messages

Often calls are received when the person required is absent from the office. The caller may ask if a message can be taken, or if the person required can ring back. If you receive such a call do not rely on your memory. It may let you down! At the time you take the message you may think you will remember. Something might distract you and you will forget. This will probably cause problems and almost certainly annoyance. Write the message down. If some details are not clear ask the caller to repeat them. A telephone message form is much better than a scrap of paper.

The message should show the name of the person who took the message in case of a query.

Freefone

A special freefone number is allocated to individuals and organisations using this service. This enables callers (e.g. firms' customers and agents) to make telephone calls without charge. The cost of the call is paid by the receiver. Calls are made via the British Telecom operator. A rental is charged and a supplemental charge for each call made. In order to encourage people to call them without cost some firms use this service when advertising for staff. The freefone number can be included in any form of advertising, including television. In addition, firms can use the Linkline device where callers can phone without charge. All such numbers are prefixed by 0800.

ADC – Advice of duration and charge

The call must be made through the operator and a request for ADC made at the time the call is asked for. On completion of the call the operator will advise you of the cost and duration. This can be useful for charging personal calls or if any visitor to the office requests the use of the telephone and has to pay the cost of the call.

Telephone credit cards

Credit cards can be obtained by any subscriber. They enable a person to make telephone calls and send telegrams from any telephone without payment at the time. This service is useful to sales representatives and business men who travel a great deal. It enables the cost of their calls, while they are away on business, to be charged to the firm's account.

Transferred charge calls

The charge for any call may be accepted by the subscriber receiving the call. The operator will ask the person called if they are prepared to accept the charge. An extra charge for this service is also borne by the receiver of the call. These calls are often referred to as Reverse Charge Calls.

Personal calls

A personal call enables a caller to name the person they wish to speak to or an acceptable substitute. The caller can ask for a particular person by name, or by quoting a reference number, extension or department. If a personal call cannot be made immediately, a message will be left for the person to whom the caller wishes to speak. He will be asked to ring the personal call operator as soon as possible. If a call is unsuccessful only the fee charged is payable by the caller and not the cost of the call. This service is useful in the making of long distance calls at peak times. On such occasions there may be doubt as to whether the person to whom one wishes to speak will be available. A normal STD call starts as soon as the person or switchboard operator answers. The charge for the call also starts then.

A personal call charge, however, does not commence until the person required comes to the telephone.

Fixed time calls

A call can be booked in advance to be connected at or about a specified time. If you have agreed to ring a customer at a certain time this can save you from forgetting, causing annoyance and perhaps losing business.

Alarm calls

The local exchange will, at the request of a subscriber, ring them at any time of day or night. This helps a subscriber who has to rise early for a journey or does not wish to be late for an appointment.

British Telecom also offer the following services (known as Guidelines)

Time. The speaking clock.

Weather information.

Motoring service. Recorded reports are available giving road conditions in many areas.

Dial a Disc. Available in many towns. A different record is played each night of the week after 6 pm and from 8 am to 6 pm on Sunday.

Recipe service, etc. Different recipes are available according to season and availability of particular foods.

Datel. Transmission of computer data.

Conference calls. British Telecom can arrange for calls to be connected between up to ten different countries if required.

Confravision

This service enables conferences to be arranged in sound and vision from British Telecom studios in London, Birmingham, Bristol, Glasgow and Manchester. Meetings can be conducted as if the people concerned were assembled in one place. A firm using this service can arrange for their representatives to attend the nearest studio. This can save a considerable amount of time and money (hotel bills, rail fares, etc) in avoiding travel to a central point.

Telephone answering set

This equipment can be used to answer a telephone and give callers a pre-recorded message. With some machines time is then allowed for the caller to leave their message recorded on an audio-tape in the machine for attention later. This can be a valuable aid to small businesses where staff may have to be absent from the office from time to time, and to freelance and self-employed people.

Telemessage

Telemessage is an electronic mail service from British Telecom. Any message telephoned or telexed into British Telecom by 10 pm (7 pm on Sundays and Bank Holidays) will be delivered the next working day. This service is also available in the USA. The message you wish to send will be placed inside a greetings card suitable to the occasion. The service is particularly useful for special occasions such as birthdays, anniversaries etc. There is one charge only for up to 50 words including the cost of the card.

Telex/teleprinter

This service provides a fast and efficient method of communication. A copy of a message is produced on a teleprinter at both the sending and receiving points. A teleprinter is a combination of typewriter and telephone. By using the dial on a firm's teleprinter and dialling another telex subscriber's number, a message can be typed out and will be printed by the receiving teleprinter. The telex service enables any subscriber to dial another subscriber. Telex directories are produced giving the name and address of subscriber, his telex number and an answerback code. The answerback code is given by the receiving teleprinter when a connection is made. This acts as confirmation that the subscriber is connected to the correct number. The service is available throughout the UK and to most parts of the world. Charges are based on time and distance as are telephone calls. The advantages of telex are:

1 Messages can be received on a subscriber's teleprinter 24 hours a day even though it may be unattended. This is useful for receiving at night messages from other countries when time differences exist.
2 Messages can be received in a foreign language and translated at leisure. This could be difficult if using a telephone.
3 A written confirmation is available at both the sending and receiving points.
4 Because the message is written it will tend to be brief and to the point.
5 Unlike a telephone call, if a person for whom the message is intended

is not available the telex message can be left for him to deal with on his return.

A bell key is pressed if an operator sending a telex message wishes to contact the operator at the receiving point. This sounds an alarm and lights a red lamp on both teleprinters. Multiple copies can be made of messages by using interleaved carbon. Providing the teleprinter is fitted with automatic equipment, messages can be prepared in advance on paper tape to be sent automatically at nearly 70 words a minute. Incoming messages, as well as appearing on paper in the normal way, can be produced on paper tape.

Where firms wish to have a private circuit, e.g. between warehouses throughout the country and head office, they can rent a teleprinter circuit for their exclusive use.

British Telecom's new teleprinter 'Puma' is a sophisticated central microprocessor for both telex and private telegraphs. The software package offers the user many facilities including:

1 *Electronic memory.* There is an electronic memory of 16 000 characters (approximately 2500 words) which is used for storage of messages for later transmission. Each stored message is automatically allocated an index number and can be easily edited.

2 *Automatic calling with delay option.* Calls can be made and messages transmitted automatically from memory while unattended to one address or more to most countries in the world. If the number is engaged, Puma tries again, at approximately two minute intervals. The equipment can be

Fig. 15.2 A Cheetah Teleprinter. Reproduced by permission of British Telecom.

set to hold incoming messages in memory; such messages can then be re-transmitted.

3 *Telex interface for electronic office equipment.* Puma offers access to telex and private telegraph networks for a wide variety of the latest and most sophisticated equipment – memory typewriters, word processors, small-business computers, data terminals. The equipment must have communication facilities and be technically acceptable for connection to British Telecom modems.

British Telecom also offers a range of teleprinters that are microprocessor-based design called Cheetah. The teleprinter consists of a keyboard, printer and integrated visual display unit. The system includes a word-processing facility to give fast and difficult message editing and memory storage.

Information services

Speedy access to information of all kinds is important to all organisations. While certain electronic information services are aimed at the businessman others are available for use in the home as well. The major services are:

Prestel

Prestel is a viewdata system operating over telephone lines. An adapted television set and an ordinary telephone line link Prestel customers to an enormous range of computer-held information. To call up an item from the thousands available you simply press the numbered buttons on a keypad the size of a pocket calculator. The information on Prestel is supplied by hundreds of independent organisations such as *The Financial Times*, British Rail etc.

The information is organised in 'pages' – a page is a screenful of information. As soon as you ask for a particular page, the computer sends it instantly down the telephone line and it appears on the screen of your special set.

The system is a two way system in that as well as receiving information, users can send messages both to each other and to information providers using response pages. Prestel is used to book hotel rooms or reserve a seat at the theatre. Salesmen who work from home can keep up-to-date with head office and key in their orders direct. Travel agents can make bookings direct with the holiday companies.

A business can set up private information networks on private prestel keeping their pages confidential to selected users. Many large companies operate their own private viewdata systems.

Ceefax/Oracle

Many of you will be familiar with the broadcasting of information via a specially adapted television set. The BBC service is called Ceefax and the Independent Television service is Oracle. This is a one way transmission system supplying information on a variety of topics to the home. Topics cover general information, news, weather and leisure and the users select the information they want from an index. This information is then displayed on the screen. Some television sets are being produced with a printer housed in the set to enable the user to obtain a printed copy.

The future use of information services such as these is tremendous for within company use, company to company and in the home.

System X

System X is a fundamentally new type of telephone exchange system which has been developed jointly by British Telecom and its three main suppliers of exchange equipment STC, GEC and Plessey. These exchanges unlike the previous exchanges of electro-mechanical design rely on the latest micro-chip technology with no moving parts. Noise and crackles will be greatly reduced and calls will be connected much more quickly. A whole new range of services is going to be available to customers connected to System X exchanges. These will be entirely automatic under customer control via a new type of press-button telephone equipped with a 12-button keypad instead of a dial; apart from the digits 1 to 0 there are two extra buttons * (star) and # (square). Simple codes are used to operate the system, an automatic voice guidance system is used to provide step by step advice and verification as required. Eight new chargeable services are envisaged for early introduction at all System X exchanges and these are:

1 *Code calling.* You can store frequently used numbers and call them quickly and easily using a short code.

2 *Call diversion.* Program your telephone to transfer incoming calls to another local number whenever required.

3 *Reminder calls.* The exchange can be programmed through your telephone to ring back at a certain time.

4 *Call waiting.* While engaged on a call, you can be notified of another incoming call and speak to the second caller while holding the first.

5 *Three-way calling.* You can hold one call, make another, and then have a three way conversation.

6 *Charge advice.* The exchange calls you back at the end of the call giving the charge.

7 *Call barring.* You can restrict outgoing calls or bar all incoming calls.

8 *Repeat last call.* The last number called can be repeated by the use of a short code.

A separate facility will be the provision of detailed call statements (at extra cost) for those requiring them.

The flexibility given by micro-processor control will enable British Telecom to continue to expand the range of services and may well include: Ringback, where the exchange keeps trying an engaged number and rings you back when free; using your telephone to record a short message at the exchange for sending on later to another person (like a spoken telegram) and being able to charge your calls from other telephones to your own account by using a personal code.

These new exchanges will be replacing the old exchanges over the rest of the century as British Telecom will be replacing the entire UK telecommunications network. The major commercial and industrial centres will be served first.

Phonecard phones

British Telecom are always concerned about vandalism and disruption to public telephone systems. In addition to the new types of public telephones designed to combat vandalism, British Telecom are introducing phonecard phones. Instead of using money to pay for a call it is possible to purchase a phonecard in 40, 100, and 200 units from shops near to this kind of telephone or in main post offices. They are simple to use. After lifting the receiver and obtaining a dialling tone insert the phonecard and make your call. As the call progresses, units are 'wiped' off the card, while a digital display on the telephone shows the remaining units. Just before the units are used up, the display will flash and a tone will sound. If a new card is inserted the call can continue uninterrupted. You can insert a phonecard at any time without making a call to check how many units are left.

British Telecom pay a commission to those selling phonecards.

Facsimile

Through electronic means using a facsimile transceiver (transmitter and receiver) it is possible via a telephone link to transmit and receive documents, photographs or microfiche. It is necessary for the users to have compatible machines and the quality of copy can be affected by the quality of the telephone line, although this problem is rare due to the increased efficiency of international services. It can be a very useful service for transmitting information such as diagrams, plans or photographs together with relevant text.

Radiopaging

It is possible to rent a radiopaging device from British Telecom. A firm can locate its employees while away from their base by telephoning a special number. This number is connected to a computer which sends out a signal over a certain area causing the device to bleep. The employee can then go to the nearest telephone and make a call to the firm. It is especially useful for contacting service engineers, delivery men and salesmen, although it can be used by anyone who travels away from their normal work base.

Telephone equipment

It is now possible to purchase telephone equipment including telephones and telephone answering machines from many different retail outlets as long as the equipment meets the standards of British Telecom and carries their seal of approval. In addition, the market is now growing for car radio phones, cordless telephones, intercom systems and many other innovations, mainly due to the advances in micro technology.

Exercises

Write the answers in your workbook
1 Where would you look for a telephone number?
2 What do the initials ADC mean?
3 What do the initials PMBX mean?
4 What service enables a firm's customers to telephone them without charge?
5 Name two types of telephone directories.
6 What is the basis for charging Telemessage?
7 What telephone service is available when you wish to speak only to a particular person?
8 What should you do to prevent your forgetting a telephone message?
9 What machine enables a person to receive telephone messages when they are out of the office?
10 What is the major difference between Prestel and Ceefax/Oracle?

Assignments

1 You work in the sales department of Anyfirm Ltd. A call is received there for Mr W Smith who is absent from the office. The caller is Mr A Williams of

J Jones & Co Ltd. He asks you to take a message. He tells you his telephone number is Middleton 83674, extension 42 and his firm had sent a request for a quotation for the supply of six wheelbarrows, four trolleys (two wheel) and six trolleys (four wheel). The quotation is urgently required. Unless a reply is received quickly they will have to go to another firm.

Write the message for Mr W Smith. Use today's date.

2 Your employer wishes to advertise for new staff. He has decided to use television as a means of advertising and wants interested people to call by telephone without charge to them. He asks you to look for a suitable telephone service and give him a report. Check the appropriate reference source and advise him what can be done.

3 So far all your firm's urgent communications have been by telephone as you do not have telex. Prepare a report on the advantages to be gained by installing telex.

4 Your employer is considering a conference of Area Sales Managers and asks you to enquire if there is a British Telecom service to enable the conference to be held without the Sales Managers attending your head office. Check from a suitable reference source and give him full details.

5 Explain the main differences between the two types of switchboards (PABX and PMBX). Give the advantages of PABX for extension users as compared with PMBX.

16 FILING

Objectives

At the end of this chapter you should be able to:

- State the reasons for having a filing system.
- File material accurately.
- Complete filing records.
- Select a suitable filing system.
- Explain the purpose of an index.
- Explain the purpose of a follow-up system.

Why have a filing system? Many people would say that one of the most effective pieces of filing equipment is a waste-paper basket. Filing is the storing of business records, including letters and documents. The purpose of an efficient filing system is to keep papers safe and clean, and to ensure that the papers can be produced without delay when required. If papers are not likely to be required again they should be destroyed, not filed.

Centralised filing

Many businesses have one department responsible for sorting and filing the majority of their papers and documents. In this case the only files kept by other departments are personal and current ones. In such a centralised filing department only the staff of that department have access to the files. Many advantages can be claimed for centralised filing, including the fuller use of equipment, and the training of staff in the filing methods employed by a business.

Departmental filing

Under this system instead of files being kept in one central location each department keeps its own files. This enables the staff of that department to use the filing methods most suitable to their needs. In addition, the files are immediately available for personal reference. This can be particularly useful in the case of a department such as the Sales department where price lists, quotations and customer details may be needed quickly, particularly during a telephone conversation.

In some cases firms combine both the centralised and departmental systems. Files which are frequently referred to are retained by the appropriate department. When not in current use they are then transferred to the centralised filing department. Whichever choice a firm makes the purposes of a filing system remain the same:

1　To store papers safely;
2　To ensure papers can be produced without delay;
3　To keep a record of any files taken out of the system.

Filing equipment

A wide variety of equipment is available. These range from very simple and cheap systems to very expensive ones. They include ring binders, box files, concertina files, filing cabinets and lateral filing units.

Classification of files

The method of filing (i.e. the method of classification or order in which files are stored), depends on the individual needs of each business. Each firm (and in some cases each department) decides on the methods most suitable for them. These include one or more of the different methods of classification available. In centralised and departmental filing different methods of classification may be used for different sections of the files.

Alphabetical filing

This method of classification uses the letters of the alphabet. It is easy to understand. Files can easily be found if the name is known. An example of the use of alphabetic order with which we are all familiar is the telephone directory. With all filing one problem is deciding the order in which files should be stored. Firms use the alphabetical method of classification when the most obvious method of reference is the name, e.g. customers in a Sales department.

Some general rules to be followed in alphabetic filing are:

1　'The' in front of a name is ignored in filing as is '& Co' at the end.
　The South Yorkshire Press Ltd would be filed
　South Yorkshire Press Ltd (The)
　W Jones & Co would be filed Jones, W (& Co)

2 Personal names: in a personal name the surname is considered first. If two or more surnames are the same, the files are stored in order according to the initials or first names of the individuals or organisations, thus:

Smith, A

Smith, D

Smith, D E (& Co Ltd)

Smith, D G

When the surname and initials are the same use the full Christian name if known, thus:

Smith, Alan

Smith, Allan

Smith, Allen (& Co Ltd)

Smith, Anthony

3 Names with hyphens: ignore hyphens and treat hyphenated names as one word, i.e. file according to the first letters of the first part of a two part name, e.g.

Stavely-Smith is filed under Sta

4 Shortest first: if most letters in a name are the same you file the shortest name first, e.g.

Smith & Co is filed before A Smith & Co

5 Impersonal names: e.g. names such as:

Express Delivery or Office Supplies Ltd

are filed in the order in which they are written, thus Express Delivery is filed under 'E' and Office Supplies Ltd under 'O'.

6 Prefixes to surnames: prefixes such as de, la, van, von, O', are treated as part of the name they prefix, e.g.

O'Brien, P

O'Connell, J

O'Donnell, W

are filed O'B, O'C, O'D.

7 Prefix of M', Mc, Mac: unless there is a separate section in the files the prefix is considered part of the surname and all are treated as 'Mac'. Thus M', Mc, Mac are filed under 'Mac' with the next letter following determining the filing order, e.g.

McCann, E

McCarthy, A W

MacCarthy, J

McDonald, D H

MacDonald, R S

Machin, M

McIlroy, A

8 The 'Saints' are filed under 'Sai' whether spelt 'Saint' or 'St'. St is treated as if spelt in full, e.g.

St Mary's
Saint Patrick's
St Paul's

9 Titles should be placed after the surname but ignored for filing purposes, e.g.

Johnson, Sir Arthur
Johnson, Professor Walter
Johnson, Rev William

10 Degrees or decorations are ignored in filing but included at the end for identification, e.g.

Williams, John BA
Williams, Malcolm, OBE

11 Abbreviations should be filed as if they were written in full, e.g.

BBC would be filed under
British Broadcasting Corporation

If an abbreviation has no real meaning, e.g. ABC Cinema then it is filed as written,

ABC Cinema
AC Company

12 Numbers in names are filed as if spelt in full, e.g.

21st as *Twe*nty-first, e.g. file under 'Twe'

13 Descriptive names: select the most important word as the filing unit, e.g.

The Hotel Majestic should be filed as
Majestic, Hotel (The)

14 Where names are identical in the case of banks or a firm with several branches, the name of the town is considered first then the street and number if required, e.g.

Midland Bank plc, *Barnsley*
Midland Bank plc, *Rotherham*
Midland Bank plc, *Sheffield*

If there is more than one branch in a town the filing unit is the street name, e.g.

Midland Bank plc, *High* Street, Sheffield
Midland Bank plc, *West* Street, Sheffield

Cross references

Even when the rules are followed occasions may arise when there is some doubt as to the filing order to be used. When such a decision has to be made, it is useful to insert a note at points where someone *may* look to indicate exactly where the papers are filed. This applies to government departments in the telephone directory, e.g.

*So*cial Security, Ministry of (entry appearing at 'So'); see Health & Social Security, Department of,

Check this for yourself in your local telephone directory. It is a good idea to insert a cross reference sheet in the files when there is a change of name, e.g. a sole trader named Alfred Brown enters into partnership with J Andrews. The new firm's name is Andrews and Brown. Put a note under Brown, Alfred saying 'For Alfred Brown now see Andrews and Brown'.

Exercise

Write the answers in your workbook

Place the following names in correct (alphabetical) filing order. Only the identifying letter needs to be written against the number, e.g. If *(q)* Lord Almondbury is first and *(p)* Rt Hon J K Dalrymple is second write 1 *(q)*, 2 *(p)*

(a) The Southern Ventilating Co Ltd
(b) The Flowerpot Garden Supplies Co Ltd
(c) A F Smyth-Jones
(d) J Smyth
(e) P McHugh
(f) M Y Plumbers Materials Ltd
(g) Rev S MacDonald
(h) S R McDonald
(j) Peter B Robinson
(k) P D Robinson
(l) P C Robinson and Co Ltd
(m) Paul Robinson
(n) Col R Smith
(o) Professor J Southern
(p) Rt Hon J K Dalrymple
(q) Lord Almondbury

Numerical filing

By this method of classification, files are arranged in numerical order 1, 2, 3, 4, 5, etc. The obvious advantage is that numbers, unlike letters of the alphabet, are unlimited. Any new file is just given the next number and inserted in the files after the last one, e.g. No 92 follows No 91. Any number given to a file can be used in references on correspondence, e.g. AJ/RF/ 684 indicates that Albert Jones, Departmental Head dictated the letter, Mrs Ruth Fielding typed it and the file reference is 684. This method of filing is useful where the number is important, i.e. licences, job numbers and the like. All numbered documents such as invoices, clock cards and petty cash vouchers can be filed in numerical order.

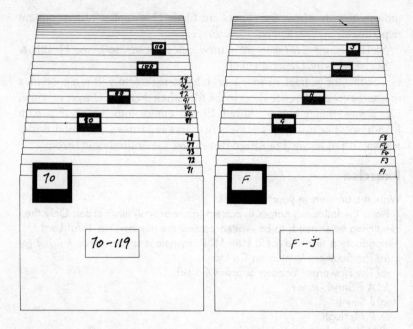

Fig. 16.1 Numerical classification   Fig. 16.2 Alpha-numerical classification

Usually an alphabetical index is used in conjunction with a numerical classification. The index can be used where the name is known but not the number. In addition to the name and file number, the index (often kept on small index cards) can contain basic information. In the case of a customer, for example, the address, credit level, and any other details can be included. When this kind of information is required the index can be used instead of referring to the file.

Alpha-numerical filing

This is a combination of both alphabetical and numerical methods of classification. The files are arranged first in alphabetical order with numbers following.

This is a useful filing method to use where there is a large amount of correspondence on a variety of subjects with the same customer. The main file is classified alphabetically with each area, i.e. sales, complaints, etc. being given a number as a means of separation. Thus the main file for J Archibald and Co Ltd would be filed under 'A', sales to the company will be A1, complaints from the company will be A2, after sales service visits A3 and so on.

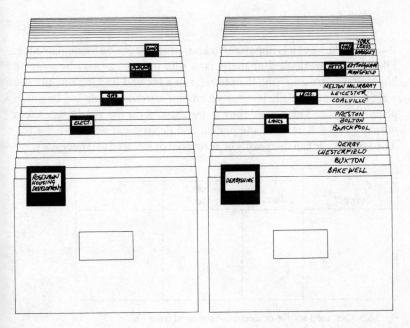

Fig. 16.3 Subject classification   Fig. 16.4 Geographical classification

Subject filing

Using this system files are classified according to the subject to which they refer. A school or college may find it much more convenient to file all correspondence relating to a subject, department or class in one file. Architects, builders and similar businesses will be involved in several contracts at one time. They may thus prefer to file all correspondence for each contract in a separate file. The main file may be classified as the 'Roselawn Housing Development' and then subdivisions created for different activities, such as electricity supply, gas, and plastering.

Geographical filing

Many firms find it convenient to arrange certain files geographically. This method of classification can be very useful for firms with customers situated both throughout the country and abroad. The files can be arranged in geographical areas according to the areas allocated to each sales representative. The usual method is to indicate the main division by countries. For UK customers the division of files will be according to counties, then towns, and finally customers in alphabetical order.

Absent folders

If a file is taken out it is important to know where it can be found if needed. Files can be overlooked or the person who took it out may be away ill. Nothing is more annoying than to refer to a file and find the one file you want is missing. If a file is removed an 'out' card or file should be put in place of the file. This should show *(i)* the name of the file, *(ii)* the date taken out, and *(iii)* the name of the person and department who have the file. The missing file can then easily be recovered or referred to if necessary.

Out Subject	Item	Issued to	Date issued

Fig. 16.5 'Out' card for file or document removed from files

Microfilm

Many firms and organisations such as public libraries use microfilm for record keeping. Documents are microfilmed and the original documents can then be destroyed. The microfilm or 'microfiches' can be stored in very little space compared with that needed to store the original documents. Microfilm can be in reels, lengths or on individual frames similar to negatives of photographs or slides. 'Microfiches' are a number of documents contained on one sheet for easy reference. Building societies often keep customers' account records in this way.

When a document or account needs to be referred to, the microfilm is placed in a reader and is enlarged to be read. Equipment is also available for producing photocopies from microfilm records. This is useful for dealing with customer queries concerning invoices or payments.

Check microfilm for yourself by looking in your local library. Many library catalogues are now kept in this way.

Indexing

An index provides an accurate and easy method of locating a file. In the methods of classification given in this chapter only the alphabetical is self-indexing. In the case of the numerical, geographical and subject methods an alphabetical index is usually necessary. In addition to assisting in the location of a file (e.g. where a customer's name is known but not their account number), the index card may also contain certain basic information. This can include address, type of customer, account number and sales representative. Often the information in an index is sufficient without referring to the file. The index cards should be kept in the order the papers will be filed, i.e. A Jones & Co would be Jones, A & Co. There is a large variety of indexing equipment including strip, visible, and card indexes, etc. (*See* pages 208–9.)

Follow-up systems

On many occasions it is necessary to check that a reply is received to a letter which has been sent out. If no reply has been received hastening action (telephone or letter) must be taken. There are also instances where it is necessary for the responsible person to be reminded that a letter or other communication has to be sent out at a particular time (e.g. sales campaign reminders). Various 'follow-up' systems for meeting these needs exist.

1 One method is the entry of details of the file to be consulted in a desk diary. This is checked daily. Any file to be consulted must be taken out on the day shown for action.

2 A tickler file or 'follow-up' file consists of a filing cabinet drawer. This is divided by guide cards for each of the twelve months – January to December. Behind the current month is a file for each day of the month. A card or note on the file concerned is placed in the respective date, and at the start of each day the cards or notes are removed. The files concerned are then extracted from the main filing system.

3 Pending files or folders labelled 'pending' are kept and copies of letters or documents still awaiting completion are kept in the folder or file.

Whatever method is used the purpose is to ensure correspondence is dealt with at the right time. Where the receipt of a reply is required there should always be action to 'follow-up' if a reply is not received.

Chronological order

This is where files are kept in *date order*, written or received. It is not normally used as a main classification of files. It is, however, the normal method of placing letters and documents within files.

File storage

From time to time organisations need to examine their files to remove old papers and documents. The papers still in use will be kept in the files and

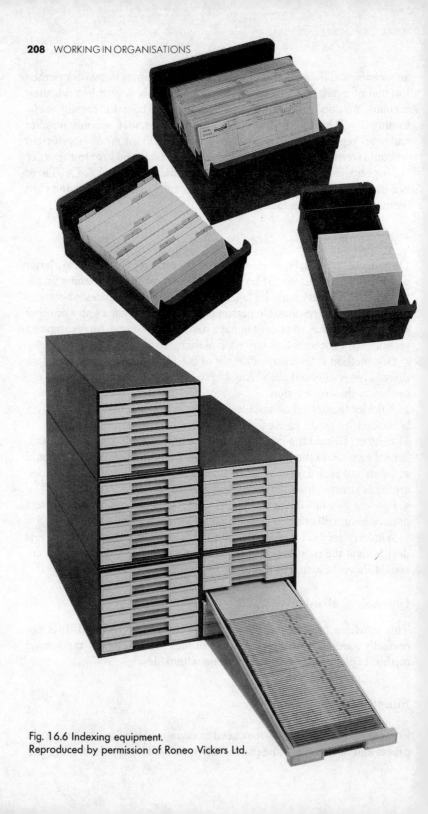

Fig. 16.6 Indexing equipment.
Reproduced by permission of Roneo Vickers Ltd.

others transferred to storage. Certain papers and documents must be kept
for a period of time. These will be stored in boxes or cartons and labelled
with the contents. Remember that microfilming of documents makes
storage much less of a problem. Papers and documents no longer required
are destroyed. This can be done by burning. The more usual practical
method nowadays is to use a paper shredder and dispose of the shredded
paper to a waste paper merchant. A shredding machine cuts the paper up
so that the contents are unreadable.

Exercises

Write the answers in your workbook
1 What is the purpose of a filing system?
2 Name two methods of classifying files.
3 Under what letter of the alphabet would you file 'The Hotel Majestic'?
4 Under what letter of the alphabet would you file the '21st Boys'
Brigade'?
5 Under what letter of the alphabet would you file 'R F O'Brien'?
6 What method enables you to store records by using much less space?
7 What would you use to indicate the location of a folder taken out of the
files?
8 What could you use to indicate where a file may be found in more than
one place?
9 What method of classification is self-indexing?
10 What is the purpose of an index?

Computer based systems

One of the essential features of any filing system is the ability to obtain
information quickly. In essence this is the great advantage of using a
computer for electronic filing. A firm using a specially designed program
can compile a database, i.e. a comprehensive file of data (information)
useful to the organisation. It is likely to include customer records,
addresses, telephone numbers and the like. In your school or college the
database is likely to include full details of each student, (e.g. the course
he is on, private address, entry qualifications, and date of birth).

There is no real limit, other than financial, to the data which can be
collected and recorded. It is important that information is arranged in such
a way that questions asked can be answered. An organisation must decide
what should be stored and what will be required of the stored data so that
the program can be written to cope with the requirements of the user.
Computers can search through files of information far more quickly than
people can. The more information an organisation needs to keep, the

greater will be the uses of the computer. For example, an organisation or an individual (say a doctor or scientist doing research), wishes to keep details of research and any publications relating to a particular topic. Using the manual method would mean keeping a comprehensive card index system. Much time would then be spent in locating different items of information. Using a database program and a computer, the information can be stored in the computer's memory. By using the computer, answers to queries can be obtained almost immediately. Additionally, more than one person or department can have direct access to the database at the same time.

Many computer database systems are in use in the world of work. The police, banks, local authorities, building societies, credit reference agencies and others keep electronic files. There are problems with such records including the difficulty in correcting errors and the maintenance of privacy. It is possible, however, to restrict access to items of information within a database, by using access codes. This ensures some control over privacy and the misuse of information.

Data Protection Act 1984

Although many firms and organisations still use the manual methods of filing described in this chapter, there has been a considerable growth in the recording of information (data) about us all on computers. The Data Protection Act came into force in July, 1984 to meet two major areas of concern:

1 That there may be misuse of information because of the ability of computer systems to store vast amounts of data (information) on individuals and to give access to this data from locations far from the place where the data is stored.

2 The United Kingdom had to ratify the 'Council of Europe Convention for the Protection of Individuals with regard to Automatic Processing of Personal Data'.

The Act creates the office of the Data Protection Registrar who has the responsibility of implementing the provisions of the Act. The duties of the Registrar are to establish a register of Data Users and Computer Bureaux and make this publicly available; to provide information on the Act; to promote the observation of data protection principles, encourage a code of practice and deal with complaints regarding the principles or provisions of the Act.

This Act will have an effect on all individuals or organisations (Data Users) who use personal data or collect personal data to be processed by computer equipment. It does not apply to manual methods. Personal data is defined in the Act as data consisting of information which relates to a living individual who can be identified from the information. If it is information on a company, that information cannot be termed personal data.

Data users must register the personal data they hold, the purposes for which they use them, those to whom they may disclose them and any place outside the United Kindom that they may transfer them. In addition, a Computer Bureau must register its name and address. Under the Act individuals have new legal rights in regard to personal data processed by computer equipment. If there is misuse of data causing damage or distress, they will be able to seek compensation through the Courts. They can apply to the Courts to correct or erase any inaccurate data or obtain access to any data of which he or she is the subject from July, 1986.

There are certain exemptions from subject access under the Act and examples of this are data for prevention or detection of a crime or where legal professional privilege (as between lawyer and client) could be claimed.

As you can see from this very brief description of the Act, it will have a far reaching effect on the protection of the individual from the misuse of data held and processed by computers.

Safety first

When using equipment such as filing cabinets and cupboards, care should be taken at all times. You may think that little can happen to cause accidents. This is not so. It is worth remembering a few points to observe in the interest of safe working.

1 Avoid overloading top drawers of filing cabinets. This prevents them falling over when the drawers are opened. Make sure that the files are spread evenly through the drawers.

2 Do not leave drawers open after use so people can trip over them.

3 Do not open more than one drawer at a time as this may cause the cabinet to fall. Some filing cabinets are made so that one drawer has to be closed before another can be opened.

4 Be careful of sharp corners, especially on metal furniture, to prevent cuts and bruises.

5 If you have to reach to retrieve or to put away a file, don't use a chair. Obtain a pair of steps and prevent a fall.

It may take a little time to do this but not so long as the time spent in recovering (or worse) from an injury.

These points are plain commonsense. But a little common sense and care can prevent many accidents to your colleagues and to yourself.

Summary

There is no 'one correct method' of filing. Each firm must set up the filing system most suitable to its own needs. All filing systems should observe certain points.

1 All documents should be kept safely. Include the use of fire resistant equipment wherever possible. With certain documents (e.g. mortgage deeds), such equipment is a vital necessity.

2 Equipment should be easily accessible.

3 The system should be simple and economical.

4 Filing should be kept up to date and not be allowed to be left.

5 Files should be kept clean and be produced quickly when required.

6 Papers for filing should be clearly marked. Any special points, e.g. the date for a file to be checked for a reply, should be carefully noted.

Assignments

1 Arrange the following in alphabetical order, rewriting them in the order they would be filed.

H Smales & Co Ltd	Dr J Elliot
K L Horsfield	Barker and Jones Ltd
Rev A Downes	P C Motor Co
Chas Redmond	Sir W Alsop
The Regency Hotel	World Wide Travel plc
T MacGill	P Macefield
J O'Brien & Co	T O'Mally
A O'Brien	A W Browne
A W Brown	Office Supplies Ltd
A Powers plc	N Power

2 You are employed as a filing clerk by Anyfirm Ltd and are responsible for alphabetical filing of customer files. Your office manager has just informed you that you are being promoted to another position and a new member of staff is to be appointed. List the rules used in alphabetical filing to assist the new member of staff.

3 Arrange the following in the order they would appear in a geographical classification:

W Jones & Co, 6 Malton Road, York, Yorkshire.
R Brown Ltd, 4 High Street, Bolton, Lancashire.
Barker & Jones Ltd, High Street, York, Yorkshire.
Office Supplies Ltd, High Street, Malton, Yorkshire.
P Appleyard, Coombe Road, Blackpool, Lancashire.
K Smith, Marine Drive, Scarborough, Yorkshire.
K Smith & Co, Leyland Road, Scarborough, Yorkshire.
A C Downes, Redbrook Road, Preston, Lancashire.
R Smales, Honley Road, Morecambe, Lancashire.
Hill & Co, Preston Road, Bury, Lancashire.

4 *(a)* Problems have occurred in your office where files are not available when required. You are asked to investigate and report on what should be done to ensure a record is kept when files are removed. Outline how this can be done. Indicate and design any documents you think should be used.

(b) You have written to a customer querying an order. It is important that you receive a prompt reply to enable you to supply the goods on time. What could you do to ensure that if a reply is not received in good time further action is taken?

5 *(a)* Look at your own firm or, if at college, contact a local firm and investigate the method of filing used. If different methods of classifying files are used in different departments find out why.

(b) List the equipment used and if any files are computerised.

6 The following are customers of your firm:

W Smith & Co	Manchester, Lancashire	Account No. 1634
R Jones	Stockport, Cheshire	Account No. 1642
A Bryant Ltd	Loughborough, Leicestershire	Account No. 1613
L Redmond & Co	York, Yorkshire	Account No. 1620
P C Motor Co	Brighton, Sussex	Account No. 1617
A W Browne & Co	Blackpool, Lancashire	Account No. 1614
A Brown	Manchester, Lancashire	Account No. 1624
J Elliot & Co	Brighton, Sussex	Account No. 1619
A Elliot & Co	Brighton, Sussex	Account No. 1640
W Alsop Ltd	Crawley, Sussex	Account No. 1635
W Allsop & Co	Leicester, Leicestershire	Account No. 1638
A Taylor Ltd	Crewe, Cheshire	Account No. 1628
M Booth & Co	Crawley, Sussex	Account No. 1623
L Smith Ltd	Lewes, Sussex	Account No. 1641
R Smales	Malton, Yorkshire	Account No. 1637

Arrange the names of these customers as they would appear in the files in:
(a) Alphabetical order;
(b) Geographical order;
(c) Numerical order;

7 Suggest a suitable method of classifying files for the following:
(a) Customers' names and addresses.
(b) Invoices issued and received.
(c) Details of suppliers including types of goods supplied.
(d) Personnel details of staff and retired staff.

17 OFFICE MACHINERY

Objectives

At the end of this chapter you should be able to:

- Describe the uses of the office machines listed below:
  Typewriter
  Dictating machine
  Word processor
  Collator/jogger
  Binding machine
  Guillotine
  Duplicator
  Electronic stencil cutter
  Platemaker
  Photocopier
  Add-lister/calculator
  Accounting machine
  Computer
- State the various basic safety precautions which should be observed when using these machines.

One of the problems facing an organisation is the variety and range of office machines available to them. It is important to establish the requirements of the organisation before purchasing office machinery. How often is duplicating machinery needed? Would it be cheaper to use a commercial printer for small jobs or have one's own duplicators? Unless the organisation is sure about its requirements a great deal of expense can be incurred and the wrong equipment can be bought. With the introduction of 'micro computers', the office is facing a revolutionary period ahead. Some of the machinery available will be referred to in this chapter. Some mail room machinery has already been explained in Chapter 13, and the use of new technology is examined in appropriate chapters.

Typewriters

There is a large variety of typewriters suitable for office work. Many have attachments for specialist work.

The main types are:

1 *Manually operated*

(a) Portable typewriters: a lightweight typewriter particularly suitable for travellers such as sales representatives and journalists.

(b) Standard office typewriters: used in most offices, and capable of a large variety of work.

2 *Electrically operated*

(a) Standard electric typewriters: the type bars are moved by an electric motor. The touch is more even than with a manual machine. As less pressure is needed, more carbon copies can be produced than on a standard manual typewriter. There are still some single element or golfball typewriters in use but all are being replaced by electronic typewriters.

(b) Electronic typewriters use micro technology. The typewriter uses a 'daisy wheel' print head and there is no carriage movement. Some have limited memory and correction facilities and can incorporate a single line screen display. They can be linked to micro processors as input devices or as printers. One system is to use one electronic typewriter as an input device and the other as the printer. When required they can be disconnected and used as independent typewriters. You may already have some of these machines in your school or college and many thousands are being installed in offices.

3 Other machines available include varitypers. These have different sizes and styles of type for making masters for printing, particularly offset masters. Special attachments can be obtained, e.g. for continuous

Fig. 17.1 EM200 Electronic typewriter. Reproduced by permission of Jones and Brother

stationery – used in typing invoices where it is not necessary to stop to reset for the next invoice. The invoices or other documents are joined together with interleaved carbon for copies. Alternatively, special paper not requiring carbon can be used. This speeds up the work as the typist types one invoice after the other. The copies are separated after they have all been typed. It is not necessary to remove each separate invoice and feed in a fresh one.

The obvious advantage of using a typewriter is to present letters and documents in an attractive style. You will appreciate that a well set out, typed letter is more impressive and readable than a handwritten one.

Dictating machines

These are electronic machines which record the spoken word for transcription by the typist. No doubt you are already familiar with tape recorders and may have one of your own. Dictating machines are similar. The person dictating uses a tape or cassette to record the message. The typist then places it in the machine and listens through headphones, typing the letter or report required. In addition to recording on tapes or cassettes, some machines use plastic discs (similar to gramophone records), belts and sound sheets. Foot controls are provided enabling the typist to stop the machine and listen again to any part of the recording. In some organisations a bank of recorders is provided in the typing pool. Anyone wishing to dictate a letter can connect to these through the internal telephone system by dialling a special number. When the dictator has finished, the tape or cassette can be removed for typing and a new one inserted for the next user.

An obvious advantage of the dictating machine is its convenience. The dictator can record at any time, e.g. out of office hours, without the typist being present. Work can be shared out amongst the typists.

The dictator should be trained in the use of this type of machine. Any instructions, e.g. number of copies required, should be given at the beginning of the recording. Any difficult spellings or technical terms should be made clear to the typist.

Word processors

A variety of automatic typewriters capable of producing standard letters and forms such as contracts, can now be obtained. They personalise letters and documents such as advertising literature, tenancy agreements, letters

Fig. 17.2 IBM Displaywriter. A desk-top information processing system with spelling verification aid for word-processing. Note the combination of typewriter keyboard, display screen and disk unit.

of enquiry, and quotations. With the advance in computer technology, word processors have been developed.

This equipment is a special purpose micro or mini computer processing words. An operator can input a standard letter or a report. This is displayed on the visual display screen and it is possible for the operator at this stage to make corrections. These include the deletion or insertion of a single letter or words, or the moving of sentences or paragraphs from one part of the document to another. When this is done adjustment to line length (i.e. margin) is made automatically. When all alterations have been made, the display can be recorded permanently in a storage unit. When copies are required the operator can recall the letter or report and have this printed on headed paper or make an offset master. Facilities also exist to enable the operator to supply variable information such as name, address, date and reference number. This variable information will be combined with the standard letter and printed in the correct place.

Letters and other recorded information can have codes attached to them. These enable only the writer to have access to them on a particular visual display unit.

With the development of micro computers and suitable software packages many firms are using the micro computer to do word processing as well as other business work including stock control, wages etc. The choice of type of equipment for word processing, whether a micro computer or mini computer with appropriate software or dedicated (purpose built) mini computer will depend on the needs of individual organisations for this kind of work.

Use of computers in business

In large and medium sized organisations hardly any commercial system today operates without the use of computers. The majority of wage slips are now produced by computer. Computers are used in stock control, accounting records, production of invoices, and costing systems, etc.

You may have heard of silicon chips. These are used widely in the production of microprocessors and, as a result, have made computers available to smaller firms. Some firms sell these to 'do-it-yourself' enthusiasts for use at home.

Whatever the size of computer, the basic components are INPUT, OUTPUT, STORAGE, CONTROL AND ARITHMETIC.

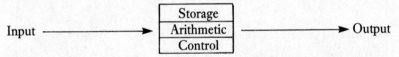

CPU = Central processing unit is made up of Storage, Arithmetic and Control Unit.

Input

This is the medium used to pass the information, e.g. hours worked by employees, into the CPU for processing. The information can be put on to:

1 Punched Cards (*see* Fig. 17.3)
2 Paper Tape (*see* Fig. 17.4)
3 Magnetic Ink Character Recognition – MICR – used by banks on cheques.
4 Optical Character Recognition – OCR. Handwritten or preprinted information from specially designed forms is read by the Optical Character Reader.
5 The Visual Display Unit – VDU – is similar to a television screen plus a typewriter keyboard. It enables information to be passed directly to the CPU without the need for converting into punched cards or paper tape.
6 Teleprinters (as above but prints on paper).

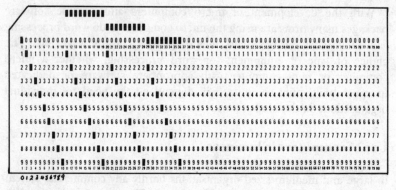

Fig. 17.3 Punched card for input to computer

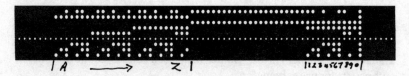

Fig. 17.4 Punched tape for input to computer

Output

Used in office work.

1 *Lineprinter*. Can print up to 150 characters per line at up to 2000 lines per minute. This is used by banks for customers' statements and by firms for payslips, invoices and statements, etc.

2 *Visual Display Unit*. Usually used to obtain 'one off' enquiries, e.g. a bank would use a VDU to obtain the balance on a customer's account on request at the counter, airlines use them for seat reservation bookings.

The uses of computers in commerce and industry are many and varied, both in administration and production. Many firms calculate wages using a computer. Throughout the book examples of the introduction of new technology and micro computers have been given, in stock control, telecommunications etc. Often micro technology exists without us being aware of it in the digital watch or the automatic washing machine.

Collator/jogger

When multi-page reports or booklets are produced, a collator can sort one copy of each sheet into a sorting bin (collate: to place in order). This

Fig. 17.5 Hewlett Packard Microcomputer includes VDU, keyboard, discdrive, and printer

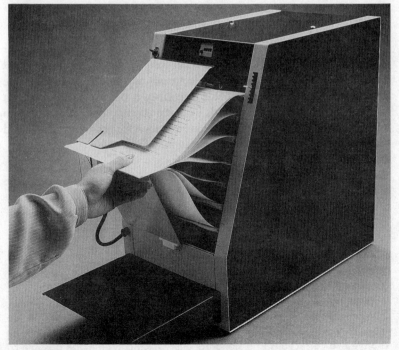

Fig. 17.6 Collator-jogger. Reproduced by permission of Gestetner Ltd.

collates the report or booklet in page order ready for binding. A jogger will straighten copies to a straight edge to ensure there are no loose sheets.

Binding machine

When multi page documents (e.g. legal documents, catalogues, and reports) are produced, a binding machine can punch them for binding to give a professional finish. Other binding machines use heat – the outer cover has glue on the spine and by using heat the glue melts and adheres to the papers in the cover. This method is often used for binding and storing computer print-outs.

Shredding machine

When papers have to be disposed of they can be shredded into unreadable strips. This paper can then be safely disposed of to a waste paper merchant. This machine solves the problem of disposal of documents, particularly those of a confidential nature.

Guillotine

It is often necessary to trim paper and card to a required size. A power operated guillotine can cut over a ream (500 sheets) of medium weight (quality) paper in a single cut. It is electrically operated and has a fail safe system which ensures that the blade is returned to the safe position as soon as the operator removes his hands from the control. The operator has to use both hands to operate the machine and therefore cannot place a hand in the machine during the cutting operation.

Exercises

Write the answers in your workbook
1 What machine can be used:
   (a) to ensure confidential documents are disposed of safely?
   (b) to sort a multi page report?
   (c) to produce a large number of standard letters?
2 Which typewriter would be useful to a person who travels a great deal?
3 Name one advantage of using a dictating machine.
4 What machine can be used to trim paper to a certain size?
5 What advantages does the electric typewriter have compared with a manually operated one?
6 State two corrections to a standard letter which can be made possible by an operator using a word processor.

Fig. 17.7 Guillotine. Reproduced by permission of Gestetner Ltd.

Spirit duplicating

This method of duplicating takes its name from the special spirit used. The spirit dampens the paper so that when a master is brought into contact with the spirit-damp paper, a carbon image is transferred to the paper (*see* Fig. 17.8). Spirit duplicators can be hand or electrically operated.

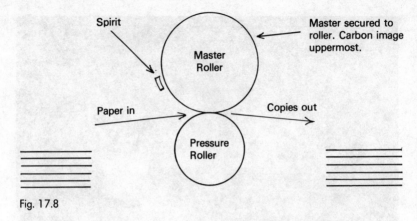

Fig. 17.8

To make copies by spirit duplicating a 'master' must be prepared. The 'master' is a piece of paper with one shiny side. The shiny side of the master paper is placed next to the shiny side of a special hectographic carbon. Its advantages are the ease of preparing a master, simplicity in changing colours when required, and cheapness.

Stencil duplicating (ink duplicating)

This used to be a popular method of duplicating and is still used in a few organisations. The duplicators are relatively cheap and simple to operate. They can be either hand or electrically operated. A stencil has to be prepared of the document or diagram to be duplicated.

Producing a stencil is commonly referred to as 'cutting' a stencil. The image to be reproduced is cut in the surface of the stencil so that ink can penetrate through the stencil where the cut has been made. As the paper is fed through the duplicator, an image is transferred under pressure from the stencil to the paper. If a stencil is required of a document already prepared, an electronic stencil cutter (*see* Fig. 17.9) can be used. A special stencil is placed on a rotating cylinder alongside the original to be copied. As the cylinder rotates the cutting stylus cuts the image on to the stencil. This is done by a photoelectric cell which senses the area of the image and is linked to the stylus. This stylus burns a series of pin-point holes in the stencil, reproducing the image on the stencil. Thermal heat copiers can reproduce an image on a special stencil.

The electronic stencil cutter shown in Fig. 17.9 can produce stencils from a wide range of black and white or coloured items. A full sized stencil can be 'cut' in just over two minutes. The electronic stencil cutter can be switched on and left. It will switch itself off when the scan (i.e. the cutting of the image) is finished.

Fig. 17.9a An electronic stencil cutter. Reproduced by permission of Gestetner Ltd.

Fig. 17.9b Stencil machine for reproducing from stencils. Reproduced by permission of Gestetner Ltd.

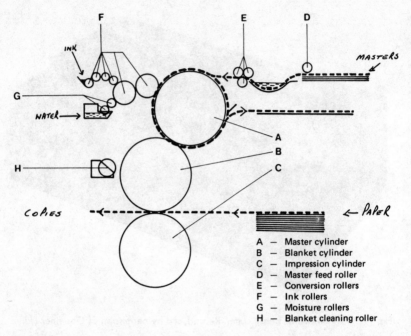

A — Master cylinder
B — Blanket cylinder
C — Impression cylinder
D — Master feed roller
E — Conversion rollers
F — Ink rollers
G — Moisture rollers
H — Blanket cleaning roller

Fig. 17.10 A diagram of the principle of offset duplicating. The image from the master is transferred to the blanket (B) and then to the paper, passing between cylinders B and C.

The duplicating paper used is semi-absorbent. This means the ink image is absorbed quickly and smearing is prevented. Several thousand copies can be obtained from one stencil. After use stencils can be stored in folders and re-used when additional copies are required. This method of duplicating produces good quality copies and is suitable for most documents.

The production of copies using more than one colour is possible. A new stencil must be cut for each colour. In addition the inking unit and ink screen must be changed for each colour or a different duplicator used.

Offset duplicating

This method of duplicating is based on the fact that grease and water will not mix. An offset master is made and the image area on the plate picks up ink. The non-image area picks up water which repels the greasy ink. The process obtains its name from the way the copy is produced. The offset master and duplicating paper are not in contact at any time.

The image from the master is transferred to a blanket roller as a 'mirror'

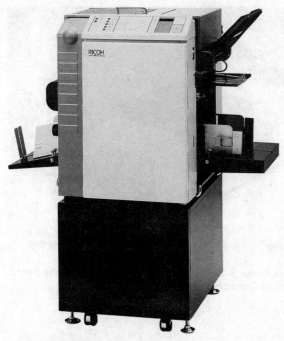

Fig. 17.11 Ricoh 3700 Offset Duplicator.
Reproduced by permission of Copystatic Ltd, Nottingham.

image. This, in turn, is transferred to the paper.

The masters can be made from paper or a thin metal. Up to 50 000 copies can be made from a single metal plate. The metal plates are made by a plate maker (*see* Fig. 17.12). This plate maker will make a metal plate in approximately one minute.

In addition to metal plates, paper plates can be produced on office copiers and by typewriter using a carbon ribbon. Special pens and pencils are available for writing or drawing. After use the plates can be stored and used again when further copies are required. Copies can be produced on a wide range of paper thickness and on card. The quality of the copies produced is extremely good. This method of duplicating can be used for many types of documents, including reproduction from photographs. Different coloured inks are available and a separate offset master must be made for each colour.

Advantages and disadvantages

When do you use a particular method of duplicating? As previously stated, organisations will choose equipment according to cost and their needs.

Fig. 17.12 Ricoh Electronic Printer S-5 and Fuser F-2 for making offset master plates.
Reproduced by permission of Copystatic Ltd, Nottingham.

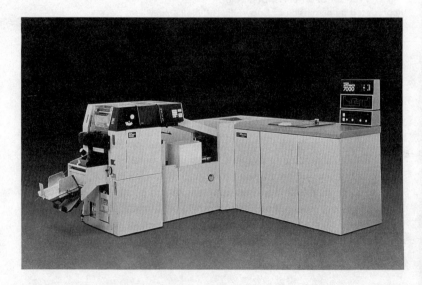

Fig. 17.13 A Ricoh 7000 Autoprinter System. A combination of a master-making module
and autoprinter offset for large volume production of 20 copies or more per
original.
Reproduced by permission of Copystatic Ltd, Nottingham.

Some of the advantages and disadvantages of each method of duplicating are:

	Advantages	Disadvantages
Spirit duplicating	*(a)* The method of preparing masters and operating machines needs little skill. *(b)* Low copy cost. *(c)* Bonded paper is used allowing copies to be used as forms to be completed in ink. *(d)* Masters easily stored for re-use. *(e)* Machines robust.	*(a)* Copies are not of high quality. *(b)* Only up to 300 copies from one master. *(c)* Copies fade if exposed to light.
Stencil duplicating	*(a)* There are different methods of producing. stencils from a variety of originals. *(b)* Both sides of the paper can be used. *(c)* Several thousand copies can be produced from one stencil. *(d)* Stencils can be stored for re-use. *(e)* High quality work.	*(a)* Not easy to change colours. *(b)* Expensive for small number of copies, i.e. less than 15.
Offset duplicating	*(a)* Up to 2000 copies on paper masters and 50 000 copies on metal plates. *(b)* High quality work. *(c)* Large range of papers of differing quality can be used. *(d)* Cheap copy cost for long runs.	*(a)* Trained operators needed. *(b)* Not suitable for few copies *(c)* High initial cost of machine.

Office copiers

There is a large range of office copiers available. These produce an exact copy of original documents. The popular name for these machines is still 'photocopiers', although the processes now available are vastly different from the original photocopiers. 'Office copier' is a more accurate way of describing them. The main methods are:

1 *Electrostatic.* These copiers can be divided into two main types.

(a) Plain paper copiers (indirect electrostatic copiers). These use a carbon based powder and copy an image on to plain paper. This is done either by heat or liquid transfer. A variety of types, colours and sizes of paper can be used. The copies from this process are particularly suitable as originals for producing spirit masters on a thermal copier which needs a carbon image. Paper offset masters and transparencies can be made on heat copiers using a powder.

(b) Direct electrostatic copiers. These copiers use a paper coated with zinc oxide supplied in rolls or sheets. The image is beamed directly on to a paper and the paper is then passed through a chemical to create the image required. These copiers can be used to produce paper masters for offset duplicating.

2 *Thermal copiers.* A special coated paper is used and a copy is produced by a heat process. Machines cannot produce copies from non-carbon images such as some ball point pens.

Fig. 17.14 An Olympia add-lister/calculator

3 *Dyeline copiers.* The dyeline process uses a special diazo-coated paper (a paper coated with a chemical). The original must be translucent (i.e. light can pass through it) or a translucent copy has to be produced. The original together with the diazo-coated paper is passed through the copier and exposed to light which bleaches the paper not covered by the image on the original. The diazo-coated paper is then passed through a chemical or vapour which develops the area left by the image, darkening it so that a copy appears. This method of copying is used particularly in drawing offices and engineering to produce copies of plans and drawings of a large size.

Whichever method of copying is used the advantage is an exact copy (facsimile) of the original. This can be very useful for *(i)* offset masters; *(ii)* letters to be seen by more than one person; *(iii)* letters for filing where copies are required in two or more files; *(iv)* copies of documents involved in queries, and all other areas where only a few copies of an original are required. Other methods of duplicating are cheaper than office copiers and should be used when large numbers are required. The copy cost of copies produced on office copiers can vary. The general rule is that the more expensive the copier the cheaper the copy cost. The initial cost of copiers is high.

Add-lister/calculator

Calculators are now a part of our everyday lives. Electronic calculators vary from the cheap, simple pocket variety to scientific models capable of the most involved calculations. To overcome the problem of not having a record of a calculation when using a visual display panel, some electronic calculators have print-out facilities on a paper roll. This is similar to the receipt you receive from the till in the supermarket. The add-lister is a useful adding machine. It provides a printed check list of all items registered on a tally roll (paper roll). This machine can be used for totalling the value of invoices, cash receipts, and the like before passing them to the accounts department for entry in the ledgers. These entries can then be totalled and checked against the summary total.

Safety first

When using office machinery you should always use great care. Some of the safety points to observe are:
1 Always switch off a machine when it is not in use.
2 Never remove or tamper with safety guards on machines. They are there for your protection.

3 If any fault occurs, switch off. Do not attempt repairs yourself. If you are not trained, send for a service engineer.

4 Always read instructions carefully.

5 If dealing with chemicals, check the instructions. Be careful when filling machines with chemicals.

6 When storing chemicals, ensure that the tops of containers are secure.

7 If you spill any chemicals on yourself wash them off immediately with cold water and seek medical advice.

8 Never leave machines switched on or plugs in sockets at the end of the day.

9 Do not allow cables to trail across walkways. They can trip people up.

10 Do not overload wiring by plugging more than one machine in a socket.

11 Store all duplicating paper and copier paper safely. Do not obstruct walkways, firedoors, exits, or stairways. The Health and Safety at Work Act 1974 places responsibility on your employer and on you to observe safe working, both for your colleagues and yourself. If you are not sure about any aspect of safety seek advice from someone who knows.

Exercises

Write the answers in your workbook

1 What is the name of the carbon used in making a spirit master?

2 How can you correct errors on a stencil?

3 Name two ways of producing a stencil.

4 Masters for offset duplicating can be made from paper and ......

5 What method of duplicating will be used when 100 copies of a three-colour diagram is required?

6 How can you correct errors on a spirit master?

7 What is the name given to the roll of paper used in an add-lister?

8 Name two types of input of material for computers.

9 Which office copier needs a carbon-based image?

Assignments

1 (a) Select the most appropriate method of reprography for the following:

2 copies of a letter just received in the mail.

150 copies of a diagram required in two colours.

2000 copies of a price list.

(b) Explain how you would prepare a spirit master.

2 You are employed as a secretary in the Grand Hotel, Newtown, with a public bar which serves meals. Each day part of your duties is to type the day's bar menu in simple list form and duplicate 30 copies.

The current day's list is:

Soup of the day

Scampi and chips

Gammon and chips

Sirloin steak and chips
Beefburgers and chips
Steak pie and chips
Ham salad
Cheese salad
Ploughman's Lunch

Sweets
Fruit pie
Ices
Cheese and biscuits

Describe what you consider to be an appropriate method preparing 30 copies of this menu.

3 Make a spirit master in two colours of a graph to show the following sales figures. Use a different colour for each year.

	19–8 £	19–9 £
January	4800	4000
February	6600	6800
March	8000	6400
April	8400	9000
May	4000	4600
June	6000	6800
July	7200	7200
August	8000	8200
September	8600	9000
October	8200	8400
November	6600	7000
December	5400	5600

Run off 6 copies as a sample.

4 *(a)* Obtain from your Course Tutor a blank order form. Using a suitable method run off six specimen copies. As should be the practice in the office, you are expected to produce an accurate and presentable copy. Therefore, carefully check what you have done at all stages.

(b) Select a suitable supplier and complete the blank order forms for the following (use your own name and address for the ordering company):

(i) A new office carpet 4 × 3 metres (red, nylon).

(ii) Two new 1 × 3 drawer filing cabinets (lockable).

(iii) 10 reams of carbon paper (A4).
20 reams of typing paper (A4 bond).

(iv) Ten black ribbons for electronic typewriter, model: Olivetti ET225.
Ten correcting ribbons for above model.

(v) Ten 11 mm spanners.
Ten 4 lb hammers.
Ten screwdrivers (large).

(vi) One standard office desk (with two drawers) and a typist's chair.

5 Calculators and add-listing machines **must** be used whenever possible for this assignment and tally rolls attached to the completed work.

(a) From the following stock list calculate the total value of stock received and stock issued:

Reference No.	Quantity Received	Quantity Issued	Price
011	288 folders	226 folders	10p each
012	12 boxes	10 boxes	90p per box
013	14 boxes	9 boxes	60p per box
014	144 packets	120 packets	30p per packet
015	72 packets	56 packets	72p per packet
016	16 packets	12 packets	40p per packet
017	129 reams	110 reams	£2.00 per ream
018	60 reams	46 reams	£2.70 per ream
019	40 reams	24 reams	£1.60 per ream
020	24 cases	16 cases	£5.00 each

(b) Calculate the value of stock left and draw up the stock list to indicate the amount of each item left.

6 Your Office Manager is concerned about safety in the office. He asks you to draw up suitable lists of safety points which staff should observe for posting adjacent to the following machines or locations:

(a) Guillotine.

(b) Offset duplicator chemical storage cupboard.

(c) The storage point for calculators and add-listers where staff pick them up to use in different parts of the office.

(d) Exit doors and fire doors.

18 SAFETY AND SECURITY

Objectives

At the end of this chapter you should be able to:

- Identify possible safety hazards in the office and suggest appropriate action in accordance with legislation concerned with health and safety at work.
- Describe and give examples of safe practice.
- Identify the need for security of equipment, stock, money, premises and information and typical procedures used to ensure it.

What are the costs of *not* having adequate measures to ensure safety and security, both in the office and elsewhere in the organisation?

1 Cash, cheques, equipment, machinery and stock may be destroyed, damaged or stolen. If the losses are very serious the organisation may have to close down for a time – perhaps even permanently. It may not be possible to complete orders on time. Custom will then be lost – now and probably in the future. Jobs may be lost – temporarily or for ever. Anticipated profits will be turned into losses.

2 There may be serious injury (even death) to employees, customers and the general public. Then there will doubtless be claims for compensation and damage to the prestige of the organisation.

3 Confidential records (e.g. correspondence, information as to debtors, creditors and stock) may no longer be available. Think of the difficulties this can cause for the organisation. Confidential information (e.g. trade secrets, production methods) may be stolen, thus benefiting unscrupulous competitors and damaging the organisation.

4 Even though insurance may have been taken out to 'cover' these various risks, some delay in the various operations is almost certain to occur. Wisely run organisations often take out separate consequential loss insurance. This compensates for revenue losses caused by the interruption of business activities due to fire or other cause. One example of consequential loss is that of profits. Again, some employees will have to be paid their salaries even though the firm is temporarily earning nothing.

Again the cost of leasing the premises will continue. Normal fire insurances cover only capital losses.

5 Various losses will result – both to the local and the national economies. Thus:

(a) Employees may be out of work and will have less to spend.

(b) Export orders, secured against fierce foreign competition may be lost. Such custom may never be regained afterwards.

Safety

Often we tend to think of accidents as only occurring in the home or while primary and secondary production are taking place. (Do you know the meaning of these terms? If not see page 273 and Fig. 20.2). Through the media we often learn of factory and mine accidents; of employees injured and killed when agricultural tractors overturn; of road crashes involving lorries carrying goods; and of fires and explosions in the home. Although not so frequently and widely publicised, many dangers do exist and accidents of all sorts do occur in offices.

Fire

Fire is probably the greatest danger we face, both at work and at home. One spark; one forgotten burning cigarette; or one electrical fault are all that is needed to start a disastrous fire. To guard as much as possible against fire, particularly in an office or other work place there must be provided the means of warning; of fighting the fire; and of escape.

Means of warning

1 *Manual.* Breaking the glass; bells; rattles; sirens.

2 *Automatic.* Smoke and heat detectors are all used. Detectors are particularly valuable at night when most premises are empty.

3 Microprocessor based central control systems are also now available. In addition to stopping unauthorised access, such systems monitor other unusual occurrences such as fires. One such system even instructs guards as to what to do.

4 The organisation must have some person(s) whose duty it is to check when there is a fire, that the building is completely empty. Again, there must be a check that all persons are assembled at arranged check out points.

Fighting a fire

Water and sand buckets; hosepipes and sprinklers must be looked at regularly to see that they are in good working order. If they are not, it is a matter of urgency to have them put right. In the event of a fire which cannot rapidly be put out, the fire brigade must be called – and quickly.

Means of escape

Their effectiveness depends on how and where they are situated. Escape routes must be well signposted and labelled. Emergency lighting should be available on all escape routes. Fire exit doors must not be obstructed or locked from the outside. Doors with 'pull down' bars (often used in cinemas and public halls) are one of the best types of exit.

Other matters relating to fires

1 All employees should be made aware of what they have to do if there is a fire. All must know their escape routes; the location of the nearest fire exit and where they have to assemble.

2 Firedoors must be kept closed.

3 Gangways and passages must be kept clear.

4 Rubbish should never be allowed to accumulate.

5 Employees *must* observe 'No Smoking' area regulations. Some firms dismiss anyone breaking such rules.

6 Inflammable items must be stored away, certainly well distant from anything that can cause them to ignite.

7 In places where people are allowed to smoke, ashtrays must always be provided. Waste paper baskets should *never* be used as ashtrays.

8 Damaged gas and electrical appliances must be reported immediately. At all times, such appliances must be used with care.

9 If you discover a fire in your office or college:

(a) Raise the alarm. If you do not know how to do this, find out **NOW**.

(b) Report the fire to a supervisor, tutor or other person with authority to call the fire brigade.

(c) Tell as many people as you can; use the escape route and wait at your assembly point. *Don't panic.* There have been numerous occasions where people have died because of being trampled underfoot by others panicking to leave the scene of a fire.

10 All fire authorities (i.e. the County Councils) have a duty to make efficient arrangements for giving advice on fire prevention; restricting the spread of fires and securing means of escape in case of fire.

The premises

The state of the premises is of vital important to all who work there – or indeed use them at any time. Thus:

1 The floors must be:

(*a*) *even* (no tiles or boards missing or patches of bare linoleum).

(*b*) *not* slippery. Highly polished floors account for many accidents.

(*c*) free from obstructions such as packing cases, old files, and new furniture.

(*d*) all openings in floors (e.g. trapdoors) must be fenced or guarded when open. Warning signs should indicate their presence.

2 Sufficient lighting must be available in every place where people walk or work. This is particularly the case where no outside light (e.g. via a window), is available. This also means that all 'dead' bulbs or fluorescent tubes must be quickly removed – and replaced.

3 Stairs

(*a*) Handrails in good repair must be provided on every staircase, particularly where there is an 'open' side. If there are two 'open' sides, a handrail on each side must be available.

(*b*) Worn edges; broken stairs; poor or no lighting and obstructions can all cause accidents on stairs. Falls account for one-third of all reported accidents.

4 The premises must be properly heated and ventilated (note a minimum temperature of 60.8°F must be maintained in all places where people work for any length of time). Windows, fans, ventilation holes must not be blocked.

5 Damaged shelves, brackets, fixtures and fittings and any article with sharp edges must receive quick attention. Loose tiles, gutterings, woodwork, plaster and brickwork must be similarly dealt with.

6 Glass doors must be clearly marked 'Pull' or 'Push'. Numerous accidents (some fatal) have occurred because people have unwittingly walked into plate glass doors and windows.

7 Adequate toilet and washing facilities and a supply of drinking water must be made available.

8 Other matters relating to the state of the premises include the following:

(*a*) They must be kept in a clean state. Refuse must be collected as frequently as possible.

(*b*) Arrangements should be made for drying wet clothing.

(*c*) Suitable seating must be provided for all employees who normally work sitting.

(*d*) Suitable facilities must be provided where employees eat meals on the premises.

(*e*) First aid boxes must be provided and be easily accessible.

(f) Note that:

(i) The Health and Safety at Work Act 1974 places on all employers the duty of ensuring as far as 'is reasonably practical, the health, safety and welfare at work of all employees.'

(ii) Conversely, employees must take reasonable care to ensure the health and safety of themselves **and** of others, who may be affected by what they do or do not do.

(iii) Legal penalties exist for employers and employees who fail to meet these obligations.

(iv) Landlords and anybody who supplies goods used at work also have responsibilities under the HSAW Act.

(g) The Inspectorate whose duty it is to ensure that the provisions of the HSAW Act are carried out has already been referred to *(see page 17, 5(b))*. In addition to issuing notices to employers, these Inspectors have a variety of other powers. Thus they can:

(i) enter premises at any reasonable time;

(ii) take measurements and photographs;

(iii) make any test they require;

(iv) enquire into the causes and circumstances of accidents;

(v) require any person to give them information relevant to the examination they are carrying out;

(vi) seize, render harmless or destroy any article or substance they regard as being a potential cause of danger or injury.

(h) All staff must be trained in safe working practices.

Remember: Whenever and wherever you work, always have the safety of your colleagues and self in mind. If you see a possible safety hazard – report it.

Better safe than sorry

Note: Because of its importance in respect of nearly all activities, safety is mentioned at different places in this book, and where it is thought most appropriate. The author makes no apology for repeating safety first rules. They are **very important**.

Exercises

1 Why is safety in the office important?
2 What are the principal things to remember about escape routes from fires, particularly in office buildings?
3 Describe fully what you should do if you discover a fire in your College.
4 Why are stairs often the scene of accidents? How should such accidents be prevented?
5 What powers do Health and Safety Executive Inspectors have?

6 List as quickly as you can, as many safety hazards as you can remember.
7 Draw a plan showing clearly, in the event of fire, the escape route from your usual College classroom or office, which you would use. Do you think it could be improved in any way?
8 Describe the rules regarding smoking in your College or the office where you work. Do you agree or disagree with them? Give reasons for your answer.
9 Name any six safety points you care to select, which relate to office machinery.

Security

Why is security important? After all most people are relatively honest. But, there always have been some people who steal, cheat and lie. Large scale theft is possibly more prevalent now than ever before. The amount of violence used in pursuit of theft also is on the increase.

Thefts of money, stock, equipment, vehicles and information, shoplifting, fraud and forgery; and sheer bad 'housekeeping' (e.g. failing to keep proper records of cash and stock movements) cost millions of pounds every year. If not checked, thefts and frauds lead to lower profits, possibly higher prices, higher costs for insurance and certainly less overall prosperity. In addition, many innocent people suffer and are caused worry by such activities.

What is to be done?
1 *(a)* Many thefts and burglaries, often accompanied by damage to property and equipment, are *not* well planned, thought out crimes. Often simple security precautions would prevent them. For example, windows and doors left unlocked or open; ladders left lying about – all help the illegal entry of intruders.

(b) Highly sophisticated microprocessor based control systems are now available. They provide for the control by card access at a single door (or a network of doors), parking places, lifts and turnstiles. In addition, they report activity by a variety of alarms – audio paper tape printout, even complete computer printouts – of everything that has happened.

Smaller organisations are not so likely to employ such systems. But simple straightforward precautions can lead to increased security.

The use of burglar alarm systems is now commonplace. As you must be aware, many private houses are equipped with them. Some of the systems used by larger firms are connected with local police stations.
2 Doors should be solidly constructed and not made in panels and faced with hardboard. Locking bars should be padlocked to the wall so that doors cannot be lifted off their hinges. It should be made impossible to pull the door frame away from the wall. Hinges should not be fitted on the outside.

3 Laminated glass is the only type of glass which, when properly fitted, resists attack. Flat roofs should, whenever possible, be avoided. Drainpipes should have barbed wire fitted on them 8 metres from the ground. Premises should, whenever possible, be illuminated at night. Skylights must not provide easy access from the roof.

Cash

1 Despite the growing use of cheques, standing orders and direct debits, (*see* Chapter 13) many transactions are settled and wages are paid in cash. From time to time there is discussion concerning the payment of wages and salaries by means other than cash. But many people still tend to be suspicious of such suggestions.

2 Considerable sums of cash are carried from and to banks and building societies. Robberies, during transportation, of such cash are only too well known. Firms exist which specialise in transporting cash and valuables. Securicor vans and guards are now a familiar sight on the streets of most towns and cities.

3 Where an organisation decides to bank its own cash certain precautions should be taken:

(*a*) Able bodied people only should be used. Those who transport the cash should not wear uniforms which associate them with the organisation.

(*b*) An escort should accompany the cash carrier and should walk a little way behind. When a night safe is used the escort must be able to provide protection whilst the money is being deposited. The cash should never be produced until the safe door has been opened. Carrier and escort should both be able to give an alarm. Whistles are often carried for this purpose.

(*c*) The routes used, and the times when cash is collected or banked, should be varied. This applies whether the cash carrier walks or travels in a car or van. Whenever possible, busy streets and roads should be used. Cash carriers and their escorts should walk facing oncoming traffic. Do you know why?

(*d*) Various kinds of security bags for the carrying of cash are available. Advice regarding them and other security matters can be obtained from the local police Crime Prevention Officer.

(*e*) Great caution is needed if a night safe has an 'Out of Order' notice displayed. Anything unusual about such safes merits suspicion. There have been cases where false fronts have been fitted to night safes.

Storing and handling cash

1 Cash left on premises overnight should always be placed in a safe. Neither cash nor safe keys should be hidden. Keys should be taken away from the premises and held by a responsible employee. Any room where there is cash (and it is not in a safe), should never be left unattended or unlocked.

2 Any safe weighing under 1000 kilogrammes should be secured to the floor. Does a week ever pass without there being a report of a safe, somewhere, being removed, opened and dumped?

3 Most organisations where cash is regularly given and received (e.g. shops) have cash registers. Regular procedures must be made known to and followed by employees handling cash in these circumstances. It is worth remembering that as we progress towards the cashless society, most of the security measures outlined in this section will be unnecessary.

Stock

1 A firm can suffer losses because of: the dishonesty of its staff and customers (e.g. at checkout points); shoplifting, burglary and fraud; poor management, e.g. failure to keep proper records of stock movements. Many of these losses are often referred to as 'leakages'.

A recent report estimated that in the case of a large multiple store, 'leakages' were due: 35 per cent to losses when goods were delivered; 10 per cent to fraud at the tills; 30 per cent to shoplifting and pilfering by staff; and 25 per cent to wastages.

2 Many leakages are caused by poor practices being used when goods and raw materials are received. 'Thanks. Just put them over there. See you next week' is just not good enough when a driver makes a delivery to a firm's warehouse. That way can lead to the organisation paying for goods which have never been received.

3 What should be done then to check these losses?

(a) All goods must be delivered only at certain stated times to the firm's delivery area.

(b) A note of damaged or opened parcels must be made on the delivery sheets.

(c) Goods must be checked against the advice note when they are delivered. They should be checked against the orders to which they relate within 24 hours of receipt.

(d) Stock, particularly where it is very valuable, must be locked in cages or secured rooms.

(e) Goods should never be left outside storerooms.

(f) Waste (e.g. packing materials) should be cleared regularly. Packing cartons should be flattened. What, do you think, is the reason for this?

(g) If there are any items missing from a delivery and where no explanation has been given, contact the supplier immediately and ask for one.

*(h)*Never sign for goods which have not been received.

(i) Stock recording, checking and control is important. See now page 117.

Equipment

Good equipment is both costly and vital to the efficient working of the modern office. Great care must be taken with its maintenance, operation and custody.

1 When any equipment is purchased, the procedures to be used when it is received are outlined on page 117.

2 The leasing of equipment is mentioned on page 249. Usually the lessor (i.e. the organisation hiring out the equipment), will insist that the lessee (who is going to use the equipment), takes out insurance to cover loss or damage. Invariably the lessee will also have to undertake to keep the equipment in sound working order.

3 Small valuable pieces of equipment (e.g. calculators) should be securely stored away at the end of the day's work.

4 Filing cabinets, desk drawers, computers and the like must be locked when work is finished. The keys must be removed and not hidden in the office. They should be held by a responsible employee.

5 Offices should be locked when they are empty. This is easier said than done. Offices have to be open when they are being cleaned, or decorated and in some cases when being repaired. Thefts are not infrequently carried out by people posing as cleaners, decorators, delivery or repair men, window cleaners and gas, electricity and telephone officials. If you see anybody who appears to be acting suspiciously, or whose presence on the office premises you cannot account for, *politely* ask the nature of their business and whether or not you can help. If you are not satisfied report the matter at once to one of your superiors. Access to many offices is still far too easy!

Documents

The storing and safeguarding of valuable documents necessitates the use of fireproof, difficult 'to crack' safes. In this connection have another look at Figs. 6.1 and 6.2 and the note relating to the Halifax Building Society.

Shoplifting

Shoplifting is a particular kind of theft and it is no less serious than others. Although it may appear to be of interest only to those in the retail trade, this is not so. Whether it is called theft or shoplifting, the results are the same. Because of it we all have to pay more for what we buy than would otherwise be the case. The following aspects of shoplifting are of general interest.

1 Retailers spend large sums of money (in staff and equipment) in their attempts to prevent it. There now exists an Association for the Prevention of Theft in Shops. Videos and advice relating to the prevention of shop thefts are available to APTS members.

2 Shoplifters, actual or suspected, have to be treated with care and caution. If the wrong person is apprehended, a retailer may be sued for any of damages, assault, malicious prosecution or false imprisonment.

3 Sales areas where there are few or no staff present; fitting rooms, blindspots and hidden areas all favour the shoplifter.

4 Goods, of all sorts, are illegally removed by a variety of methods. These include slipping articles into pockets, carrier bags and handbags and using coats with several inside pockets. On occasions the shoplifter will place some of his own possessions on top of the stolen items. 'Ticket switching' (i.e. placing a low price ticket on a more highly priced item and then paying the lower price), is also used by thieves. Sometimes shoplifters work in co-operation with an employee (maybe a friend or relative who is a till cashier). They then pay far less for the goods they are 'buying' than they should do. Recently, there has been a growth in the use of shoplifting gangs one of whose members will distract the employee's attention whilst the others remove the goods. There seems to be no limit to the ingenuity of shoplifters.

Credit card fraud

Credit cards (*see* page 146), when they fall into the wrong hands, can be used falsely to obtain credit.

1 The payee should always check the signature on the top copy against the signature on the credit card.

2 Where there are any good grounds for suspicion, the police should be contacted and attempts made to keep the customer in the shop. Where larger sums are involved the salesperson will have instructions to phone the credit card organisation.

3 The use of a passport type photo would be another possible safeguard. None of the credit card organisations yet use this technique.

4 Credit card companies are usually willing to reward anyone who prevents a person from falsely using one of their cards.

Information

The importance of information cannot be overestimated. Through tales of fact and fiction, most of us are familiar with spy trials, where the security of the state appears to have been threatened. Our concern here is with a less exciting type of information – and its safeguarding, i.e. commercial and trade information. The 'leaking' of a firm's trade secrets (e.g. its production processes) to its competitors, either at home or abroad, may seriously affect its performance – and its profits.

1 Much information is still contained in files and filing cabinets. The safeguarding of such data has already been mentioned (*see* page 243). Nowadays, and on an ever increasing scale, computers are used to store information of all kinds. This can range from personal details about employees to financial accounts; from records of stock and wages to those relating to debtors and creditors. If such information is stolen, lost or destroyed, the consequences may be disastrous.

2 Where computers are in operation, certain precautions for the safeguarding of the information they hold must be taken. These include:

(a) Ensuring that only the staff responsible for the information are permitted to operate or change the computer programmes.

(b) Making sure that copies of all such vital information are kept on tape or disks. Such copies are known as 'backups'. Whenever the information held is changed, the backup copies must be similarly altered.

(c) Having a system of secret codes and passwords, available to, and only to be used by the computer staff. This helps to stop unauthorised persons gaining access to information.

(d) Arranging for all computer installations to be securely kept. Locked doors; operation behind windows with blinds and strict fire precautions are all used. Visitors are usually denied access to any rooms where computers are used.

3 Despite the existence of patents and trade marks, we still have some way to go to ensure the protection of new ideas and inventions. These are a form of property. They are intellectual property and they can be bought and sold. This country has a tradition of leading the world in inventions and ideas and we rely heavily on getting value from such assets.

An example of how brilliant young inventors are in danger of being left unprotected by existing laws is in the field of computer games. Stories of young software writers earning large sums often receive wide publicity. Regrettably more than one of these young people has been 'ripped off by the sharks of the software trade' (David Dawson, researcher for radio's 'The Chip Shop'). However, a number of the more reputable companies have drawn up a comprehensive code of conduct. This includes an agreement to treat programmers fairly.

4 Small enterprising firms and individuals need protection when their ideas are being commercialised (i.e. incorporated in saleable goods and services). Large organisations can look after themselves. They can afford top rank legal help. Not so the 'little man' or firm. They can have their ideas stolen. Even though they may have taken out a patent or registered design in the UK they often have not the cash to protect their rights through the country. The UK government is considering introducing into Parliament an Intellectual Property and Innovation Bill. It is hoped that such a Bill will allow for the introduction of a registered inventions scheme. This should give a more readily accessible type of protection, particularly to the individual or small concern.

5 There is, however, another side to this coin of the security and protection of information. Lord Scarman, formerly one of our most eminent judges and a member of the House of Lords, as long ago as 1978, criticised government attitude towards official secrets. He argued that both the judges and the public needed some declaration of principles regarding the general right of access to official information. The Freedom of Information Act in the USA virtually commands, with only a few exceptions, government departments to make information available to the public.

6 The Data Protection Act, which came into force in 1984, gives people the right of access to information about them which is held on computers (*see* page 211). This would allow them to check its accuracy. There have been a number of cases in recent years where computer information about the credit worthiness of individuals has been wrong. The result has been that these individuals have been denied credit where they should have been allowed it. Incorrect information in computers can mean that a person is not allowed hire purchase, insurance or banking facilities. This can mean injustice for the individual, possibly injury to his business prospects and a grave (and false) slur on his reputation. The whole topic of safeguarding computer information and the individual's right of access to it, is one of great importance. Try and keep a lookout for any references to it in the media.

Personnel

Some of the best methods of safeguarding an organisation's possessions revolve around the staff.

1 Efficient managers will do their utmost to make all employees mindful of the importance of security. Involving staff in decisions which affect them and are related to their jobs; treating people as more than numbers; setting a good example – all help towards the creation of morale. If staff morale

is high, loyalty is likely to be high too. Employees who are loyal are not so likely to pilfer.

2 Staff training; the operation of incentive schemes relating to security in sound supervision and constant alertness all lead towards better security.

3 Initial recruitment of staff is obviously of importance. The vast majority of job applicants are honest. This does not mean that an applicant's references and academic certificates should not be carefully scrutinized. More than one job has been obtained with forged documents.

When there is any cause for suspicion, time spent at an interview, in ensuring an applicant's honesty, may be more than repaid.

Inefficiency

Not all losses incurred by an organisation are caused by criminal activities. In many instances, losses may be down to bad practices, carelessness and general inefficiency. Here are a few examples:

1 Clerical errors (e.g. not checking goods properly when they are received. This can mean paying for non deliveries).

2 Careless treatment of stock and equipment. This may mean items being declared obsolete and 'written off' before they should have been.

3 Failing to sell, even on occasions at a loss, older (and deteriorating) stock. Think here of the importance of 'cash flow'.

4 Insufficient care being taken when change is being given. Many modern tills indicate cash total of items purchased and, after payment has been offered, the change due.

5 By accident giving overweight – where this is done deliberately it is pilfering.

6 Finally, the way customers are treated by any organisation can lead to incalculable losses. Whether someone is buying goods or services, it should never be forgotten that the customer is the lifeblood on which the organisation depends.

Here are just a few examples, all based on real life incidents. They have resulted in customers walking out and unless there is no alternative, never patronising the organisation in question again. No doubt you will be able to think of other examples, probably based on your own experience.

(a) Being promised the delivery of an article or the arrival of a tradesman to do a job, altering one's arrangements so you will be there – and then nobody arriving at the arranged time. To make matters worse, in a number of instances, no explanation, apology or forewarning is volunteered.

(b) Waiting to be attended to at some office or shop counter and being ignored. Meanwhile the employee(s) behind the counter have private telephone conversations or chat to colleagues.

(c) On telephoning an organisation being switched from one extension to another and not being able to reach the correct person or section.

(d) Being treated rudely or suffering sarcasm when you ask a polite question (even though it may seem stupid to the other person).

(e) Being subjected to long, acrimonious and embarrassing arguments when faulty goods are returned. 'What can you expect when you only paid £x for it' is scarcely calculated to retain a customer's goodwill.

(f) Employees being busily engaged in stocktaking or labelling whilst a customer waits (if he does for very long) unattended.

Most large scale organisations (but not all) do manage to avoid such things happening. These are usually the ones which take their staff training very seriously.

7 It is more than likely that on some occasion or other, you have suffered treatment of the sort described. Such incidents inevitably cause the loss of future (and possibly present) custom. Consumers who are badly treated tell others. The ultimate overall losses to the organisation can be serious.

Exercises

1 If most people are relatively honest, why do we have to spend so much on security?

2 What should be done to ensure the security of office or college premises?

3 What precautions should be taken to ensure the safety of cash when it is being banked?

4 What are leakages? How would you prevent them?

5 What should be done to safeguard valuable documents (e.g. confidential correspondence, share certificates)?

Assignments

1 Using the index at the end of this book, make a note of the pages where safety is mentioned (in addition to this chapter). Study them and list the danger 'spots' mentioned in the text which you do *not* think are shown in the office in the illustration opposite.

2 Describe as fully as possible, any three accidents which you think might occur in the office shown opposite.

3 You have just started work in a local office. On the first morning, after explaining your duties to you, your head of department mentions briefly the importance of safety in the office. You are given a copy of the picture opposite, and a list of questions relating to it. You are told to spend the afternoon studying the picture and the questions and to report at 2.30 pm with your answers.

The questions on the paper are as follows. Prepare answers to them:

(a) Make a list of what you consider to be hazards and dangerous practices in the office in the picture. Note all the points as briefly as possible and number them separately.

Fig. 18.1 ROSPA (Royal Society for the Prevention of Accidents) illustration showing hazards and dangerous practices in the office.

(b) An accident happens to one of the male office workers in the picture.

   (i) Describe the accident and the circumstances surrounding it.

   (ii) The nurse in the company's First Aid Room decides that the injured office worker should go to hospital because of the serious nature of the injury. This man is not on the phone at home. His wife does not go out to work. The police are contacted so that the wife may be informed of the accident. Write out the message which would be given by telephone to the police.

4 Accidents in offices are sometimes caused because of inadequate space in which people can move about. The desks and tables shown in the picture are all 122 cm long, 66 cm high, and 61 cm wide. The filing cabinets are 138 cm high, 61 cm deep, and 46 cm wide.

   (a) Calculate the total area of floor space occupied by this office furniture.

   (b) Provide your own dimensions for the tea trolley and the cabinet next to the door. What do you consider should be the length and breadth of the office shown in the picture — to provide a reasonable and safe amount of space in which people can move about?

(c) According to the company's Accident Report Book, which it is obliged by law to keep, you are told that during last year, in the company's factory, accident details were as follows:

Major accidents: 7 head injuries; 12 eye injuries; 9 broken limbs; 24 injuries to the back; 12 removals to hospital.

Minor accidents: 95 cuts; 40 bruises; 60 torn clothing; and 50 falls. Removals to hospital: 5.

Construct a bar chart to illustrate this information.

5 Over a period of a week and using whatever sources of information you like (press, journals, news items on TV and radio) select as many items as you can relating to security in shops and offices. State what common features (if any) they have. Can you suggest how, in the items you have chosen, greater safety or security might have been obtained?

19 THE ORGANISATION AND THE PROVIDERS OF FINANCE

Objectives

At the end of this chapter you should be able to:

- Describe the methods used by sole traders, partnerships, limited companies, co-operative societies, local authorities, and public corporations to finance their activities.
- Give examples of the obligations of these organisations towards the providers of finance.

Credit

How much more simple everything would be if we could buy anything and everything we wanted, exactly when we wanted it and pay for it without a second thought. As you well know, life is very different from that. The money that individuals and organisations have is limited. They have to choose between different ways of spending it. Often they will want to buy some goods or services but cannot afford to pay immediately. To meet this difficulty *credit* is given to them. All this means is that they can obtain the possession, and use (and sometimes legal ownership), of what they want and pay later.

Most individuals need credit when they make a large purchase. The biggest purchase most people make is when they buy their own house. Very few individuals, when they first get their own home, can pay for it immediately. They go to a building society usually, which advances them a loan with which to buy the house of their choice. This is often described as 'taking out a mortgage'. The loan is repaid to the building society, with interest and by instalments, over a fairly lengthy period (usually 20 to 30 years). The house does not belong to the borrower until the original sum and interest have been paid. Club trading with a mail order firm; using credit cards such as Visa and Access; paying for newspapers and milk at the end of the week; buying furniture on hire purchase – are all examples of buying on credit. A person or an organisation may have a large number of debts – all falling due for payment at roughly the same time. In such circumstances, time to pay, or credit, may be asked from some or all of the creditors. In some cases credit arrangements will have been made when the purchase was made.

Whether or not credit is granted depends often on the creditor. Some organisations and people will give only limited credit (say a month). To put pressure on a person to settle outstanding debts, particularly when willingness to pay by regular instalments has been shown, may turn future business away. Also, legal action to recover debts can be costly and result in instalments being paid over a long period of time.

The word *credit* has many other meanings. It is used in book-keeping and accounting, and is a technical term used to indicate some sorts of entries in a firm's book of account. *Credit* also is often used to refer to a personal quality – somebody's reputation. For instance, you might hear someone say 'Your son does you credit, Mrs Jones'. That hardly has anything to do with finance. On the other hand if we say a person's credit is good, it means he can be trusted to pay his debts, i.e. to pay for the goods he has bought on credit. This is very important for if A is about to give B credit (time to pay) for some purchase B wants to make, and he finds B has the reputation of being a bad payer, he will be far more cautious than he would have been otherwise. Indeed, he may decide not to give B credit (time to pay) at all. Organisations exist to give traders information about customers' credit worthiness, and thus protect traders from giving credit to people and firms with bad payment records (e.g. HP Information Ltd keeps a record of instalment agreements).

Notice that often where credit has been granted the debtor has to pay for the extra time he has been given in which to pay, i.e. he pays interest, as in a hire purchase agreement. In many instances if a debtor pays immediately, or very quickly, a cash discount will be given. This means he will pay less than the original purchase price. The reason for this is that the seller has use of the money owing to him sooner than if the debtor took time to pay.

Credit is something you will come across very often when studying the world of work. It exists at every stage of the chain of production (*see* Chapter 20) and is used by all types of organisation.

This chapter aims to examine how an organisation obtains the necessary cash or credit to start in business and to carry out its various activities. This means a survey of how it is financed and the obligations the organisation has to those who have financed it. 'Finance' does not just mean having the money in the safe or being loaned the cash. It also includes being able to buy goods or services on credit.

There are two major providers of finance for an organisation – its owners and its creditors.

Obligations of private sector organisations to their owners

Sole traders

The *sole trader* usually finances himself, or at least in part, from his own resources. He may use his savings or give up (surrender) an insurance policy and get the cash from that. Where he is a house owner, and his house is paid for, he can use the title deeds in order to borrow funds to help start his business. Of course, this new mortgage will have to be paid off eventually.

Partnerships

As you already know (*see* Chapter 4) a sole trader wishing to expand his business may decide to take in one or more partners. They bring in cash or other assets and share the responsibilities. The partners have obligations to each other. No partner may make a secret profit on his own at the expense of the partnership. Every partner is entitled to be dealt with, by his fellow partners, with honesty and good faith. These are important matters. If the business fails because of the activities of one partner, all may become bankrupt. As you have already read, it is best if the rights and obligations of the partners are put in a legally binding agreement. The obligations then of the partnership (i.e. the organisation) are to pay agreed salaries and interest on capital to the partners, provided these matters have been stated in the agreement.

In a limited partnership, the organisation's obligation is to pay the limited partner(s) their share of the profits and to let them inspect the books. A limited partner may not take part in managing the business.

Both sole traders and partnerships may be helped in financing their future development and expansion by using profits they have kept in the business. The organisation which does not spend everything it earns shows the same wisdom as the individual who puts something away for a 'rainy day' – or as the farmer who ploughs back some of his crops to improve the fertility of the soil.

Limited companies

Whereas the sole trader and partnership usually obtain their starting capital from their own savings or other resources of their own, the owners of a company buy shares in the business. Re-read carefully page 57 and notice again the distinctions between private and public companies. In particular remember that the public company can invite the public to buy shares. The private company cannot do this.

The special obligations of the public company towards its shareholders are that before anybody buys shares they must, via the prospectus, be given information (*see* page 61). The law relating to this information is aimed at avoiding the misleading of investors by unscrupulous company promoters. At one time it was not compulsory for the company to reveal the sum of money it needed to cover initial expenses and provide enough cash with which to run the business. If the company failed 'to get off the ground' and start trading, the promoters usually avoided loss. They made sure that they got hold of the cash already received for the assets they had sold to the company. Now, if the total from the shares which have been applied for is *below* the amount stated in the prospectus as being necessary to enable the company to start operations, all application moneys received have to be returned. Thus, when offering shares to the public a company will make a contract with underwriters. In return for a commission the underwriters agree to buy part or all of the shares which have not been purchased by the public. If the issue is highly successful, the underwriters have got their commission virtually for nothing. If the issue is not a success, they have the obligation already mentioned to buy the unsold shares.

The following obligations apply to both private and public companies.

1 Provided the payment of a dividend is recommended by the directors and the Annual General Meeting (AGM) agrees, there is an obligation on the part of the company to pay dividends according to the rights of the different classes of shares. Formerly dividends *had* to be paid out of profits. No restriction then existed concerning *when* the profits had been made, or whether losses had been incurred after the profits had been made. Now, dividends can only be paid out of accumulated realised profits less accumulated realised losses. Furthermore, dividends can only be paid when the total of the firm's assets is not less than the total of the called up share capital and undistributed reserves. The payments of dividends must not reduce the assets below that figure.

2 One of the main objectives of company law has been to ensure that money entrusted to the company by its owners (i.e. the shareholders) has been properly used. Publicity as to what the company, and particularly the directors have been doing with the shareholders' cash, is essential. Thus, the company must keep proper books of account and send various documents every year to the Registrar of Companies. There they can be inspected by anyone – not only the shareholders.

3 The Annual General Meeting is another example of a company fulfilling its obligations to its owners and keeping them informed of the company's activities.

During recent years various arrangements have been made by central government to help companies which have been short of capital. In 1973, Finance for Industry Ltd was created. It aimed to cater particularly for organisations requiring large sums, but which could not show a quick return on capital. Equity Capital for Industry was formed in 1976. It aimed to provide Ordinary share capital for companies of medium size. The National Enterprise Board was set up in 1975. Among other things, it was asked to increase capacity in major sectors of manufacturing industry; to help increase exports and save imports; and to extend the public ownership of industry. Later the NEB was merged with the National Research Development Corporation to form the British Technology Group.

Since 1979 the government has paid particular attention to the small firms sector, which it has endeavoured to help in various ways. The Business Start Up scheme was introduced in 1981. It is designed to encourage outside investors, i.e. individuals other than the proprietor and his associates, to take up equity (i.e. risk capital) in enterprises at the difficult starting up stage. Investments under this scheme must be in new, independent companies which are genuinely starting up new business ventures, or which have started up within the preceding three years. Some worthwhile projects fail to find adequate finance, because the potential borrower has no 'track record' (i.e. no previous record of success in a business venture). Through the Loan Guarantee Scheme, government guarantees have been made available to financial institutions in order to encourage additional lending.

In 1983, the Business Expansion Scheme was introduced. This was to apply to investment in new and existing trading companies. The Business Start-up Scheme has also been extended to include a large number of existing unquoted trading companies. Certain tax and VAT concessions have also been made to help small businesses. The Small Workshop Scheme is intended to encourage the construction of small industrial buildings. The Manpower Services Commission sponsors training for people considering starting their own business. The Enterprise Allowance Scheme which provides financial assistance during the first 12 months of working for yourself has encouraged many to take the step into self employment. Help, advice and financial support for a tourism project can be obtained from the National Tourist Boards in England, Scotland and Wales.

It has been estimated that the UK has approximately 1.3 million small firms. This figure may appear to be large but compared with other industrialised countries it is really quite small. For instance, the Netherlands, with only a quarter of our population, has four times as many small businesses as the UK.

If the opportunities available in the small firms sector are to be fully exploited, there must be more flexibility in lending to them and some fundamental changes in attitudes and organisation.

Obligations of private sector organisations to their creditors

Sole traders and partnerships

1 In addition to their own resources sole traders and partnerships may borrow from relatives, friends or the bank. The conditions attached to any such loans will be agreed between the two sides. Usually the obligation will be to pay interest at the rate agreed. Sometimes a close friend or relative will make the loan without any interest on it being payable. The lender may have his loan 'secured' – so that if the business fails his loan must be repaid before any other of the sums owing.

2 Another way by which sole traders and partnerships may be financed is to get their stock, or part of it, on credit. But usually payment in such cases cannot be long delayed. If creditors do not get paid on time they may immediately stop further supplies and also take legal action to recover the debt.

3 In some cases, equipment will not be bought. It will be leased instead. In effect, an annual rent (hiring charge) is paid. If this debt is not met, the equipment or machinery will be removed.

4 Hire purchase and credit sales are both methods whereby an individual, or an organisation, can obtain goods on credit. Because of the interest charges, hire purchase can often be a costly means of financing the purchase of assets.

5 Until payment is made for goods or services supplied on credit, the

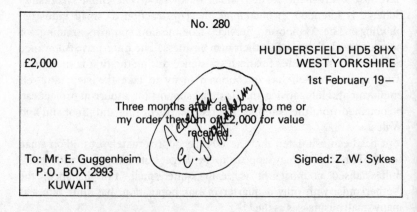

Fig. 19.1 A foreign Bill of Exchange

money owing is of no use to the creditor. One way by which the creditor can gain effective use of the money owing to him is to draw what is called a bill of exchange on the debtor. What happens is this:

(*a*) The creditor Sykes (*see* Fig. 19.1) draws up (i.e. drafts) a bill of exchange on the debtor (Guggenheim). This requires the debtor to pay the amount owing to the creditor on or before a particular date. In this situation the creditor is known as the 'drawer' of the bill and the debtor as the 'drawee'.

(*b*) The creditor then sends the bill to the debtor. If the debtor agrees to its terms, he writes 'Accepted' on the bill and signs it. Now he is known as the 'acceptor' and the creditor is known as the 'payee'. The acceptor then returns the bill to the payee. In law, the bill is then proof that the debt exists.

Because of the problems arising from transactions over a distance, bills of exchange are more frequently used in international trade than in home trade. Fig. 19.1 is an example of a foreign bill.

(*c*) The payee can now do one of three things:

(*i*) He may negotiate it (i.e. he signs it over) to someone else in payment of a debt. In turn, this second person may negotiate it to a third person – and so on. Whoever has the bill when it becomes due for payment will present it to the acceptor (i.e. the original debtor) and request payment.

(*ii*) The payee may discount the bill with his bank. This means the bank takes the bill and regards it as money deposited in the payee's account. It is just the same as if he had paid a cheque into his account. The bank then holds the bill until it becomes due for payment. They will then present it to the acceptor for payment. The bank will charge the payee for this service. This is known as a 'discounting charge'.

(*iii*) The payee can hold the bill until the due date and present it for payment when it is due.

In (*i*) and (*ii*) the creditor is receiving the money due to him (less the discounting charge in (*ii*)). It is almost as if the debtor had paid him straight away. The debtor is also given time in which to pay.

6 A large part of bank profits results from loans to customers. In addition to the methods of financing themselves which have already been mentioned, sole traders and partnerships often turn to the banks for loans. The interest on a bank loan is charged on the whole sum from the time it is borrowed. Alternatively, a bank may agree to provide an overdraft. In both cases the usual practice is for the borrower to provide some form of security. A 'security' is something of value given to the bank. The bank holds the security, and if the customer fails to pay back what he has borrowed then the security can be realised (sold). The bank then takes that money as a payment of part (or whole) of the money borrowed by the customer. Unlike a bank loan, overdraft interest is only charged on the

amount actually overdrawn. The bank places a limit beyond which the customer cannot overdraw on his account. Unless a customer wants to use the whole of a bank loan immediately, it is obviously cheaper, in terms of interest payments, to obtain an overdraft. But, an overdraft may be more difficult to obtain. Usually it can be recalled more quickly than a loan in times of difficulty.

Limited companies

1 Borrowing from relatives and friends; getting stock on credit; hiring equipment; using hire purchase and credit sales and bills of exchange; obtaining finance from a bank; all these (except the first) are employed to a greater or lesser extent by public companies.

Many private companies are also financed by *all* these methods.

2 Debentures are a means of finance used only by companies. A debenture is a type of loan. A debenture holder is a creditor and *not* an owner of a company. He is entitled to receive a fixed rate of interest. Interest to debenture holders *must* be paid, whether or not the company has made a profit. Some debentures have a 'charge' against the assets of the company. This usually means that if the company comes to an end and is 'wound up' then the debenture holders get paid before other creditors. The nature of 'charges' do however vary widely between companies.

3 In recent years, the private sector organisations have increasingly used the services offered by finance companies. The term 'finance company' is not an easy one to define. It is sufficient to remember that they get their finances from various sources – their own shares, bank overdrafts, bills of exchange and deposits from the public. Much of their business is concerned with using their resources to make finance available on long terms for industry and trade.

Much hire purchase business, particularly that undertaken by retailers, is financed by these companies. Thus, when a customer visits his local TV retailer, it is the finance company, and not the retailer, who lends the money to the individual to help him make his purchase. The finance company concerned may itself be controlled by TV manufacturers and dealers. Many motor car sales on credit are financed in the same way.

4 Leasing of office equipment and machinery (*see* pages 255-256) is also becoming popular. Again, it is a method used by sole traders, partnerships and companies. The main reason for the growth of leasing business is that instead of having to find all the money straight away to buy the machinery, office equipment and so on, only the money for the instalments has to be found. Also, when a lease runs out and is renewed, the most up to date equipment can be obtained. This rarely happens if a company has bought its equipment outright, because a company is less likely to replace

equipment paid for, if it is still working. Leasing is also regarded by the tax authorities as an expense when tax is calculated and this is an advantage for some types of business assets.

Exercises

1 Define credit.
2 What is a discounting charge?
3 Why does a prospectus have to contain certain information?
4 How does a share differ from a debenture?
5 What is the main difference between a bank loan and an overdraft?
6 Why do organisations lease instead of buying equipment?

Assignment

In your workbook draw a table similar to the one shown opposite. In each of the appropriate boxes write:
1 Who owns each type of organisation.
2 By what methods each of them obtains credit.
Example: The owner of a sole trader type of organisation is the sole trader or proprietor himself. Therefore in box 1A you will write 'The sole trader'.

Before you write the answers to this assignment in the table in your workbook, it would be a good idea to do the whole piece of work in rough first. Then you will be sure to leave enough space in each of the boxes when you come to rule up the table.

	Sole Trader	Partnership	Private Company	Public Company
	1	2	3	4
A Who owns the organisation.				
B The methods by which credit is obtained.				

Co-operative societies

1 Reference to Chapter 6 will remind you that a retail co-operative society obtains its capital from its members' shareholdings (maximum £5000 per person). A society's members are then its owners. There are no limits to the amount any member may loan the society, nor to the number of members there may be. Remember though that whatever his shareholding, or however much he may have loaned to the society, a member is only entitled to one vote at meetings of the society. Until recent years a

substantial part of the profits was returned to the members in the form of a cash dividend proportionate to their purchases. Nowadays, faced with the competition of multiple retailers and supermarkets and the increasing costs of administration, most societies have scrapped the payment of dividends. Instead, trading stamps are issued at the time of purchase. These can be exchanged for cash or goods at the customer's convenience. Alternatively, any sum due for trading stamps, can be left with the society to accumulate with interest. Stamps are issued to customers whether or not they are members of the society.

2 Members are entitled to repayment of their shares and interest virtually on demand. Contrast this with the shares of a public limited company which have to be sold by the shareholder. Notice also that the society's obligations include this payment of a fixed rate of interest on shareholdings. These interest payments are cumulative, i.e. they are carried forward from one year to the next until paid.

3 Local societies are controlled by an elected board of directors. In some cases they are known as the management committee. Members' meetings are held, usually half-yearly. At these meetings the directors account to the members for their management of the society.

4 In the same way that individual members provide the capital for the local retail society, so also do the societies supply the capital for the Co-operative Wholesale Society. Similarly, the CWS is controlled by its retail society members, just as the retail society is accountable to its individual customer members.

The public sector

Our study of the finance of public sector organisations is directed towards local authority and public corporations.

Local authorities are financed from:
1 the rates;
2 grants from central government;
3 sales, fees and charges;
4 activities such as the rent of land and buildings;
5 loans from the public and from institutional investors.

The obligations of the local authorities to these providers of finance differ.

Rates

Rates are a type of local tax. They are based on the rateable value of houses, non-agricultural land, industrial and commercial premises, and public buildings.

1 The rent at which each property might be let, if the landlord paid for

maintenance and the tenant paid the rates, is called the Gross Annual Value. From the GAV is subtracted, in each case, a figure for repairs. The result is the rateable value of the premises or land.

2 Assume a house has a rateable value of £220 and the local authority's general rate for the year has been calculated at £1.55 in the £. (Don't let this term 'in the £' confuse you. It means 'per £ of rateable value' but the wording used is still 'in the £'). This means that for every £ of rateable value of the house, the occupier pays £1.55 to the local authority. Thus, in this particular case he will pay 220 × £1.55 = £341. In addition, he will probably have to pay a water rate of say 50p in the £, i.e. 220 × 50p = £110. The water rate now is not paid via the local authority as it used to be. It is paid direct to the Water Authority (*see* page 68). The occupier's total payment for general rate and water rate is thus £451 (£341 plus £110). These sums may be paid in instalments.

3 The rate in the £ varies every year as the local authority's estimate of the money it will require to provide its services, and to meet alterations in prices, changes. No rates are paid on churches and agricultural land. Premises used for charitable purposes only pay 50 per cent of their normal rates. People with limited incomes can also get rate rebates. From its total estimated expenditure, the authority will subtract what it is to receive from the government in grants.

4 Study now the information given in Fig. 19.2. It has been extracted from information leaflets sent to all the ratepayers in the area of the Kirklees Metropolitan District Council in West Yorkshire. All authorities differ in the totals of the rateable values and in their expenditure. Nevertheless, the principles on which they operate are similar.

Note: (see Fig. 19.2), that *from* the General Rate of 176p in the £ the sum of 18.5 p in the £ is to be deducted as domestic rate relief. This sum is general throughout England, except for a number of London authorities. The rate income lost to the local authority when it makes this reduction is offset by a central government grant called the Domestic Rate Relief Grant. Thus, the rate in the £ for the Huddersfield area of Kirklees was 176p minus 18.5p = 157.5p in the £. In addition, of course, ratepayers have to meet their water rates.

Assignment

Using the headings shown in Fig. 19.2, find the statistics for the local authority in whose area you live.

Accounts

The Council is accountable to the electorate at all times. Councillors hold regular 'surgeries' which are advertised in the local press and people in

1984/85
Where the money comes from and how it is spent
Kirklees Metropolitan District Council

A Where the money comes from			£.m
8%	1.	**Sales, Fees and Charges.** The cost of many of the Council's services is met in part, or in full by the people who use them eg school meals, trade refuse, car parking, and leisure facilities	14.5
66%	2.	**Government Grants.** *Block Grant* £87.8 m; *Specific Grants* £24.2 m; and *Domestic Rate Relief* £3.1 m. Block Grant is received towards the net cost of all services. Specific Grants are to meet the cost of particular services. Domestic Rate relief is to compensate for the subsidy to domestic ratepayers of 18.5p in the £	115.1
	3.	**Ratepayers.** *Domestic owner occupiers* and tenants £17.8 m; *Commercial* Shops, offices, restaurants £6.8 m; *Industrial* Factories, mills and other workshops £6.3 m; *Other* Mainly public buildings eg hospitals and schools £7.2 m	38.1
26%	4.	**Balances**	2.0
	5.	**Other income** arising from such activities as the rent of land and buildings, interest and services for other Councils	4.8

TOTAL £174.5m

B How the money is spent			£.m
59%	1.	**Education.** Over 4600 teachers and lecturers for 79,000 pupils and students in 234 schools, 2 technical colleges and Huddersfield Polytechnic. 45,000 school meals per day. Careers advice and support for Youth Clubs	103.5
12%	2.	**Social Services.** Care and support for the elderly, children, handicapped and ill and help for families in difficulty; 49 residential homes and 5 day nurseries. Home help. Meals on wheels	20.4
5%	3.	**Housing.** Assistance towards rent payment for over 27,000 private and Council tenants. Environmental improvement. Assistance for homeless	9.0

Fig. 19.2

			£.m
4%	4.	**Environmental Health.** Collection of about 120,000 tonnes of refuse from 146,000 domestic and 4,000 trade customers. Cleaning of 1,100 miles of roads. Management of market halls and open markets. Inspection of premises to enforce health and hygiene standards	7.0
7%	5.	**Recreation and Amenities.** Over 1,100 acres of parks and open spaces. 6 sports centres, 5 swimming pools and a golf course. 2 crematoria and 13 cemeteries. 3 museums, 2 historic houses and 4 art galleries	11.2
1%	6.	**Development and Technical Services.** Control of building developments. Improvement of the environment	1.9
10%	7.	**Resources and Planning.** Administrative and financial services. Management of the Council's commercial and office accommodation. Magistrates' Courts. Special measures for the unemployed	17.4
2%	8.	**Contingencies.** The amount set aside to cover pay and price increases up to March, 1985	4.1

TOTAL £174.5m

C What the money is spent on

			£.m
	1.	**Employees.**	101.4
	2.	**Running Expenses.** Maintenance and running costs of all Council buildings. Purchases of books. Postage, telephone and office expenses. Housing benefit and Rate Rebate payments	54.4
	3.	**Financing charges.** The repayment of and interest on loans raised to finance major capital projects	14.6
	4.	**Contingencies.** The amount set aside to cover pay and price increases up to March, 1985	4.1

TOTAL £174.5m

D Rate in the pound for 1984/85

	Rate in the £ p
Kirklees Council	129.0
West Yorkshire Metropolitan County Council	47.0
General Rate	176.0

The total rateable value of all properties in Kirklees is £33.171 million. A rate of 1p in the £ is expected to raise £319,000.

their area (constituents) can contact them by letter, telephone calls or by personal contact. On such occasions the councillors can be consulted by people from their own area, usually on matters of interest to the individual (e.g. a complaint regarding dustbin clearance) or other local problems. It is at election times, however, that financial matters are raised most frequently. 'Taxes are paid in sorrow; rates in anger' is an old phrase. Nevertheless, on occasions a relatively small item of expenditure – if it catches the public eye, can attract interest and publicity out of all proportion to its real importance. Local authority accounts are also subject to audit. They are scrutinized by district (central government) auditors or by private auditors. Nowadays a body known as the Audit Commission tells the local authorities whether they are to have the district auditors or if they have to appoint private auditors. The public have the right to inspect the accounts and to make representations to the auditors.

Central government

On a national basis, central government provides approximately 50 per cent of local authority annual revenue finance. Of the various grants the most important is the Block Grant (*see* A2 in Fig. 19.2). Grants are accompanied by a number of controls. Thus, local authorities have to reach certain minimum standards in providing their various services. They are subject to inspection (e.g. education). Certain accounts, statistics and information have to be provided to the appropriate departments of central government.

In addition, where a local authority's expenditure on any item is considered to be excessive or otherwise unlawful (i.e. *Ultra Vires* which means 'beyond its powers') there are powers whereby application can be made to the Court for an order. This order requires those responsible for the expenditure to refund the appropriate amount in whole or in part from their own pockets. This is referred to as 'surcharging'.

Central government also advise councils of their capital allocations. This is the amount they are allowed to spend on major projects such as new schools or houses. A local authority will then usually borrow the money to finance these schemes. In some cases, local authorities have obtained loans from abroad. Such loans are secured on the authority's rates and revenues.

Finally, note that some local authorities gain revenue from trading activities. In other cases transfers from the rates to meet deficits from municipal trading have occurred. Examples of such trading include lotteries, an oyster fishery at Colchester and plant for recovering wool grease from fleeces and its conversion into industrial soaps at Bradford and planning applications for building or extensions to buildings, etc.

Rate capping
From 1985/6, it is proposed that more central controls are to be introduced. The government will then be able to fix the maximum level of expenditure for an authority and the maximum rate it can levy.

You may think that rather a lot of attention has been paid here to local government finance, and particularly to the rates. But most readers will eventually be ratepayers. Indeed, some may already be paying rates. Of all our taxes, probably the rates are the most discussed (and the most disliked). It is important therefore, for you to know what you are paying for and how your rate bill has been calculated.

Public corporations

Read page 67 again to remind yourself what we mean by the term 'public corporation'.

These bodies are financed in a number of ways. In some cases when industries were nationalised, the compensation paid to the former owners and their further capital needs, were financed by selling government stock with Treasury guarantees. Some public corporations raised their own finances. They sold their own stock. Treasury loans have also been provided from time to time. The nationalised industries have been criticised over the years because they made losses. More recently most of them have tended to make considerable profits. Remember though that making a profit is not always a sign of efficiency. Whether it be in the public or the private sector, and particularly if it provides an essential good or service, a monopoly is more than likely to make a profit. At times, government policy has forced the nationalised industries to hold down their prices, when other prices and costs have been rising. In 1984 the government compelled the nationalised electricity industry to *increase* the price of electricity by 2 per cent. Also the nationalised industries have had to pay interest on the stock held by former owners, whether or not they had a surplus of income over expenditure.

Ultimately it is the public, as both customers and taxpayers, who provide most of the finances of these corporations. You should already know that the corporations account to the public for their activities in various ways. If you have forgotten, have another look at page 67. To your knowledge of these controls, you should now add the following information.

Notice first the clash between two of the major principles on which the corporations were built. One was the decision that the corporations should have enough freedom to act as commercial bodies. The other was that they supply essential goods and services such as railways, coal, and electricity. Also they were given monopoly powers by Parliament. Hence it was felt that they must, in certain ways, be accountable to the public for their activities and serve the 'public interest'. Sometimes, these two basic ideas have been in conflict. For example, during the 1960s a survey of Britain's railway services was made. As a result a number of stations and branch lines were closed because they were not profitable. In some cases there was strong public protest, particularly where people living in remote areas were left without any form of transport (e.g. those without cars who were dependent on the railway). Later, the government decided to allow certain train services to operate even though they made a loss. These were met by subsidies from the government and local authorities. The clash occurs because operating as a commercial organisation and aiming to make a profit, is not the same as providing a necessary service at a loss. Notice that each corporation is expected, over a five year period, to pay its way – taking an average of good and bad years.

Another means of control which is worth a mention is the system of examining the finances of these bodies by committees of the House of Commons. The first is the influential Public Accounts Committee, which has powers to examine all kinds of public expenditure. Secondly, there used to be the Select Committee for the Nationalised Industries. Now scrutiny is undertaken by ad hoc sub committees from two or more of the Select Committees dealing with Energy, Environment, Industry and Trade, Scottish Affairs, Transport and the Treasury. Select Committees have been much criticised. They have been described as watchdogs that never bark. It has been said that they are starved of money, talent and information. But these are largely matters of opinion.

A network of Consumer Councils also exists. They deal with complaints from the public and give advice to the corporations. In general, their influence has not been great. Few people seem to know of their existence. Even fewer visit them with their complaints. Of those old enough to remember the days when local authorities provided services such as gas and electricity in certain areas, many probably preferred the way they could then complain to their local councillor.

Whether or not all the methods described have been effective, or are even desirable, is a matter for debate. Nevertheless they do represent more consumer control than is found with private sector organisations. But the reply to this is that they are monopolies, created by Parliament. It is only fair that the public should know more about them than is the case when the customers buy from a limited company. But perhaps you don't agree? Discuss it with your friends.

Exercises

1 If you wanted to withdraw money you had invested in your local co-operative retail society, how would you go about it?

2 How would you withdraw money you had invested in a public limited company?

3 From which sources does a local authority obtain its finances?

4 A man owns a house which has a rateable value of £200. The general rate of his local authority is £1.80 in the £. The water rate is 80p in the £. What is his total rate bill for the year?

5 Why do councillors hold 'surgeries'?

Assignment 1

Consult the current handbook of your local authority. A copy will be in your local library. From it find:

(a) How many councillors there are on your local council.

(b) The name of the Director of Finance or Chief Financial Officer.

(c) The services provided by your local council.

(d) The services provided by three nationalised industries.

(e) The total rateable value of your local authority.

(f) The estimated product of a 1p rate for your area.

Assignment 2

Consult the financial page(s) in any of last week's issues of your newspaper. Be sure to state the date of the issue you have selected.

1 What is the Bank base rate?

2 How many US dollars would you get for £3.50?

3 What is the figure given for the FT All Share Index?

4 Quote the prices for Barclays Unicorn Income Trust and Save and Prosper High Yield. (Both these are Unit Trusts).

5 What is the price of lead per tonne? (Look under 'Commodities').

20 THE ORGANISATION AND ITS RESOURCES

Objectives

At the end of this chapter you should be able to:

- Describe the basic material needs of man.
- Define the term 'standard of living'.
- Appreciate the importance of scarcity.
- Describe the factors of production and explain the role played by each of them.
- Illustrate the interdependence of mankind and give an example of the chain of production.
- Define specialisation.
- Be aware of the services rendered by commerce.
- Define barter and explain its disadvantages.
- State the functions of money.
- Describe the 'mixed economy'.
- Describe the 'information society' and the 'cashless society'.
- Be aware of some of the forces now shaping our future.

The aim of this book has been to help you to understand the nature and functions of different organisations so that you will appreciate their roles and importance. In particular it has been concerned with the interrelationships within organisations of different departments and in helping you to gain an ability in the basic skills of the office.

Certain basic features of the world in which we work now follow: they are the essential background.

Despite all the progress man has made, the basic material needs stay unchanged. We have to have food and drink. We need some clothing to keep warm and dry and to protect us from the sun. We also require some type of shelter against the heat, cold and damp. Without food, clothing and shelter, however simple, man soon perishes. It has always been so.

If you make a list of what you now eat, drink, and use, notice how many items there are which you take for granted (e.g. TV, cars, computers) which even a century ago, were unknown. We say that the standard of living is now much higher than it was then. Your standard of living means what you can get with the money you have. It obviously refers to food, housing, clothes, travel and entertainment. But it also includes the various services available to you. Roads, a water supply, education, libraries, provisions for sickness, unemployment and old age are all services, without which your standard of living would be lower than it is. You may have a large money wage. If prices are also high, your standard of living may be no better than when wages and prices were much lower.

Don't forget either that millions of people still, in African, Asian and other countries, obtain only enough to keep alive. Many others die of hunger.

Scarcity

'Scarcity' is a term which is easy to remember when we see photographs of starving children in the East. How is it that we hear of 'scarcity' in the West when our shops are bulging with goods of all sorts? It is because all goods and services are scarce *relative* to what people want. We should all like to have more (and often better) possessions than we now have – whether they be houses, furniture, clothes, holidays or means of transport. Our wants are many. They never end. As soon as we have satisfied one want, another one presents itself. But the resources (i.e. raw materials, labour power, factories and so on) for making all we would all like to have, are limited – or scarce. One of the best examples today of scarcity is energy. We need energy to run our industries, make our homes comfortable, and enable us to travel from place to place. Our demand for one of the most important sources of energy – oil – is almost without limit. In a few years, because of the speed with which the world is now using up its oil supplies, we shall be virtually without it. New sources of energy will have to be found – and fairly quickly.

The factors of production

Land

In trying to satisfy his wants, man uses his hands and brain in changing the form and place of all the resources Nature has given him. Thus, trees are felled, cut into suitable lengths, transported to a factory and made into furniture. Cocoa beans eventually are made into chocolate. Wool is taken from sheep and ultimately becomes clothing.

Natural resources include coal, gold, silver and copper and all the other substances found in the ground; the fish in the sea; all the things that grow on the land such as trees, fruit, barley and wheat; the animals and birds which man both rears and hunts. Don't forget the air, sunshine and rain without which life, as we know it, could not continue. Nor should you overlook nuclear energy – the only energy form known on earth which owes nothing to the sun. This is a natural resource we have only recently started to use. All these resources are lumped together under one word: *land*.

Labour

What is important for you to remember is that it is man, working in all the various ways he does, who changes these natural resources so that they can be used to meet his wants. In many instances it is the services which people provide which satisfy others' wants. 'Production', which is the satisfying of people's wants, conjures up the idea of making or creating something tangible which we can see and touch, e.g. a wardrobe, a motor car, a suit of clothes. What we are really doing is bringing together different materials. We are altering their form – or we are moving them from one place to another. We don't alter the form of an apple but it has had to be picked, packed, and transported to the shops where we buy it. Anyone who helps in any way towards meeting needs or wants – and for which people will pay for either their goods or services (i.e. their work) is a 'producer'. Thus the providers of services are as much 'producers' as are the factory or agricultural workers. From all this you will appreciate that phrases such as 'There are far too many non-producers today' are a long way from the truth.

Capital

You already know that in the making of many goods, machines are used. Along with factories, lorries, reservoirs, offices, roads and the like, they are called *capital*. Indirectly they help us meet our needs. With them we can produce goods more quickly and more efficiently than if we worked with hand and brain alone. Think of the early man who suddenly realised that if he shaped a stone into a rough hammer, he would be able to perform simple tasks he had not been able to tackle before. He probably eked out his food stocks and made two days' supply last for three days. He could have used that extra day to hunt or fish. Instead he made his hammer. That hammer was capital. It was wealth he had saved (two days of normal food supply being made to last for three) – in order to make future production easier and more efficient.

Practically every type of organisation needs capital. The window cleaner needs a ladder, bucket and wash leather. The owners of a small factory need machinery and raw materials before they can make and sell anything.

The bigger and more complicated the product, the more capital is needed before a start can be made (e.g. motor car production).

Enterprise

In any size or type of organisation somebody has to bring together and organise (i.e. make work together) the natural resources, the labour power (manual and mental), and the capital. In a small business the owner of the capital often provides the organisation as well. In large limited companies the capital is provided by the shareholders (and sometimes by the government) and managers provide the organisation. The four productive resources are known as the factors of production. They are:

1 Land (all the resources of nature)
2 Labour (of all kinds)
3 Capital
4 Enterprise (or 'organisation' as it is often now called).

The total production of any country depends on the quantity and quality of its factors of production.

The interdependence of mankind

How many of the things you now enjoy did you make for yourself? Did you grow the coffee, make the bread, rear the hens and pigs which all help to provide your breakfast? Did you build the roads, provide the water supply to your house or make the radio you use regularly? The answer is NO. Primitive man may have had a very low standard of living compared with yours. But they did meet most of their needs by their own efforts. They caught or grew their own food. They provided the raw materials for their family's simple clothing. They built the hut or cottage in which they all lived. We call this *direct production*.

Contrast this with what happens today. Very few people now satisfy their own wants directly. Money has made it possible for people to work and be paid for their efforts. They use the money they have received as wages or salary to buy goods and services which others have provided. In the same

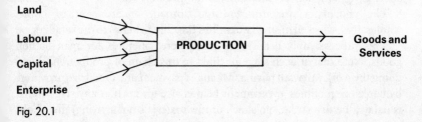

Fig. 20.1

way, these other people have received money for what *they* have helped to produce. These others also buy the goods and services *they* want and can afford. Nowadays people work in order to get the means to satisfy their own wants. At the same time, their efforts are helping others to satisfy their wants. Thus, we are all producers and consumers at the same time.

Most people do only one job. Often that job is but one of a large number of processes. With the constantly improved machines which we have, more and more people do not need to work in the making of goods. They can provide services for others, such as transport, banking, and insurance.

People such as teachers, doctors, entertainers and solicitors provide direct services. Another group – HM Forces, the police and the prison services, ensure that there is some law and order so that life can carry on in a fairly orderly way. Because most of us only do one job, we all depend very much on each other. You only need to think of any strike involving railway or lorry drivers, refuse collectors or machine tool operators to appreciate this simple fact.

The chain of production

The making of even simple things requires the work of many people. Each one adds value at some stage of production – from the collection of the raw materials to when the article is in the shop and can be bought. The making of a bar of chocolate shows how this system works.

The stages are:

1 Cocoa beans grown in West Africa.
2 Planters sell beans to cocoa marketing board.
3 Export to UK arranged.
4 Beans transported first to the African coast – then to the ships – to the UK – from the port in the UK to the warehouse – to the chocolate factory.
5 Cargoes, ships and lorries have to be insured.
6 Other products used in the manufacture of chocolate are also brought to the factory. They include sugar, nuts, coconuts, paper and aluminium foil.
7 The chocolates are made. Machines are often used. The factory employs roasters, tasters, carton makers, packers, chemists, office and advertising staff, delivery men and many other workers.
8 The chocolates are exported (go abroad) or are sent to home wholesalers, who sell in small quantities (i.e. 'break bulk') to the retailers.

This process, only briefly described here, operates for many other goods. Note that at each stage or 'link' in this chain of production, those doing the work will want paying. Means of payment and credit are provided by banks. Sometimes government help is also given. If at any stage there is delay (due to a strike, 'go slow', or raw materials not arriving) the whole

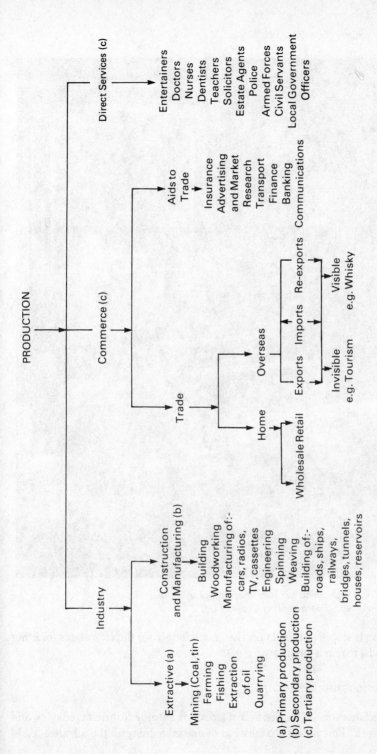

Fig. 20.2 The branches of production

Fig. 20.3 High speed machine wrapping of chocolates
Reproduced by permission of Cadbury Ltd.

chain is stopped. It will take that much longer for the chocolates (or other
goods) to reach the shops.

Specialisation

Specialisation, or the division of labour, is a strong feature of today's world
of work. This means that instead of one man doing all the jobs needed in

making something or providing a service for somebody, the jobs or processes are 'divided up'. One man does only one job. Remember as well, that many jobs are now being done by machines instead of by humans and that it will soon be possible (even if it does not happen!) for most of us to work only a relatively few hours a week. If you don't believe this find out all you can about computers, word processing and the silicon chip. Without industrialisation, specialisation would be largely impossible. It is because we live in an industrial society that we can enjoy the range and quantity of goods and services which we now do.

Specialisation, however, does not operate only in making things (manufacturing industry). It applies to those who provide services as well. Even entertainers specialise as singers, dancers or comedians! Very few do all three.

Advantages

1 Skill and knowledge grow when a person does only one job. Constant repetition leads to the tasks becoming almost automatic for the worker. Think of some of the working skills seen in television programmes about jobs and you will realise how true this is.
2 Specialisation also means that people do not waste time changing from one job to another – nor in 'settling down' to each new process when they start it.
3 When expensive tools and equipment are used, specialisation makes their continuous use possible. They are not 'resting' whilst the worker uses another piece of equipment.
4 Specialisation and the increasing use of machines have made possible our present high standard of living. If everyone wanted hand carved chairs or individually tailored shirts then most of us would have neither chairs nor shirts. There is not enough time, nor a large enough supply of skilled craftsmen. Specialisation aims at turning out the greatest number of articles and services at the lowest possible cost.

Disadvantages

1 But a price has had to be paid for all this. Boredom usually results from doing the same process all the time. The worker often comes to regard himself as merely a cog in a machine. 'I just close my eyes and stick it out. I think about the kids and the next premium being paid' wrote Huw Beynon in 1973, referring to his work on a car assembly line.
2 If a highly specialised worker (e.g. a blacksmith) becomes redundant, his chances of getting another and a different job will be more difficult than if he had done several jobs. Facilities for continuing education and training are provided, not only to help people do their jobs more efficiently, but to prepare others for new jobs.

3 Some people criticise this system. They say everybody has the same type of house, clothes, furniture and so on. But there is still a good deal of variety in mass produced goods. Usually more than one firm produces them. In any case one firm will usually try and make a range of products.

Standardisation (the making of thousands of exactly similar articles or parts), means the cost per article is lower than if every article was individually made. Standard parts can easily be used in a number of similar articles. Every TV set, whoever makes it, must have circuits and a tube. Many countries also specialise in producing certain manufactured articles and raw materials. A country with no gold deposits is not going to be able to concentrate on gold mining. Oranges can be grown in hothouses in the UK. It is far cheaper to bring them from California, USA where they grow easily out of doors and far more cheaply.

To some extent early man learned how to specialise. The best hunter in a tribe would meet his own family's needs first. He would then exchange whatever meat he had left over with a neighbour who was best at fishing or growing crops. There is no real difference between this simple specialisation and exchange and the system we now have. In our different ways, we all add to the national supply of goods and services. *We all very much depend on each other.*

Exercises

1 What does the phrase 'standard of living' mean?
2 Make a list of the shops in the main street of your local town or city. State which of them specialise in one type of commodity and which sell a variety of goods.
3 What are the advantages and disadvantages of specialisation?

The services of commerce

'Industry' is a term often used to describe the processes involved in making goods for use at home and overseas. Industry cannot manage without the services of commerce to enable it to carry out its functions. Commerce has many branches. They can be divided into two main groups:

1 Trade – both at home and overseas.

(a) At home goods come from the manufacturer to the wholesaler, then to the retailer where we buy them.

(b) Overseas trade consists of imports (goods and raw materials brought into the country) and exports (going out of the country).

2 The main aids to trade are transport, communications (including advertising), insurance, finance and banking and warehousing.

Barter

You already know how people use the money they receive, to buy the goods and services they want, which have been provided by others. Contrast the situation where money is used with that which faced very early man. He satisfied his own wants. Sometimes he would have more of something (e.g. fish he had caught) than he wanted for his own and his family's use. He would then exchange this surplus fish with a neighbour who would give him something in return. This process of 'swopping', of giving anything except money in exchange for some goods or service, is known as *barter*. It is still used. Schoolchildren exchange stamps and comics. Vegetables may be exchanged by neighbours in return for simple household jobs. In primitive communities barter is still sometimes used – although various forms of money are often found in such places too. What are the snags with barter? Why is it not used on a wide scale today?

Try and solve this riddle by exchanging goods and services:

Joe is a decorator. He wants kitchen cupboards.

Ron grows vegetables. He wants his kitchen decorated.

Charlie fits cupboards. He wants a TV set.

It's difficult isn't it? The phrase, 'The hungry hatter looking for the hatless baker,' should help you to remember the snags with barter. How many cupboards or vegetables equal the decoration of one kitchen anyway? What an enormous number of vegetables would have to be exchanged for one TV set. You could scarcely give a fraction of a TV set in exchange for the few potatoes and cabbages you wanted for Sunday lunch.

Money

How were these difficulties solved? Man started to use money. Anything can act as money if it is regarded as money. Pieces of leather, cowrie shells, chips of bark, cattle have all been used (and still are in some places) as money. We use metal coins, banknotes, cheques and credit cards. They are all money. Anyone who accepts money in any form has to know that when he wants to, he will be able to use it to buy what he wants. Money then acts as a medium or means of exchange and as a measure of value (e.g. £1 = 20 cigarettes = 1 steak). Money is a type of lubricant. It enables Charlie to fit cupboards for others, get paid for his work and use his money to get what he wants, i.e. a TV set.

The mixed economy

1 When trying to satisfy their needs, people throughout the world face the same problems of choice and resources in limited supply. In meeting these difficulties people arrange and organise their activities in different ways. We call each main different way a 'system' or an 'economy'. Don't let these terms worry you. There are only two major differences between the different systems. First, who owns the resources? Secondly, who decides on how they shall be used and to what end? Again, the different systems tend to use different types of organisations although some very similar organisations are found in all systems.

In Chapter 22, page 287 you will read that we have a 'mixed economy' in this country. Some of our resources and organisations belong to, and are controlled by, the government; others belong to private individuals and are run by them. Many countries now have 'mixed' economies. In some cases there is a larger public sector than private sector. The reverse is also found. The important feature of them all is that the system is a mixture of both types of ownership and organisation.

2 It is argued that ownership and control by private individuals (called free or private enterprise) is the most efficient way of satisfying consumers' wants.

If people demand any good or service, the organisation will try to meet their demand. Land, labour and capital will be brought together to produce whatever is demanded. Note that 'demand' means more than just wanting something. It means being both able and willing to pay for what you want.

3 Under free enterprise, resources are used in ways people want them to be used, because production responds to or follows demand. Prices and profits act as a sort of barometer. If an organiser forecasts correctly regarding people's demands, then the goods or services he produces will sell well. A profit should result. But don't forget that advertising is a powerful force in influencing people in their decisions about what to buy. The opposite happens if people do not want the goods and services which have been produced. Few people will buy them. A loss will follow.

In a market economy, production shifts to meet changing demands. It is consumer demand, working through the mechanism of prices and the market, which is all important. Private enterprise caters for this demand.

4 The incentives to work hard and use one's initiative are encouraged in a market economy. Profit is the goal. Success comes to those who satisfy consumer wants.

5 Critics of the private enterprise system argue that:

(a) The needs of many ordinary people are not met. Why? Because they do not have the incomes effectively to demand (i.e. to pay for) the goods and services which would meet these needs (e.g. housing).

(b) Because there is little or no profit to be made from meeting the various needs, the appropriate goods and services will not be produced (e.g. clothing at a price many pensioners can afford).

(c) Because income distribution is unequal, luxury goods are produced to meet the demands of the wealthy, whilst the real needs of the less fortunate go unsatisfied.

6 The nearest to a market economy we have ever had in this country, was during the first half of the nineteenth century. Government activity then was limited to foreign affairs, defence and internal order.

7 The mixed economy is said to be 'the best of both worlds'.

(a) Thus some goods and services are provided according to the 'pull of the market', by demand and supply, e.g. foodstuffs, clothes, cosmetics. Other services are regarded as being of such basic importance to the mass of the people that some measure of public control is needed (e.g. coal, electricity).

(b) In a number of public sector services the competition which used to exist was regarded as wasteful (e.g. if three different organisations provided gas in the same street). Thus, public monopolies ('mono' meaning 'one') were established.

(c) It is also unlikely that most of us would enjoy some services (e.g. libraries) if we had to rely on profit making activities for their provision. Note that some services are provided by both the public and private sectors (e.g. TV, airways).

8 Critics say that the public corporations are too big and too powerful (the same thing can be said of some limited companies of course). Others ask, 'Where do you go for some commodity or service if you do not like what the one and only supplier provides?' But remember that monopolies exist in both sectors.

Exercises

1 Describe the ways in which man uses two of the following gifts of Nature to satisfy his needs: coal, trees, water, the sun.
2 Name the factors of production.
3 What are the arguments for and against the private enterprise system?

A word or two about the future

Have another look at Fig. 20.2 under 'Aids to trade'. You will see, right at the bottom of the list 'Communications'. Its position in the diagram in no way reflects its importance. Carrying information from place to place and from individual to individual has been very important for a long time. Specialisation is impossible without communication. If a manufacturer did not receive notification of the goods his customers wanted to buy, he would not stay in business for very long. The payment of your student grant may be delayed because of a communication failure, e.g. a lost application form. How will you feel if your wage increase or overtime pay is delayed because of a communication breakdown?

Recent technological developments, however, are resulting in communication being of greater importance than ever before. Videotext; teletext; satellites; cable TV; robots; lasers; data networks. These and many other associated words are now being added to our everyday language. They indicate that we have now reached a stage where we are using completely new methods of storing, dealing with and conveying information. So powerful are these developments that the term 'Information Society' is now being used to describe this new situation.

All sorts of possibilities are opening up before us. Already there exist homes, equipped with two way cable television. This means that without stepping outside, individuals can order goods and services from shops; talk to various organisations and people and even vote in local elections. Rapidly we are moving towards the Cashless Society. After all, money is merely a way of showing that somebody has the ability to pay. You will also have heard of the office of the future as being one without paper. Furthermore, the number of people engaged in communication (the Information Industry as some people call it) is on the rapid increase. Meanwhile the percentage of the workforce involved in manufacturing industry and agriculture is rapidly declining.

Assignments

1 If a man's wages are twice as high now as they were ten years ago, does it mean his standard of living has doubled? Give reasons for your answer.
2 'Manufacturing is productive but so is insurance'. Explain this statement.

21 THE EFFECTIVE USE OF RESOURCES

Objectives

At the end of this chapter you should be able to:

- Understand the importance of financial control.
- Explain the need for financial and management accounting.
- Understand commonly used accounting ratios.
- Illustrate ways of presenting financial information to employees.

In Chapter 20 we looked at how organisations raise finance and use their resources. What any organisation must do is check that it is making the most effective use of its resources. Failure to do so can lead to loss of profits or even business failure, and the consequences of closure for the owners and employees.

Accounting

Accounting is concerned with giving information of an economic type about business or organisations. Economic information is information that can be measured in money terms. The information is in two major areas:

1 Information about the resources used. This can cover a wide range of resources from land and buildings to the amount of typing paper used.

2 The second type of information in accounting is concerned with the organisation's performance. How effective has it been in using its resources? Has the business made a profit or a loss? Accounting statements cover the performance of an organisation for a year and comparisons can be made from one year to another. An organisation's performance will be of interest to many, including investors, employees and government. The keeping of accounting records is equally important to those organisations which do not operate for profit. Organisations such as the National Health Service still need to measure their resources and assess performance over time. Accounting which is for those outside the business is called Financial

Accounting. Accounting which is prepared to help managers run their business efficiently is called Management Accounting.

Financial accounting

The use of book-keeping to record transactions and the preparation of final accounts of different types of organisations such as partnerships and limited companies are outside the scope of this book. Such skills, however, are very important to an organisation so that the economic performance and situation of a business can be stated. When this information is presented it is useful to have a method of analysis to make decisions. Fig. 21.1 shows details of a few of the many accounting ratios available to examine key areas for success of the business.

Examples of Parties with an immediate interest	Type of Ratio
Potential Suppliers of goods on credit; Lenders, e.g. Bank managers and debenture holders; Management.	*Liquidity (Credit Risk):* Ratios indicating how well equipped the business is to pay its way.
Shareholders (Actual and Potential): Potential take-over bidders; Lenders; Management; Competitive firms; Tax Authorities; Employees.	*Profitability:* How successfully is the business trading.
Shareholders (Actual and Potential); Potential take-over bidders; Management, Competitive Firms, Employees.	*Use of Assets:* How effectively are the assets of the firm utilised.
Shareholders (Actual and Potential); Potential take-over bidders; Management; Lenders and Creditors in assessing MSK.	*Capital Structure:* How does the capital structure of the firm affect the cost of capital and the return to shareholders.
Shareholders (Actual and Potential); Potential take-over bidders; Management.	*Investment:* Show how the market prices for a share reflect a company's performance.

Fig. 21.1

Turnover/market share

Organisations must be concerned about the sales and their share of the total market available. There is little point in a firm entering a market with a new product if the total sales available are insufficient to recover the resources used. Equally, it must always examine the market to ensure that its products are competitive and it maintains or, if possible, increases its share.

Return on capital

If you invest your money in a bank deposit account or a building society you will expect to receive interest. If anyone invests in a business whether it is as a sole trader, a partnership, or a private or public company they will expect to receive some interest on the money invested. This can be in the way of profit for the sole trader or partner or as a dividend for an investor in a large public company. The success of a business can be measured by the return by profit or dividend to the investor of capital. If you were investing in shares in a company one of the measures of confidence you would have in the management of that company would be the level of dividend received.

Interpretation of accounts for employees

An employee is very easily put off if too much detail is presented to him. Most firms attempt, therefore, to give a much more limited amount of information and to present it as imaginatively as possible in a special employee report. It is always far better to get over a limited amount of important information than to include so much detail that the message is obscured. Those who are interested can look for more detail in the main published accounts.

Firms have developed many different approaches in preparing their reports to employees. Many succeed by capturing interest through good graphics and design. Care must be taken, however, not to make these reports appear too trivial or condescending. Some examples of graphical

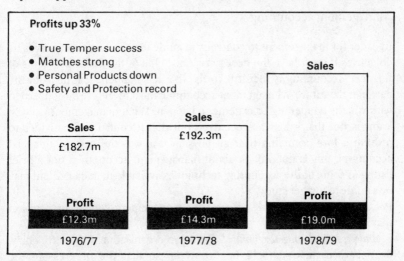

Fig. 21.2

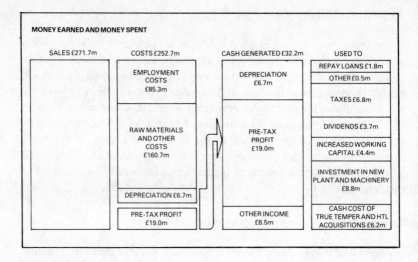

Fig. 21.3

illustrations which are also used in the main published accounts are shown on pp. 283 - 5 below. There is, however, a very wide range of approach between different firms, many of which include cartoons and 'comic-strip' types of presentation to capture interest. Space is not available here to do justice to this type of presentation. Try to find examples of company reports in libraries.

Management accounting

In order for management to control and guide the organisation towards its objectives it must have the necessary tools. One of the major problems of financial accounting is that it records what has happened; it deals in the past, not the future. Management accounting must therefore be concerned with what is happening or is going to happen. What management need to know is not that a loss has occurred but that it controls its activities to prevent a loss occurring if at all possible. As was the case in financial accounting this is not a book about management accounting, but a brief listing of some of the accounting techniques available to management may be a guide to further study.

1 *Cost accounting.* A study of costs for management control or decision making.

2 *Budgeting and budgetary control.* When an organisation's objectives have been agreed, plans should be drawn up so that the progress of the organisation can be directed to achieving these objectives. The people in

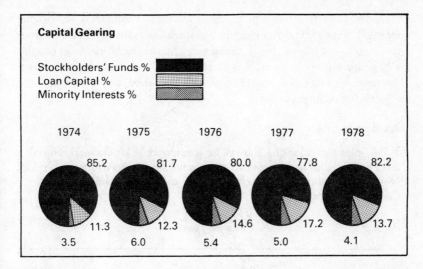

Fig. 21.4

any organisation should be actively involved in drawing up budgets to ensure a sense of being involved rather than budgets being imposed upon them. There are different budgets for different activities within the organisation, i.e.

(a) production budget

(b) cash budgets

(c) sales budgets

The setting of budgets leading to a master budget is often co-ordinated by a committee. There is little point in setting a production budget to produce more goods than can be sold or if in fact cash is not available to finance the production.

If budgets are set on, say, a monthly basis, it would be possible to monitor the actual results with forecasted figures in the budget, and if there are variations then management can establish reasons and if necessary take corrective action.

3 *Break even analysis.* A method of measuring how much revenue has to be earned (sales) before a profit can be made.

Computer-based systems

If management are to make effective decisions, it is important that the information they receive should be clear and accurate. Many firms, large and small, have computer-based accounting systems. The use of a computer and its ability to process information quickly ensures that management can have information (data) readily available. The computer can be used in forecasting if changes need to be made, i.e. level of sales – how many more items have to be produced? – what would be the cost? – how much more cash would be needed and when, and what would the effect be on company profits?

Assignment

1 The Sales Manager of J Shaw & Co is responsible for the marketing of three products. He is concerned to increase the market share for each product. Normally, the firm price their goods at cost plus 50 per cent profit. Currently sales are:

Product	Unit selling price £	£
A	30	45 000
B	12	30 000
C	6	54 000
		129 000

(a) What is the unit cost of products A, B, and C?
(b) What is the total profit on the sales of £129 000?

2 In order to increase the firm's market share the sales manager would have to lower the price and give you the following projected figures

Product A   Cost + 40%   Expected Sales 2400
Product B   Cost + 60%   Expected Sales 2500
Product C   Cost + 30%   Expected Sales 9500

Assume costs remain constant as given.
(a) What would total sales be?
(b) What would the total profit be?
(c) Would it be in the best interest of the company to attempt to increase its market share from a profit basis?

3 What considerations other than profit might make the company want to improve its market share?

22 THE ORGANISATION AND THE ECONOMY

Objectives

At the end of this chapter you should be able to:

- Describe the relationship of organisations in both the public and private sectors to the country's economic structure.
- Relate the activities of the education service, particularly the institution at which you are studying, to that structure.
- Construct a diagram demonstrating the interrelationships of organisations belonging to both the public and private sectors.

Resources and the mixed economy

The term 'economic structure of the country' refers to the methods by which we all work in satisfying our material needs, and how we use and share out what has been produced. Before we consider the ways we use our resources, we must bear in mind that these resources are scarce, and that people's wants are unlimited. By 'resources' we mean the land on which we live; the things that grow on it – and we take from it (and from the sea); and the air, sunshine and rain without which life would be virtually impossible. By using our hands and brains, and in many different ways, we change these resources in order to satisfy our wants.

What would most people in this country ask for *if* they were given a completely free choice and were told they could have anything at all they wanted? Most of them, no doubt would ask for a Rolls Royce or a Mercedes, their own private plane and yacht, a beautiful house, fine furniture and the very best of food. Unfortunately, very few people can have all these things. There just aren't enough of them to go round.

What we are looking at is how our society organises and uses its resources in trying to meet our needs. In this country we have a 'mixed economy'. This means, quite simply that all of our organisations belong *neither* wholly to the government *nor* all to private individuals. Some belong to and are operated and controlled by the government, by local authorities and by semi-public bodies. Others belong to private individuals – or to groups of private individuals working together, as in a limited company. Because in this country we have some of each of these different types of organisation, it is called a 'mixed economy'.

Markets

Every organisation, large or small has to operate in its own market. These markets tend to be specialised, although very large national and international companies can, and do, operate in many different areas of the economy. They are often involved in both the national and international economy. Examples of separate markets are:

1 *Raw materials:* where raw materials are sold to dealers and manufacturers, e.g. cotton, metal ores, etc.

2 *Manufactured goods:* where manufactured goods are sold direct to the retail trade or through wholesalers.

3 *Financial:* specialist markets dealing in money, raising finance, foreign currency and precious metals such as gold.

4 *Retail:* the market place most of us are familiar with. The 'High Street' store or the local retail market or corner shop where we buy the finished product of many activities.

Let us look at the part different organisations have to play in the economy.

The organisation of business in a mixed economy

Sole traders* and partnerships

These smaller types of business organisations are found in a wide range of activities.

The most usual type of sole trader is probably the small shopkeeper. Undoubtedly he plays an important role in our economy. He is the final link in the chain of distribution. The ordinary consumer often gets the majority of his requirements through this type of organisation. Other sole traders, such as window cleaners and odd job men, also meet consumer needs. They also leave the people for whom they work free to get on with their own work. It may seem 'far fetched' but really it isn't, to say that a person's performance at work may be affected if he has to worry about repairing a leaking roof in his own home. It is better in most cases for a skilled repairer to do the job. 'Every man to his trade' is another way of describing specialisation. 'Do it yourself' may have become popular in

*Sometimes described as 'Sole Proprietors'.

some areas, e.g. home decorating, but there are limits to it. Climbing on a roof is something that most people like to avoid!

Another group of individuals who are in the sole trader category (though you are not likely to use that phrase when referring to them) are all those people who provide direct services. Their relationship to the economy is that they all, in their different ways, meet a variety of consumer needs. A solicitor, for example, gives legal advice and represents clients' interests. He certainly pays a vital part in economic matters such as the buying and selling of houses and in legal actions to recover unpaid debts. Without accountants, many of whom are in partnership with others, much business information would not be available. More than one concern has been ruined by a lack of accurate records and forecasts as to how it was progressing. Accountants also advise clients on taxation problems.

Limited companies

These are involved in a variety of activities which affect our economy. As a nation lacking so many of the gifts of nature (oil and coal excepted) we have to 'pay our way' by producing goods and services for export. Remember that this does not mean only sending goods abroad (e.g. woollen manufactures, whisky, cars). We earn foreign currency whenever tourists come to Britain, or we 'sell' commercial services, like insurance, overseas. The limited company is the form of organisation now used in so many economic activities, from garages to glass manufacture, from chemicals to cleaning and maintenance services. Have a look at the Yellow Pages directory. Note how often the limited company type of organisation is used. Limited companies are also frequently employed in providing leisure services such as bingo halls. Many clubs are registered as limited companies.

Public corporations and regional authorities

These provide vital energy supplies (e.g. electricity, coal) and transport services (e.g. rail, buses). Without them industry could not operate. Certainly our personal lives are very dismal when we are without these services. The Post Office and British Telecom provide a network of communications which make business activities possible between organisations and individuals both at home and abroad.

The National Health Service not only helps to make life happier for those who are sick; it also has a tremendous effect on the economy. It helps keep disease at bay. This in turn means production is not lost because workers are absent through sickness. The BBC and IBA (Independent Broadcasting Authority) provide entertainment and education – both of which should help towards a more efficient work force. Weather reports help farmers, fishermen and others.

Local and central government

The government provides a host of services which have an impact on our economic system. The provision of services concerned with defence and with law and order mean that peace and stability are more or less secured. Without these two essentials, no economic system can operate for very long. Think of the political disturbances in various overseas countries in recent years where, on occasions, the economy has been in danger of grinding to a halt.

Education and training

Education, a service with which you are familiar, is most often provided by local authorities who receive much financial help from central government.

During recent years, increasing attention has been paid to vocational preparation and training. Considerable sums of money have been directed, by the government, and through the Manpower Services Commission, into a variety of schemes. The Youth Training Scheme (YTS) for example is aimed at providing vocational preparation for young people. Greater emphasis is also now being placed on technical and vocational education in secondary schools. To this end, schemes such as Technical and Vocational Education Initiative (TVEI) have been established. Funded through the MSC, this scheme aims to provide a more meaningful education for pupils of all ability levels and equip them for life in an advanced technological society. The Certificate in Pre-Vocational Education (CPVE) has now been introduced to enable young people not committed to sample several vocational areas as well as developing the basic skills.

What is the relationship of the organisations providing education and training with the economic structure? First, in the schools children are taught, among other things, how to read and write. Without these skills their possible use as employees would be severely limited. People have to be able to read and write if they are to understand simple instructions (e.g. on how to operate a machine). Technical training should lead to a more efficient workforce. Industry and commerce must have trained personnel in fields such as business, construction, engineering, food and fashion. Many of the old routine jobs (e.g. lifting, carrying, moving, copying, adding up and the like) have now disappeared. Machines have taken over where the jobs are fairly simple and repetitive ones. In more recent years however, they have been able to undertake more complicated tasks. A computer in ten minutes can now do the same quantity of work as a clerk, who used to do only calculations, might have been done in his 40 years of working life. However, many people do jobs other than simple, clerical work. It is only the repetitive type of work that a computer can take over. A computer, for example, cannot deal with the customer who comes into a shop to buy a dress and is doubtful as to whether or not the colour suits her, or whether it is too long. On the other hand the computer can work out her bill very quickly indeed.

A sizeable proportion of the young unemployed have no qualifications of any sort. The urgent demand today is for workers at the 'middle' level – the technicial, supervisory type job. Such posts demand education. Without these junior officers of industry and commerce the economic system will not only fail to reach top efficiency. In certain instances it will not operate at all.

The education service has another impact on the economic system. It provides employment, not only for teachers, but also for those who supply the supporting services (e.g. technicians, canteen ladies, cleaners, caretakers, suppliers of stationery and books). The purchasing power of students and staff belonging to a large educational institution (e.g. university, polytechnic or large college of further education) is certainly a considerable influence on the local economy of the neighbourhood where it is situated. Ask the owner of any garage supplying petrol, or of a sweet and tobacco shop situated near a large college, about the effects of holidays on his sales!

Exercises

1 Of what use to the economy are the services of an accountant?
2 'The tourist and whisky industries are both exporters'. Is this true? If so, why?
3 What are the relationships between education and our economic system?

Government controls

Whilst carrying out their various activities, no organisations are completely free to do exactly what they want. All must obey the laws of the country. In various ways most organisations and individuals pay various taxes to both local and central government to help finance their activities. Again, certain controls are provided by the government to ensure that goods and services reach required standards of quality. A consumer is then protected if he buys faulty or impure products. The environment has to be protected – for the sake of citizens' health and incidentally, that of the economic system too. The production, use and disposal of products such as asbestos and nuclear energy are therefore controlled, though some people would say – not closely enough!

Other organisations affecting the economy

What of other organisations whose operations affect the economy? Building societies make it possible for people to buy their own houses before they are fully in a position to pay for them. This helps to create employment not only in the building industry. It also stimulates demand for all those goods required by householders such as furniture, curtains, and electrical goods.

The most powerful organisations today are possibly the Trades Union Congress (TUC) and the Confederation of British Industry (CBI). They are frequently consulted by government particularly when matters such as wages, salaries and prices are under consideration. A major disagreement involving these bodies can almost stop the whole economy dead in its tracks.

Two more examples will show you how the activities of organisations are related to the country's economic structure and operation.

The Stock Exchange

If you save your money and loan it to a building society, or merely leave it in the bank, you can get it back virtually on demand. This is not the case if you have invested in the shares of a limited company. You cannot expect that company to repay to you the cash you have invested in it. The reason is simple. The company will have used your money (and that of other investors) in buying the assets it uses in the business (such as buildings, machinery and vehicles).

If you could never recover the money (or part of it) which you have used to buy shares in a limited company, then obviously you would probably have decided not to buy the shares in the first place. Fortunately you can sell your shares to other people, and it is these people who will give you the money for them. The money for the shares does not come from the limited company itself.

We can look at the exact way this is done. In the case of a public company being formed, the shares will be sold direct, by the company, to members of the public who may wish to buy them. This would also be the case when, possibly after a few more years, the public company decided to issue (sell) some more shares. When shareholders decide later to sell their shares they can do this by asking a stockbroker to sell them for them. Quite often a shareholder will not know a stockbroker and will ask the bank manager to sell the shares. This is done by the bank manager then asking a stockbroker who deals in shares on behalf of the bank.

The place where the shares in public companies are sold is the Stock Exchange. This exists for selling shares which have previously been bought by members of the public. It is, in fact, a type of 'second-hand market' for shares. The stockbroker *selling* the shares for the client will sell them, via the people who work in the Stock Exchange, to another stockbroker who will have been asked by another member of the public to *buy* some of these shares. The Stock Exchange therefore assists the movement of capital through the economy. Without the Stock Exchange public companies could probably never start up, as people would not want to invest in them if they could never get their money out again. This means that firms can be set up, some of them very large firms indeed, and these firms can help to supply the goods and services which are demanded at any time.

Shares in private companies however, cannot be sold on the Stock Exchange, and so the sale of them from one person to another is done privately. As most private companies are relatively small, and as the shares are sold mainly between people who are acquainted with one another, the sale of shares is managed without recourse to any such organisation as the Stock Exchange.

The British Technology Group

The British Technology Group (BTG) also influences the economy. It supports the development and exploitation of British technical innovation by:

1 Investing in companies of all sizes which are active in areas such as computers and microelectronics.

2 Licensing technology which has come from UK public sources such as universities.

3 Investing in companies operating in parts of the country where it is hoped to foster new industry (e.g. areas of heavy unemployment).

BTG was formed by merging two bodies – the National Research Development Corporation and the National Enterprise Board.

This brief survey should have shown you how the few organisations to which we have referred affect the country's economy. Try working out how the activities of other organisations, large and small, also affect it. Not one of them works in isolation. If some of them stop operating, their employees will become unemployed. They, in turn, will no longer be able to demand nearly so many of the goods and services as they once did. This will lead to difficulties for other organisations – and maybe to yet more unemployment. Nor will the country be able to export as many goods and services as formerly. This will lead to a reduction in what we can afford to import (i.e. to buy from abroad). This interdependence is also apparent in the field of production. If one link breaks, the whole chain will be stopped.

Figure 22.1 aims to show you the different kinds of organisations and how their activities overlap and affect each other.

The outer circle A represents the United Kingdom. The small shaded portion or segment (F) illustrates how some of the public companies have activities in both the United Kingdom and in other countries, e.g. ICI, Shell, Unilever, Lonrho.

Circle C includes sole traders, partnerships, public and private companies, clubs and societies.

Circle B includes all the public sector organisations and the 'middle' range too, such as co-operative and building societies.

ORGANISATIONS

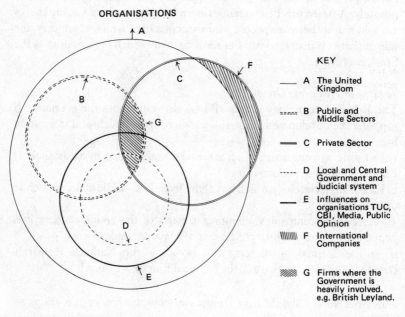

KEY

A The United Kingdom

B Public and Middle Sectors

C Private Sector

D Local and Central Government and Judicial system

E Influences on organisations TUC, CBI, Media, Public Opinion

F International Companies

G Firms where the Government is heavily involved. e.g. British Leyland.

Fig. 22.1

This diagram can be altered in certain ways to show public sector involvements outside the United Kingdom (e.g. overseas aid, sales of arms) in addition to the activities of international companies.

As you know, in some cases, companies have received assistance from the Government, e.g. Austin Rover. It is not easy to say whether these can now be classified as public companies, or as a new type of public enterprise.

Hence the overlap between Circles B (public sector) and C (private sector) marked by the shaded portion G.

Notice how Circles D and E cut across (intersect) all the others. D represents all those activities of central and local government which affect other organisations. These include taxation, both central and local; laws and regulations (planning, control of pollution) and the whole judicial system, i.e. the courts – from the highest to the lowest. Circle E represents all various 'outside' influences on organisations such as the TUC, CBI, the media (press, radio and TV) and public opinion.

Watch your newspapers! There is rarely a day passes but one of these influences is not at work changing, or trying to change, decisions made by other organisations. Examples include TUC and CBI influence on the economy (e.g. pay policy); the Friends of the Earth, the National Viewers and Listeners Association, and the political parties. There are dozens of examples such as this. John Donne said 'No man is an island' – nor is any organisation.

Exercises

1 The Stock Exchange and the British Technology Group both influence the economy but in different ways. What are they?
2 Name any two ways in which the BBC and IBA influence other organisations.
3 In Fig. 22.1 there is a segment outside the largest circle. What does it represent? Why is what it represents not within the large circle?

Economies of scale

Although there is, at present, a positive effort to encourage the setting up of small firms, it is the large companies and public organisations that provide the major employment and investment in our economy. There has been a growth in this century of very large organisations, often with many nationally-known firms being part of one combine or holding company (owning other companies known as subsidiaries). The advantages obtained by the growth in size of firms are often called 'economies of scale', where the benefits listed below are claimed.

1 More intensive and economic use of land, buildings, plant and equipment.
2 Purchase of raw materials in bulk, therefore obtaining better price.
3 Easier to raise capital.
4 Able to afford expensive equipment for large scale production.
5 Employment of staff with specialised skills.
6 Investment in new technology.

7 Investment in research and development for new products.

There can also be disadvantages with growth in size.

1 As size increases management becomes more complex and can lead to inefficiency.

2 Communication between organisations and departments can become difficult.

3 Jobs often are reduced to repetition (production lines) and lead to boredom. Employees become just numbers.

Many small firms still continue to flourish in our economy, often providing goods and services to larger firms, which have found them not worth doing or providing for themselves, or, in the retail trade where convenience is often a factor, such as the corner shop.

Change in the economy

The nature of industry and commerce is changing in many ways other than size. With the closure or reduction of many of our traditional industries, e.g. coal, steel, shipbuilding, there is the growth of the new technology industries, e.g. computers, and the growth of the service industries, e.g. leisure and catering. The types of employment available are changing and the demand for new skills means many of us will have to consider changes in our working lives. The growth of many industries in the industrial revolution was as a result of geographic features, e.g. cotton, steel. With the growth of modern communications, the need to locate industry near to natural resources is no longer necessary.

Assignments

1 In any period of four days you care to select, make a note of all the examples you can from both press and TV to illustrate how one or more organisations try to influence and/or change other organisation(s).

2 'The Government interferes too much in the country's life'. With the help of your teacher and four of your classmates, organise a debate. There is to be a chairman and two speakers from each side. At the end of the debate draw up a table in which the **for** and **against** arguments are briefly stated.

23 MARKETING AND ADVERTISING

Objectives

At the end of this chapter you should be able to:

- Understand the use of market research.
- Give examples of media for advertising.
- Describe the roles played by the Advertising Standards Authority (ASA) and the Independent Broadcasting Authority (IBA) with regard to advertising.

Chapter 24 deals with the organisation and the customer/client, but how does the organisation find its customer clients? Much of what is produced by manufacturers is produced in anticipation of demand. The successful organisation is the one which is successful in its anticipation of that demand.

Identifying the customer/client

Each organisation has to identify its position in the market place. If it is in manufacturing will it sell direct to the public, to wholesalers, to retailers or to all of them? If it is a service industry will it supply its services to other organisations or to the householder? In the preceding chapters we have discussed many different types of organisations – sole traders, partnerships, private and public companies, public organisations and many others. All of them have to cater for the many differing wants and needs of their customers and clients. In order to try and identify these needs and wants, organisations often employ market research.

Market research

Many firms try to establish actual and potential demand for their products or services by the use of market research. This is particularly useful when a new product or service is to be introduced. The intention is to find out as much information as possible to enable management to make the right

decisions and a number of methods could be used including:
1 Giving out free samples and obtaining the user's reaction to the sample.
2 Conducting surveys by using questionnaires: would you buy the product? etc. You may yourself have been asked to take part in such a survey.
3 Selecting a trial area of the country to establish the consumers' reactions with a view to introducing in other areas.
The information they would attempt to obtain would include the present competitors, the potential size of the market, the willingness of the customer to buy, and the price.

Advertising

Very few organisations do not use advertising. We are all familiar with the advertising on television, local radio, newspapers and magazines, but there are many other methods. These include:
1 Display boards and hoardings on buildings at sports events and by the roadside;
2 Wrapping paper for products;
3 Plastic carrier bags;
4 Circulars, catalogues;
5 Special offers and free gifts (e.g. sale of petrol).
There are many other methods of advertising and firms select the method they feel will enable them to best reach their customers.

FAIR TRADING ACT, 1973

BUSINESS ADVERTISEMENTS (DISCLOSURES) ORDER, 1977

Under-A-Fiver is strictly for the use of private individuals disposing of their own personal property and not for traders, dealers or their representatives, selling goods for profit.

The publishers accept advertisements only on this distinct understanding and advise readers who have reason to believe that they have been misled concerning the true status of an advertiser to inform the Classified Manager (Huddersfield 38321) and the Consumer Protection Department (Morley 536111).

Fig. 23.1

Advertising is one of the major means through which we learn of the existence of goods and services we may want to buy. Individuals may want to sell something of their own. Local newspapers usually carry small adverts catering for the needs of such people. Sometimes such adverts are free, limited to say 16 words and the amount the advertiser may ask for what they want to sell (e.g. under £5). Such adverts usually have to be submitted on a coupon which only appears in the newspaper in question. This helps to sell the paper. (*See* Fig. 23.1.)

It also helps the advertisers to sell something which otherwise it would not be worth their while to advertise.

Consumer protection

But the adverts with which we are all most familiar are those aiming to sell a well-known product – be it a car, a brand of chocolates or a new make of kitchen furniture. Advertising is a costly business. As you will note it is a powerful force in influencing people in their decisions as to what to buy. Most goods are produced in anticipation of demand. If the supplier has 'guessed' wrongly, they may suffer serious loss. Obviously, then producers will try to influence demand. And they usually try to do this through advertising. Obviously anybody trying to sell something will invariably try and present it to any possible buyer in as good a light as possible. It is important then that the customer should be protected against grossly exaggerated or untruthful advertising. Also, if action is not taken against the small minority of dishonest advertisers, the reputations of the honest majority may well suffer.

There are a variety of organisations which aim to help the customer (*see* Chapter 24). Insofar as advertising is concerned, the customer is particularly assisted by the Advertising Standards Authority (ASA) and the Independent Broadcasting Authority (IBA). The BBC also offers programmes from time to time, which aim to expose cases of trading malpractice often involving deceptive advertising.

The Advertising Standards Authority (ASA)

The ASA was not created by law. It has no legal powers. It was established by the advertising industry to make sure that the system of self control, which advertisers are supposed to follow, is genuinely working in the public interest. The British Code of Advertising Practice covers newspapers, magazines, cinema commercials, brochures, leaflets, posters, circulars and commercials on video tape. It does not cover TV and radio broadcasting. These are the concern of the IBA.

The General Rules of the ASA state that all advertisements should be legal, decent, honest and truthful. Another rule is that advertisements should not without justifiable reason, play on fear.

Suppose a security firm sent a leaflet through the post which said 'I'm a burglar, and I can get into your house as easily as this leaflet'. This could terrify an older person living alone, and ASA would do everything within its power to put a stop to it. Another rule in the Code states that 'advertisements should contain nothing which is likely, in the light of generally prevailing standards of decency and propriety, to cause grave or widespread offence'.

Finally, here is one of the many examples, (names withheld) taken from one of the ASA's Monthly Summary of Complaints! Two members of the public objected to a national press advert which claimed exceptional results had been reported by doctors in scientific tests for a device to reduce car sickness. The ASA did not consider the evidence in support of the claim, which had been furnished by the advertisers, was sufficient to support such a claim. The advertisement was withdrawn after notification of the complaint.

The Independent Broadcasting Authority (IBA)

The IBA has issued a code of advertising Rules and Practices for Television. In addition, there are Guidelines for Independent Local Radio Advertising. Remember that the BBC does not advertise. Among other things, this Code aims at protecting the consumer from attempts by advertisers to exert undue influence by 'swamping' programmes with adverts or by too closely relating advertising to the material used in

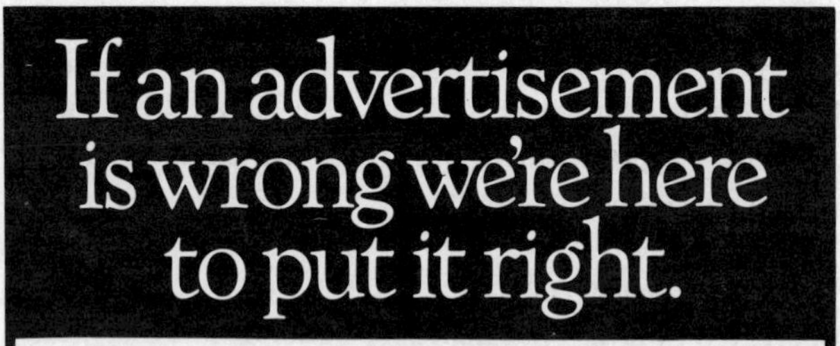

Fig. 23.2

programmes. Thus the IBA Code outlines a number of matters relating to TV advertising such as:

1 Who are not acceptable in adverts, e.g. news readers.

2 The circumstances under which an advert has to be separated from a programme. Thus, products which are incidentally featured in programmes are allowed in the breaks *before* or *after* such programmes though *not last* in the break *before* or *first* in the break *after* the programme.

3 Adverts shall not be inserted in the course of any broadcast of a religious service, a formal Royal ceremony, programmes designed and broadcast for reception in schools, and plays of ½ hour duration or less.

4 Adverts can only be shown at the beginning or end of a programme or during 'natural breaks'. Three pages of the Code are spent in defining a 'natural break'.

5 Some commodities may not be advertised in intervals immediately before, during or after certain programmes. Thus, alcoholic drinks may not be advertised before, during, or after children's programmes. Again, children's medicines may not be advertised before 9 pm.

6 Finally, note that the IBA may give directions to a programme contractor with respect to the times when adverts are allowed, and the amount of time to be given to them.

Public image

Many organisations use advertising and sponsorship (sporting events, athletes, etc) to create a public image. If you watch some advertisements on television they are not aimed at a particular product but the company's image. The intention is to create an image for all its products, not just one. Many advertisements for products now carry the message that the product is one of many from a large group of companies. This trend may well grow as diverse companies come under the umbrella of a large combine or holding company. Publicity is good for the company as long as it is good publicity.

Assignments

1 List as many of the different methods of advertising which you have encountered personally or have heard or read about. Give at least one example to illustrate each kind of advertising you mention.

2 Classify the kinds of products and services which you see advertised in any one issue of a newspaper (and TV channel) of your choice. State why, in your opinion you regard any three of the adverts you select as good or bad. Include in your selection at least one example of an advert of which you are critical.

3 Select any two advertisements from television and explain what you think

the company is trying to achieve. Give the method used by the company to reach the customer, i.e. humour, factual, image, etc.

4 Select a new chocolate bar product to be introduced on the market. Give it a name and design and draw a poster to be used to advertise the new product.

5 Cut out the advertisements from any three issues of the newspaper(s) of your choice. Ignore small personal advertisements.

(a) List them as to the types of goods and services offered, e.g. foodstuffs, clothing, household requirements, holidays.

(b) Which types appear most frequently?

(c) To which sector do the firms which have inserted the advertisements belong in each case (i.e. private or public)?

(d) What do you think are the essentials of a good advertisement?

24 THE ORGANISATION AND THE CUSTOMER

Objectives

At the end of this chapter you should be able to:

- Explain why consumer protection has been strengthened in recent years.
- State the essentials of a valid contract.
- Give examples of the seller's obligations in a sale of goods.
- Outline the rights of buyer and seller when hire purchase and credit sale arrangements are used.

First notice the difference between what the customer may expect (e.g. a helpful staff) and the obligations of the organisation which are enforced by the law. The old rule of 'Let the buyer beware' does not now operate as widely as it once did. A number of laws have been passed, particularly in the last 30 years, aimed at protecting the consumer. These developments are due to:

1 A growth of interest in consumer affairs.

2 An increase in the number of TV and radio programmes aimed at giving the consumer more information about goods and services.

3 The fact that not so long ago customers could see and handle most goods before buying them. They were usually able to discuss purchases with the shopkeeper. Nowadays this is not always so. Today more goods are packaged than used to be the case. The coming of supermarkets has meant that the only employee most shoppers ever come into contact with is the person at the cash desk.

4 Many items we buy now are highly technical. How is the ordinary person to know that the digital clock radio he buys is of good quality and soundly made?

There are other factors than laws which should protect the consumer. No organisation, however large and powerful, welcomes a court case involving its products or services – together with the resulting publicity. It is said that one weapon the buyer always has, if dissatisfied, is to go elsewhere. This is not always true.

For certain reasons a customer may want to avoid Brand X, but there are no convenient shops which sell Brand Y – to which he or she would like to switch. The customer may be old, have no car and suffer a poor bus service.

The organisation also has obligations to provide reasonable working hours and conditions for its staff. These different obligations may clash. Employees may like a five day week. A customer who can only conduct his business at the weekend may not share their opinion.

Remember that the majority of organisations are reasonably honest. Many have very high standards in their dealings with customers. There is another side to the coin. The extension of credit has meant a growth in the number of bad debts. It is easier now to live 'beyond one's means'. Shoplifting has increased because of the open shelves – now so common a feature of modern shopping. The practice has grown of making lists with information concerning the paying habits of customers. Occasionally, customers have had their names wrongly included on such lists. A trader refusing a customer credit can be asked for the name and address of any credit reference agency he has used to find out about the customer's credit worthiness.

The obligations between the organisation and customer/client exist:
1 In shops of all sorts, from whom most everyday requirements are bought.
2 Where services are provided:
(a) Solicitors, doctors and accountants (Professional).
(b) Car servicing, electrical contracting work (Technical).
(c) By the central government and its agencies, e.g. Social Security, the Probation Service.
(d) By local government, e.g. refuse collection, food safety and hygiene, libraries and sports centres.
The quality and quantity of central and local government services is mainly determined by the opinions and policies of elected representatives. The obligations are stated in a mass of laws and regulations such as the Education Acts.

If you are not satisfied with a local government service which directly affects you, first complain politely to the people who are doing the job. If nothing happens, go (or write or phone) to the offices of the department concerned in your local town hall or civic centre. If you fail to get satisfaction there, consult your local councillor.

For most people, the obligations of the greatest importance seem to occur in their dealings with commercial organisations, mainly in the private sector, like shops. Before these are examined, remember the legal obligations which fall on the organisations involved where customers may be exposed to risks to their health and/or safety. Prosecutions and the award of damages can result from failures in this field. Every year people are killed when bricks fall on them from scaffolding. Perhaps the organisation's premises are being altered. Particular care has to be taken to protect customers from injury in such cases. See also Chapter 18 for further details regarding the health and safety of people other than employees.

There are two main types of obligation:

1 The 'square deal, value for money' group.

2 Protection of the customer when he uses credit in settling his bills. (*See* page 309.)

Value for money

Every day, people make social and personal arrangements with each other, e.g. attending a disco or a soccer match together. If one side does not turn up, there is no question of 'going to law' about it. These are not legally binding agreements. Contrast such arrangements with contracts, where one side pays, or agrees to pay money, in exchange for goods or services supplied by the other side (or 'party').

'Contract' perhaps conjures up in your mind some technical document with a lot of sealing wax on it. Some contracts are of this sort. The majority, particularly for small everyday transactions (like buying some groceries) are made without any writing. Often very few or no words are used.

For a contract to be enforceable at law there must be:

1 Something of value, however small, given and received by both sides, e.g. A agrees to sell B a three month old music centre for £15. The price is low. Provided A is the legal owner, a contract can exist for there is a consideration, i.e. A parts with the music centre and receives £15 and for B the reverse happens.

2 The parties to the contract must be able ('have the legal capacity' is the phrase used) to make a contract, e.g. an insane person cannot make a contract. Anybody who is under 18 years of age can, only under certain conditions, make a contract.

3 There must be unconditional offer and acceptance. In the example above if B had said 'Yes, I'll give you £15 for the music centre provided you give me two LPs as well' – there is no offer and acceptance. In effect, B is now making the offer. A can accept or not, as he chooses.

The sale of goods

The most common kind of contract is probably the sale of goods for money. It is so important that Parliament has made laws relating solely to such transactions (e.g. Sale of Goods Act 1979).

The contract may be one to sell existing or future goods. The main point is the buyer pays, or agrees to pay money. The sale of goods does not apply to the sale of a house or a contract for hire (e.g. a motor car where the hirer remains the owner).

Consumer law

A number of factors operate in a contract for the sale of goods.

1 There is an implied condition that the seller is the legal owner of the goods. If he is not, the buyer can return the goods and recover what he has paid. In some cases, he can also get damages.

2 What is sold to the buyer must be reasonably fit for its normal purpose, considering the price and how the goods were described. This is what is meant by 'merchantable quality'.

If you buy a TV set and when it is plugged in you can get no picture at all, you have the right to return it and get a full or part refund. Exactly what you would be entitled to, depends on how long you have had the goods and the kind of fault. In this case it is likely that the shopkeeper would either send the maintenance engineer or give you another set.

3 If you buy anything in a sale, look out for any card or ticket telling you what is wrong with the goods (e.g. 'shop soiled). But they must still be of merchantable quality. If you buy an electric fire and the price is reduced because it is scratched, it must still serve the purpose of such a fire – i.e. the element must operate and give out heat.

4 If you told the seller why you wanted the goods, then they must meet that particular need. The goods must do what they are described as being able to do, whether the salesman tells you, or there is some note on the goods with a statement to that effect. If you ask a pharmacist for something to colour your hair brown, then whatever he gives you must do just that, for you are relying on his skill and judgement.

5 If the buyer merely describes the type of goods he wants (e.g. 'a white shirt') then the goods must correspond to that description. The contract has been broken if when you get home and unwrap the parcel, you find a blue shirt.

6 In all these cases you can return the goods and get a refund of all or part of your money or you can demand their repair or exchange. Sometimes a retailer offers you a credit note (which you can 'set against' the cost of another purchase). You are *not* obliged to take a credit note. If you do take a credit note, then unless the seller agrees, you may not later change your mind and get a cash refund.

7 You may decide to look at a sample and then order goods in bulk based on it. If you do, the bulk must correspond (or be similar to) the sample.

You also have to be given the chance to compare the bulk with the sample.

8 If you are sold faulty goods it is no excuse for the seller to blame the manufacturer and suggest you return the goods to him. The retailer must exchange the goods or refund your money.

9 Again, if you examined the goods before you bought them and the seller pointed out their faults to you (or after a reasonable examination you should have seen them) you cannot legally demand a refund.

There is an obligation on the buyer to take care. Caveat Emptor ('Let the buyer beware') says the law. Obviously it would create an impossible situation if a buyer could return goods to a shop three months after purchase just because he had changed his mind.

Consumer rights

All these rules apply when you buy from a trader in the normal course of their business. If you buy from an ordinary individual after reading an advertisement **or** if you buy second hand goods – take particular care, for the rules already stated do not apply. **But**, if you are told something that is important but untrue about second hand goods, you can return the goods and demand a refund.

Some traders used to try and avoid their obligations to their customers. They would get the buyer to sign a document which, in effect, removed the buyer's legal rights. This can no longer be done.

Don't depend on any guarantee given with any goods you buy. If there is a guarantee however, sign it and send it off. A guarantee cannot limit your rights but it may give you extra ones.

The Supply of Goods and Services Act, 1982, implies similar terms, as those above, to contracts where the Sale of Goods Act does not apply. One of its main purposes is to bring together and to clarify the basic rights that consumers have when they obtain a *service*, e.g. contracts for the hire of goods, supply of a service, and contracts for work and materials. This means that the work should be carried out with reasonable skill and care, within a reasonable time, and at a reasonable cost.

The Trade Descriptions Act, 1968, added to the law some important safeguards for the buyer. A trader can now be fined or imprisoned if he tries to mislead the public by making false claims (spoken or written) about his goods.

Suppose that from his local supermarket Charles buys a can of steak pie. The picture on the outside leads him to believe that he is going to have a pie full of rich meat. When he opens the can, he finds a lot of pastry and two small pieces of poor quality meat. Charles should see his local Trading Standards Officer. If the officer finds that what happened to Charles is not the only such case, it is likely that he will prosecute the supermarket.

Buyers are also now protected from false price reductions. Before the Trade Descriptions Act, some traders, particularly in their January and July sales, used to make extravagant and untrue claims about the price reductions they were offering. It is now an offence to do this, unless the goods have been offered at the higher price for at least 28 consecutive days during the previous six months. If this happens to you, see your local Trading Standards Officer. He also checks that the standard measures by which goods are sold are accurate, e.g. that when you buy a pint of real ale, that you are getting the pint to which you are entitled.

It is an offence to describe food falsely, as it is to make misleading claims about its quality and nutritional value. Ingredients and accurate weight must be stated on the can or container.

Premises have to be clean and hygienic. Running water and hand basins must be provided for employees. No smoking is allowed where food is handled. The packer's name and address have to be given. This permits the source of any unfit food to be traced.

The sale of 'dangerous goods' is carefully controlled. This means goods which can cause death or serious injury and relates to items such as oil heaters, electric blankets, celluloid toys and the paint on pans used for cooking. It is a criminal offence to break any of the regulations relating to these matters.

A practice which was growing until the Unsolicited Goods and Services Act was passed in 1971, was that of sending goods through the post to people who had not asked for them (e.g. books and office carbon paper). Anyone now receiving goods in this way should write to the sender and ask for the goods to be collected. If they are not collected within 30 days they can be thrown out. The period is six months if you don't write. After six months the goods are your property.

Exercises

1 Consumer protection has increased substantially in the last 30 years. Why do you think this has happened?

2 Is there a contract betwween the parties in each of the following situations? Give reasons for your answer.

(a) Anne is given a radio by her aunt for Christmas. The radio does not work.

(b) John asked Susan to go to a disco with him. Susan said she would go and John bought a new suit to wear to the disco. Susan did not turn up.

(c) Tony purchased a bar of chocolate from a vending machine.

3 Find out where your local Citizens' Advice Bureau and Consumer Advice Centre are situated. Make a visit to the location of each. What are your opinions of their design, appearance and availability to the consumer?

4 All the refuse bins in your neighbourhood, except yours, seem to be cleaned regularly and efficiently. What should you do?

Buying goods

When buying larger items (e.g. a car or furniture) many people nowadays pay for them over a period of time. Credit cards, trading checks, budget accounts, bank overdrafts and personal loans are all used to finance purchases. The buyer has to pay interest for being given more time in which to pay.

One method is that of 'credit sales' being paid for by instalments. This means the seller has no chance of getting the goods back if the instalments are not paid or if the buyer has sold them to somebody else.

Instalment buying is now very common. Hire purchase is the method most often used. Over an agreed period of time (say 12 months) you pay the purchase price, plus interest charges by means of a deposit followed by regular payments or instalments. Under hire purchase, until the debt is paid in full, the goods do not belong to the buyer.

If the buyer cannot 'keep up' the payments in a sale by hire purchase, they can return the goods. They still have to pay up to half the total purchase price plus a sum for any damage done to the goods. If one third of the total purchase price has been paid a court order has to be obtained before the seller can recover the goods. If the seller gets the goods back without a court order, the buyer can recover everything they have paid and need not pay any more.

A hire purchase agreement must be signed by both parties. The cash price and the hire purchase price must be stated. This allows the hirer (the buyer) to know exactly what interest they are paying. A copy of the agreement has to be given to the hirer within seven days.

If the goods are sold by hire purchase 'on the doorstep' (i.e. anywhere other than the seller's place of business) a copy of the agreement has to be given to the hirer when they sign it and a copy must also be sent to them within seven days. If required, the buyer can cancel the agreement within five days of receiving the second copy.

It is easy to criticise hire purchase because it allows people to buy more than they can afford. But, it has allowed those with low incomes to have goods they otherwise might never have had. The system encourages sales and thus also helps to keep people in employment.

Organisations to aid the consumer

These include
1 The Office of Fair Trading is a government department. It is

responsible for the administration of a number of Acts of Parliament including the Fair Trading Act, 1973; the Consumer Credit Act, 1974; the Estate Agents Act, 1979; and the Competition Act, 1980. It is under the supervision of a Director General of Fair Trading. The main job of the OFT is to watch commercial activities in the UK. It aims to protect consumers against unfair practices. Its five main areas indicate its functions viz–consumer credit, consumer affairs, anti-competitive practices, monopolies and mergers and restrictive trade practices. The OFT has been responsible for various publications, such as the leaflet 'How to cope with door to door salesmen'.

2 Consumer Councils for the Nationalised Industries.

3 Citizens' Advice Bureaux give help on all kinds of problems, not only those involving purchases.

4 Consumer Advice Centres help with genuine complaints and give pre-sales advice.

5 The Consumers' Association is a private organisation. It issues a monthly magazine *Which*. The 'best buy' on all types of goods is given in *Which*.

6 The British Standards Institution lays down minimum standards. Any product meeting them carries its standard of approval – a kite mark.

7 The Design Council gives its label to products which are well made, good to look at, and practical.

8 The media, e.g. items in TV programmes such as 'Watchdog'.

9 The Mail Order Publishers' Authority protects those who have sent cash by mail and the firm has gone out of business before the goods are received. Refunds are made if application is made to the Advertising Manager of the newspaper or periodical in which the advert appeared.

10 Many manufacturers and shops are members of trade associations. With assistance from the Office of Fair Trading, some of these associations have drafted codes of practice. These aim to give customers a 'square deal' by laying down standards for goods sold or serviced. Joan, for example, is not at all satisfied with the transistor radio she has just bought. The shopkeeper is unwilling to do anything about it when she complains to him. If the trader belongs to the RETRA (the Radio, Electrical and Television Retailers' Association) and displays their sign Joan should contact that body. It is, by the way, very unlikely that any member of a trade association would not do his best to meet a customer's complaints. Not all traders belong to their relevant association. Nor are all makes of goods 'covered' in the code of practice. Nevertheless, it is worth knowing that these codes of practice exist for travel (particularly package holidays abroad), footwear, shoe repairs, cars, electrical goods, goods bought by post, laundry and dry cleaning.

Each association has its own distinctive symbol. Your local Consumer

Protection Department, Consumer Advice Centre, or Citizens' Advice Bureau should be able to give you advice on these matters, or tell you where you can get further information.

One final reminder. The term 'organisation' includes all kinds of sellers – from sole traders to limited companies and nationalised industries.

Don't assume that the retailer is always the sole trader type shopkeeper.

ii Instances have occurred of individuals unjustly suffering both inconvenience and embarrassment because computer data concerning them has been inaccurate. For example, wrong (and detrimental) information about a person's credit worthiness may be stored in a computer. As a result, that person may be refused credit when he should be allowed it.

Parliament has considered computer privacy, and rights of access to computer information, on more than one occasion. Parliament passed the Data Protection Act in 1984 (*see* page 211). Amongst many other things, it requires that:

(*a*) a register of data users and computer bureaux is maintained;

(*b*) the unauthorised disclosure of data by computer bureaux is forbidden;

(*c*) an individual who has suffered damage by reason of inaccurate data will be able to seek compensation through the courts.

Developments in this field, dealing with information concerning us which is held both by the government and by private bodies, concern us all. They are worth watching.

Legal tender

If creditors were allowed to refuse to accept money when debts were being settled, confidence in the currency would very soon diminish. Accordingly, governments make it compulsory for everybody to accept certain types of money when payment is being made. The money offered in the form laid down by law is called 'legal tender'. In this country the exact sum due must be offered and no request for change must be made *if* the conditions regarding legal tender are to be complied with. In these circumstances a creditor must, by law, accept it. If a legal tender of money is refused by a creditor, the tenderer is not discharged from his obligation. But, if without delay he pays the money into court, he has a good defence if an action for non-payment is made against him. Also, the debt will not carry any interest. In many transactions, of course, change is asked for and is given. Legally however a creditor is not bound to accept payment in such form.

In Scotland and Northern Ireland only Bank of England notes are legal tender. Scottish notes are not legal tender. Nevertheless, in practice in Scotland such bank notes enjoy a new status equal to that of Bank of England notes and they are generally accepted by English banks. The commission which English banks used to charge on Scottish bank notes has now been abolished.

In the United Kingdom the regulations regarding legal tender are as follows:

1 Bank of England notes of £1, £5, £10, £20 and £50 denomination for any amount.
2 There is no limit to the number of £1 coins which may be preferred as legal tender.
3 The limit for coins of 5p and 10p denomination is £5.
4 The limit for coins of 20p and 50p denomination is £10.
5 The limit for bronze coins (2p and 1p) is a total of 20p.

Assignments

1 On a piece of paper (A3 size preferably) prepare a map of a shopping area with which you are acquainted. Give five examples of how customers are protected in shops in the area you have chosen.
2 Working with fellow students describe, through the medium of a short play, the visits to a Consumer Advice Centre of at least three citizens who are seeking advice on the (different) problems they have encountered as consumers — and the advice they were given.

25 THE ORGANISATION AND THE ENVIRONMENT

Objectives

At the end of this chapter you should be able to:

- Explain possible dangers to the environment;
- Be aware of the need for control to protect the environment;
- Be aware of the organisation's responsibility to the environment.

Organisations exist to satisfy the needs of man. They are made up of human beings. The organisation then should act in a responsible way concerning the environment. For those organisations and individuals who do not appreciate their moral responsibilities, a variety of laws and regulations have been made, to protect the environment and to penalise those who do not respect it.

The remainder of this chapter deals with the various dangers to the environment and how we are trying to deal with them.

The dangers to the environment

1 *Smoke.* Over 80 per cent of smoke at ground level comes from household fires burning coal. Local authorities now have powers to set up Smoke Control Areas in which only smokeless fuels can be burned. Fines, and on occasions imprisonment, can be imposed for failure to obey these rules. The emission of smoke from furnaces is also strictly limited (emission: the giving of or out). Planning permission now has to be obtained from the local authority before a new factory can be built.

2 *Sulphur dioxide* is formed when fuel containing sulphur is burned. When dissolved in rainwater it produces a weak acid which corrodes metals, attacks stonework and harms plants.

3 *Grit and dust* come mainly from industry and are a considerable nuisance. Think of the money and effort we spend in fighting them, from the washing and dry cleaning of clothes, to the use of the vacuum cleaner.

4 *Hydrocarbons* are unburned chemicals which follow combustion. Car exhaust fumes are a good example. Many countries have strict anti-pollution laws for vehicles. Often these are stricter than ours.

5 *Carbon monoxide* is poisonous and results from fuels not being completely burned. Road vehicles using petrol engines are one source of this gas which is found in busy city streets and underground carparks.

6 Certain *smells* spoil our enjoyment of our surroundings though they don't harm our health. The local authority has to give permission to carry on trades such as glue making and tripe boiling.

7 The import and production of *radioactive substances* is now licensed. Ministerial consent is needed before a new nuclear site is built.

8 *Dirty air* is costly. It attacks stonework and corrodes metal. It reduces the sunlight available to us, thus causing higher lighting bills and stunting the growth of crops. Paint is affected by dirty air as are curtains and textiles. Above all, air pollution is an important cause of chronic bronchitis. Some pollutants may be a cause of lung cancer.

9 More research is needed into:
(a) Developing alternative sources of power (e.g. solar and wave power).
(b) A pollution free vehicle.
(c) Improved methods of combustion.
(d) Means of removing sulphur from fuels.

10 If you have any complaints or queries, see the staff of your local Environmental Health Department.

Exercises

Attempt after you have read the whole of this chapter.
1 Give three reasons why it is important for us to know as much as possible about how we treat our environment.
2 What are the dangers arising from polluted air?
3 In a college debate you are to speak for the motion – 'That the motor car should be abolished'.
What arguments would you use?
4 *(a)* Minor noise nuisances such as . . . . . (give four examples) can be controlled by local authorities.
(b) If the person or organisation responsible for the noise fails to stop or reduce it, the local authority . . . . . (complete this sentence).

Noise pollution

Noise has been described as 'sound which is undesired by the recipient'. There are many reasons why noise is not wanted. People want to read, study, get to sleep, relax after a hard day, or they just don't like it. In some work places, excessive noise can lead to deafness.

Noise can be classified as follows:

1 From road traffic. Nearly two fifths of our urban population, whilst in their homes, suffer from undesirable levels of traffic noise. Vehicles can be quietened. Roads can be directed away from residential areas. Houses can be insulated. Fines can be imposed by the courts in respect of vehicles making excessive noise. The use of motor horns is also controlled.

2 From air traffic. Many are the complaints made by people living near major airports or under the flight paths of large aircraft. Understandably they also fear the dangers arising from air crashes. The night movements of jet aircraft near to airports, such as Heathrow and Manchester, are restricted. In some cases the Secretary of State for Trade can require the management of an airport to limit the amount of noise.

Other noise nuisances

By-laws made by local authorities often control minor noise nuisances. These include noisy animals, power boats, fireworks, model aircraft, radios and TVs, music near houses, churches and hospitals. If those responsible for the noise fail to stop or reduce the nuisance, the local authority can be asked to send them a notice. Legal proceedings can follow continued refusal to stop or reduce the noise. The use of loudspeakers is controlled by the Control of Pollution Act 1974. Only the police, ambulance and fire brigades can use loud speakers in the streets between 9 pm and 8 am.

Noise on construction sites is also controlled by local authorities, who may designate certain areas as Noise Abatement Zones. This aims to control noise particularly from industrial premises. The consent of the Secretary for the Environment is required before such a zone can be designated.

Water

1 Regulations and Acts of Parliament exist to stop chemical waste, anything poisonous, ashes and the like being put into a river or stream. Fines can be imposed and imprisonment ordered in serious cases.

2 Anything calculated to poison or injure fish must not be put into the water.

3 The discharging of sewage into the sea, and of oil and industrial waste from vessels at sea is closely controlled.

4 A well or water container, from which domestic supplies are drawn, must not be situated so that it becomes contaminated.

Other aspects of the environment, where the organisation has both interests and obligations, relate to:

1 Buildings of architectural and structural interest. They are 'listed' and cannot be altered or demolished without consent.

2 Developments (e.g. town centres) where planning permission is needed. These are often the cause of public enquiries, much publicity and disagreement.

3 The felling and replanting of trees, over which there is a number of legal controls.

Some final points

The improvement in our standard of living is often associated with an increase in the production of manufactured goods and in the supply of services. Such developments can result in more pollution, and more waste. If we are constantly adding to our controls over the environment shall we be faced with fewer goods and services and a lowering of our standard of living?

Are there too many controls already – or too few?

Scarcely a week passes but the media make a reference to an environmental problem. One example is the alleged effects of airborne lead and carbon monoxide. Both these come from the exhausts of motor vehicles. It is agreed that brain damage to children and chest troubles result from them.

Assignments

1 Select any three organisations in your town or city. In what ways do their activities affect the environment? Points to look for – Factories causing dirty air or dumping effluent into rivers and/or sewers; roads jammed because of loading and unloading of goods – and consequent road blockages; danger of explosions and fires from certain activities; parked cars of employees almost completely blocking roads; noisy activities.

2 Take a walk round your nearest town or city centre. How do you think the environment might be improved?

3 A government document contained this sentence: 'New roads do improve the total environment, although inevitably amenity* is reduced in some areas and for some people' (*the quality of being pleasant or agreeable). Do you agree or disagree? Give reasons for your answer.

4 'Environmentalists are killjoys'. Do you agree?

INDEX